# AGITPROP IN AMERICA

### *agitate*

To weaken support for established social, economic, moral, and
political practices and beliefs through incessant discussion, speeches,
indoctrination, rallies, marches, and protests, for the purpose of
promoting alternative beliefs and practices.

### *propagandize*

To disseminate often deceptive concepts, information, or doctrines
in newspaper pieces, pamphlets, essays, books, and electronic
broadcasts to further one's own cause or damage the cause
of an opponent.

### *agitprop*

Of or for a combination of agitation and propagandizing, a strategy
created by the Marxist revolutionary Vladimir Lenin; who in
founding the Union of Soviet Socialist Republics in 1922 included
among its departments a bureau for agitprop.

# AGITPROP IN AMERICA

## JOHN HARMON McELROY

ARKTOS
LONDON 2020

TO

*my uncommonly lovely and accomplished
Cuban-born-and-bred wife*

& IN MEMORY OF

*Cuba's Escambray guerrillas who died fighting
Fidel Castro's Marxist tyranny in the 1960s*

You can live with the loss of certainty,
But not belief.

— "The End I," a poem by ROBERT REHDER

# TABLE OF CONTENTS

## PART IV
# THE FUTURE OF CULTURAL
# MARXISM IN AMERICA

# A Brief Word to Readers

THE FOLLOWING discussion of the history of the Counter Culture/Political Correctness Movement in America from the 1960s to the election of Donald Trump has a perspective no other commentary on this movement has: a definition of culture, which is indispensable to understanding Political Correctness as the attempt to "transform" America's culture that it is, using agitprop as the means of transformation.

Please avail yourself of the blank pages at the end of the book to note the location of passages that particularly interest you.

JOHN HARMON McELROY

# Foreword

WILLIAM S. LIND in *The American Conservative* for May/June 2018 identifies Political Correctness as a Marxist movement dedicated to eradicating Christianity in the United States and America's culture. I agree. The Marxist agenda wherever found has always been (and remains) the same unequivocal formula which can be summed up in three words. Destroy and Rebuild. Agitprop has been the method for destroying America's culture and rebuilding it as Cultural Marxism.

My own interest in the nature of culture goes back to 1968–1969 in Spain when, as a Fulbright Professor of American Studies at the University of Salamanca, I was asked to give a course on the "The Cultural History of the United States." That course began my development of an understanding of culture as a set of historical belief-behaviors, which eventually led to my writing a series of books. *Finding Freedom: America's Distinctive Cultural Formation* (1989). *American Beliefs: What Keeps a Big Country and a Diverse People United* (1999). *Divided We Stand: The Rejection of American Culture since the 1960s* (2006). *America's Culture: Its Origins & Enemies, A Synopsis* (2016). And now, the book you have in hand, *Agitprop in America*.

This book contends that since the 1960s Marxists and their sympathizers in America have been using agitprop (an integration of intense agitation and propaganda invented by Lenin) to destroy America's culture and build Cultural Marxism. To do this, agitprop has changed American speech and manipulated American cultural values and beliefs. For instance, Christian charity in America; the middle-class

American desire not to offend others; the deeply rooted American beliefs in equality and freedom. A major activity of agitprop in America besides changes to American speech has been rewriting American history to make it into a Marxian tale of unmitigated oppression: the conspiracy of "the haves" (as Marx called the rich) against "the have-nots." Agitprop has changed the perception many Americans have of their country. Where America was once regarded by almost every American as a land of freedom and extraordinary opportunities, which in its four-hundred-year history attracted ambitious immigrants by the tens of millions, it is now seen by many Americans after five decades of agitprop as a land of oppression, of "victimization." In the agitprop version of American history, nothing remains of America's uniqueness as a country replete with persons grateful for the freedom, equality, and opportunity America has given them, who want to "give something back" (hence the extraordinary charitableness of Americans and their proneness to volunteer to perform community service).

Fifty years of agitprop attacks is replacing the American cultural belief that every person has an equal, God-given birthright to pursue happiness with a Marxian-socialist demand for government provided happiness for classes.

But if American history is not exceptional and is just the most egregious instance (as Marxists say) of Marx's concept of history as the conspiracy of the rich against the poor, how can the indisputable facts that America has attracted more immigrants than any other place on earth and has produced history's largest, wealthiest middle class be reconciled with that assessment? If agitprop has persuaded you that the word "victimization" does epitomize the history of America, how did America's unprecedented distribution of wealth in the world's largest middle class occur? Are there examples of evil in American history? There are. America has been populated by human beings, not flights of angelic beings, and is the world's third-largest nation in population and area. Of course wickedness can be found in its history. But show me any sizeable nation where wrongdoing is not part of its history. Show me another large nation which has had a better ratio of personal success to failure. Where else than in America have the needy (Marx's "have-nots") been treated with greater charity; where else is the desire to redeem wrongdoing more evident? The Marxist "narrative" about America denies the self-determination that pervades American history, and substitutes a Marxian narrative of class struggle for it. America's history of immigrants from many nations, religions, and languages and their descendants working hard to achieve personal success, while at the same time cooperating with one another for reasons of self-interest to create a highly prosperous, future-oriented culture, is being transformed into a tale of one biologically defined ruling class (straight white males) "victimizing" all other biologically defined classes: the class warfare which is the Marxian theory of human history.

Part I of *Agitprop in America* is a sketch of the historical context of agitprop in America. Part II illustrates the many changes agitprop has made to American speech to alter the perceptions of Americans. Part III discusses concepts agitprop is imposing in America. (Biological Class Consciousness, "Social" Justice, Mandatory "Diversity," A Standard of Double Standards, "Sensitivity" Above All, "Correct" Free Speech, A Culture without Belief in God.) Part IV considers America's soaring deficit spending and national debt, intolerable trade deficits, and the perilous condition of U.S. public schools which must be addressed if the downward slide of American culture into Cultural Marxism is to be stopped. This concluding fourth part of the book also considers the significance of the Soviet Union's collapse in 1991 and Donald Trump's election as president of the United States in 2016.

The people of the States of the United States appear at last to be rising up in opposition to the alien dogmas of Political Correctness, and the strong-arm tactics of agitprop which impose them, because these dogmas are causing the destruction of America's exceptional culture.

JOHN HARMON McELROY

PART I

# THE CONTEXT

# Historical Background of the Counter Culture/Political Correctness Movement

I F YOU ASK a traveler in the United States whether Political Correctness exists where he comes from, you will receive, I daresay, an answer in the affirmative; and if you talk awhile with him about Political Correctness in his country, you will discover how many of the ideas and how much of the language of the movement where he lives exist also in the United States.

Marxism is the only political movement in modern times with that sort of international uniformity and reach. Richard Pipes, a Harvard professor who specialized in the history of Soviet communism, compared communism and the other totalitarian socialist movement of modern times, fascism, this way: "The principal difference between totalitarian regimes of the Communist and 'Fascist' varieties lies in the fact that the former thought globally while the latter focused on the nation" (*Communism: A History*, Modern Library Chronicles, 2001; p. 106). Communism is a totalitarian form of socialism that purports to be a scientific concept of history and human nature of benefit to mankind as a whole. Fascism, on the other hand, is a form of totalitarian socialism that derives from the history and needs of a particular nation and aims to benefit that nation, as the fascist movements in Germany, Italy, Spain, and Japan did in the 1920s and 30s, the decades

1

in which communism was taking over the Russian empire and organizing the first Marxian regime the world had ever seen.

Political Correctness has an international uniformity of language and dogma because it is a Marxist project. It started in America on college campus in the 1960s as the domestic front the Soviet Union opened inside America to prosecute its Cold War with the United States. It called itself "the Counter Culture." American opponents of the Counter Culture in America renamed it "Political Correctness" in the 1970s because they saw in it the same dogmatism and intimidation that Mao Zedong's "Cultural Revolution" manifested in China. And Mao, the chairman of the communist party of China, called the politics of his Cultural Revolution "Political Correctness." The method of attacking the existing culture in both the American and the Chinese "cultural revolutions" has been agitprop. The attacks on America's culture inside the United States have been continuous since the 1960s.

The dissolution of the Soviet Union in 1991 had no effect on the purpose of the politically correct movement in the United States. By 1991, Political Correctness was firmly entrenched in America and functioning autonomously. Its purpose of destroying America's influence in the world by replacing America's culture with Cultural Marxism was institutionally established. Indeed, the destruction of the USSR in the U.S.-Soviet Cold War seems to have strengthened rather than weakening the PC movement in America by making it more determined than ever to destroy the United States in revenge for the collapse of the Soviet Union.

From its inception, the CC/PC movement in America has promoted revolutionary "change." Political Correctness wants to replace the beliefs of American culture with these Marxist dogmas. (1) All human problems are material in nature and have only material solutions. (2) Human beings are only one more species of animal that has evolved on this planet without intelligent design. (3) The environment determines human behavior, as it does that of every animal. (4) The purpose of government is to control the social, economic, political, and natural environment to produce correct human behaviors; therefore, everyone must defer to the decisions of government experts who have the knowledge, command of resources, and authority to control the socio-politico-economic and natural environment. (5) Anyone who rejects these propositions deserves to be treated as an enemy of human beings.

Many American intellectuals in the 1920s and 30s regarded the Union of Soviet Socialist Republics as "the wave of the future," the model for a more humane, economically just, internationally oriented world government that would end nationalism and war. They believed the USSR, which Lenin created in 1922 after the Red Army had quelled the counter-revolution that attempted to undo the Bolshevik takeover of Russia in 1917, represented the dawn of a new era for mankind in which wealth would be produced collectively and distributed according to a fully rationalized plan for universal "social" justice.

The Union of Soviet Socialist Republics was the first Marxist regime in the world. But it was not a nation. It was the empire of the Russian czars under Marxist control. That the Soviet Union was not a nation but an empire of conquered nations was shown by its 160 nationalities speaking 131 languages using five different alphabets and spanning eleven contiguous time zones. When the United Nations was organized in 1945, two of the fifteen republics that constituted the Soviet Union (Byelorussia and the Ukraine) had their own seats in the UN General Assembly as if they were separate nations, which the Soviet dictator Stalin declared they were whenever it suited him. The USSR thus became the only "nation" with three votes in the General Assembly of the United Nations: one for the Soviet Union, one for the Soviet Socialist Ukrainian Republic, and one for the Soviet Socialist Byelorussian Republic.

As Lenin and his successor Stalin in the 1920s and 30s carried out the program of domestic terror in the Soviet Union which Lenin in his book *State and Revolution* (1917) proclaimed was necessary to establishing and maintaining the authority and discipline of the

Communist Party of the Soviet Union, the brutal nature of the world's first communist regime became apparent to everyone who was not a doctrinaire, believing Marxist. In 1991, after a comparatively short existence of seventy years after its founding, the Union of Soviet Socialist Republics disappeared from the world's political map and was replaced by the Russian Federation, a much reduced, but still imperial territory comprising 6.6 million square miles. Canada, the world's second-largest political entity in area, is only a bit more than half the size of the Russian Federation; the United States is third in size; China, fourth; Brazil, fifth.

Most of the impetus for the "Counter Culture" movement in the United States in the 1960s came from a Marxist-oriented organization with the name Students for a Democratic Society (SDS) which issued a manifesto (the "Port Huron Statement") denouncing the culture of the United States and its post-World War II foreign policy of containing the spread of communism in the world. The pro-Marxist nature of the SDS mission statement was expressed by one backer who characterized it as "four-square against anti-Communism, eight-square against American culture, twelve-square against sell-out unions, one-hundred-twenty square against an interpretation of the Cold War that saw it as a Soviet plot" (quoted in *The Sixties: Years of Hope, Days of Rage* by Todd Gitlin, Bantam Books, 1987, pp. 109–110). As far as Students for a Democratic Society was concerned, the Cold War was an anti-Soviet, American plot. For SDS members, Fidel Castro and "Che" Guevara whose Marxist takeover of Cuba occurred in January 1959 were international heroes of boundless stature because of their anti-American Marxist politics. The very name of the organization, Students for a Democratic Society, was a condemnation of the United States in accusing it of not being a "democracy," and the name called upon American college students to make the United States a "democracy." Politically correct agitators and propagandists in America are still making that charge, that the United States lacks a truly democratic government.

The Preamble to the Soviet Constitution in effect when the Soviet Union collapsed in 1991 (the so-called Brezhnev Constitution) indicates what these young Americans who belonged to Students for a Democratic Society probably had in mind in their concept of democracy. "[The Soviet Union] is a society of true democracy, the political system which ensures effective management of all public affairs, ever more active participation of the working people in public life, and the combining of citizens' real rights and freedoms with their obligations and responsibilities to society." In countries such as Cuba that continue to cling to the Soviet model of government, this is called "participatory democracy," a form of government in which every citizen is forced under penalty of law to vote in elections and only the communist party gets to nominate candidates for office. In Marxist theory, communist-ruled countries are true democracies because they hold "elections" in which everyone votes. The communist party nominees in such one-party, one-nominee-per-office "elections" always "win" (not surprisingly) by margins of 95% or more of the vote.

Such absurd Marxist "elections" serve two purposes. They condition human beings to participate in the Party's practices, no matter how nonsensical these are. Such "elections" also reaffirm the revolution that gave the communist party the authority to stage such one-party/one-candidate-per-office charades. Thus, according to Marxist theory, the people of Cuba (not the Communist Party of Cuba) "elected" the head of the Communist Party of Cuba, Fidel Castro, to lead the Cuban government for forty-nine straight years, a world-record dictatorship. The Marxist legal system in Cuba would have penalized any Cuban voter who did not show up at the polls to vote for Castro, the only candidate on the ballot for president. The Communist Party of Cuba felt no embarrassment bragging about how "popular" Castro "*el lider maximo*" (the ultimate leader) and the communist regime were with the Cuban people as shown by the enormous percentage of "votes" the Cuban people gave Castro at every "election," where he was the sole candidate for the office of president. Marxist "elections" are grounded in the supposition that Marx's doctrines are "science," and therefore unassailably and permanently valid. Indeed, the preface to the Constitution of the Union of Soviet Socialist Republics in effect when the Soviet Union collapsed in 1991 stated that the government of the USSR was based on "science."

In full-fledged Marxist regimes, wherever they occur, the authority of the communist party in charge of the regime exerts a control that is both omnipotent and omnipresent, or total. The Party regulates everything through its control of government and its "organs." Art. Banking. Commerce. Communications. Education. Elections. Employment. Entertainment. Food Production and Distribution. Healthcare. Housing. Justice. Labor. Leisure. Manufacturing. The Media. Police. Politics. Prices and Wages. Religion. Sports. Transportation. Travel, both foreign and domestic. Etc. Etc. Every activity is politicized. The ownership of property of any significance is a matter for the Party to assign to a government bureau and is administered in the name of the people. This theory of social ownership is why corruption is the rule, not the exception, in communist regimes; why supplies of food and other necessities and amenities of modern civilization such as electricity, soap, and toilet paper are erratic. In countries run according to orthodox Marxist theory where "society" owns the land, food is rationed. Again to use communist Cuba as an example, food has been rationed there ever since all agricultural land was confiscated for "social" ownership. That's sixty successive years, three generations, of food rationing. How many generations does it take to admit the failure of Marxist agricultural theory? (Or is food rationing in Cuba a means of political control?)

Toward the end of Soviet control of the former Russian empire, the necessity for food forced the Communist Party there to allow limited production of food on private plots of land. In 1985, "1.6 percent of the Soviet Union's agricultural land" produced 60% of the potatoes consumed in the USSR, 32% of other vegetables and meat, 30% of the eggs, and 29% of the milk. There were 35 million of these private plots which averaged half an acre in size. (Hedrick Smith, *The New Russians*, Random House 1991, pp. 208–209.)

An orthodox Marxist economy simply cannot be as productive as a free market economy because there is no private initiative and private ownership of property in societies governed by the dogmas of Marxism. In such societies, the state plans everything, and the right to make economic decisions based on a personal assessment of the market and its risks simply does not exist.

In the United States during the 1960s, Students for a Democratic Society and other Marxist front organizations planned and led continual street demonstrations against "American imperialism," which is to say against U.S. military defense of non-communist South Vietnam from military seizure and incorporated into communist North Vietnam. SDS leaders referred to these street demonstrations as "bringing the war home." Sympathetic coverage of the "protests" in the U.S. press and on television and the media's incessant, unfavorable reports on U.S. military actions from the battlefields of South Vietnam were the centerpieces of agitprop in America in the late 1960s and early 70s. The riots of 1968 at the Democrat national convention in Chicago by politically radicalized American youths marked the beginning of that political party's conversion to Political Correctness. A recent piece in *The Wall Street Journal* by one Ted Van Dyk, who attended the 1968 convention and continued to work for Democrat presidential candidates for the next forty-some years, confirms that the Democrat Party has become the party of what he termed "political correctness and conformity" (see Van Dyk, "The Democrats' Biggest Problem Is Cultural," *Wall Street Journal*, July 29, 2017, p. A15).

The withdrawal of U.S. military forces from Vietnam in March of 1973 was a stupendous victory for agitprop in America; and those Americans who made that victory for Marxism in the United States possible by embracing and abetting the foreign policy of the Soviet Union were behaving as dedicated Marxist agents. Even if they were not card-carrying members of the Communist Party USA, their actions implemented policies Moscow wanted implemented. They acted as if they were members of the CPUSA.

It is essential for Americans today, especially younger Americans who were not alive fifty years ago, to understand that the goal of Marxist agitprop in America during the 1960s was not just to force the U.S. military to withdraw from Vietnam. To be sure, that was the immediate pro-Marxist aim of the Counter Culture Movement. But as its name, Counter Culture, suggests, this anti-America movement also had a long-term goal: to replace American cultural beliefs with Marxist dogmas because they unified the people of the States of the United States and were the basis of the foreign policy of the U.S. government to contain communism's global expansion. Ever since its organization and launching on American campuses, the Counter Culture Movement of the 1960s, which was given the name "Political Correctness" in the 1970s *by its opponents*, has striven to create division in American society. Like every one of the communist revolutions of the twentieth century, agitprop in America has as its final aim the replacement of an already-formed, existing culture, in this case America's culture, with the dogmas of Cultural Marxism.

The revolution which has been going on in America for the last half-century, however, is employing a quite different strategy from earlier Marxist revolutions. Instead of overturning the U.S. government by force and taking comprehensive control of the United States all at once, the Counter Culture/Political Correctness Movement has been engaged for the last fifty years in gradually but relentlessly transforming the United States from within little by little, by co-opting its institutions and destroying existing cultural beliefs slowly and methodically, and replacing them with the dogmas of Marxism. This has been a prolonged, incremental revolution. It has been likened to stealing a salami a slice at a time instead of grabbing the whole salami or killing a frog in a pan of water by raising the water's temperature ever so slightly and meticulously. The frog gets used to the slowly rising heat, does not realize it is in deadly danger, and does not jump from the pan as it would if it sensed the danger it is in.

❧

At the end of World War II, two starkly different understandings of history and the nature of man were espoused by two militarily powerful nations, one having a socialist and supposedly "scientific" regime and the other having a capitalist, Christian, constitutional culture. The fundamental inherently different cultures put the Union of Soviet Socialist Republics and the United States of America on a collision course. The ends and the means of Soviet communism and the American way of life were so at odds, and Soviet foreign policy was so aggressive and all-encompassing, that these two immense political entities, one (the Union of Soviet Socialist Republics) an empire of conquered nations extending over the northern half of Asia and all of eastern and half of central Europe and the other (the United States) a nation comparable to the whole continent of Europe in size, which was to become the largest nation in population after China and India, were bound to clash. From its inception in 1922, the USSR had a foreign policy that proposed, as Marxist doctrine said, to "liberate" other countries from the "chains" of capitalism and the "opiate" of belief in God, which inherently made the Soviet Union and the United States cultural enemies. Marxism theoretically intends to bring peace to the world by making its philosophy of materialistic determinism regnant, along with Marx's so-called "scientific" theorems on history and human nature. The United States, conversely, from its inception in 1776 had a culture centered on belief in man's unalienable birthright to life, liberty, the pursuit of happiness, and government by consent of the governed which Americans attributed to the will of God, the omnipotent Creator of heaven and earth and everything in them. The United States hoped other countries would embrace its God-based culture because of America's political and economic success; the Soviet

Union intended to coerce mankind into embracing Cultural Marxism through agitprop and revolution.

When World War II ended in 1945, the United States was the world's third-largest nation in size (considering the Soviet Union to be a nation instead of an empire of conquered nations) and the fifth-largest in population. Today America ranks third in both categories. The United States had then and still has the biggest, most productive national economy the world has ever known. In 1945, America had been politically independent for 169 years and had a culture whose formation predated by several generations its declaration of independence in 1776. The Marxist regime of the Soviet Union, on the other hand, had only been in existence for twenty-three years (1922–1945), though its culture was rooted in the sixteenth-century autocracy of Ivan the Terrible, the first Russian ruler to call himself a Czar, or Caesar. That culture had concentrated all governmental power in the person of the czar in Moscow and had begun the conquest of the largest contiguous empire centered in Europe the world has ever known: the eastern third of Europe and the entire northern half of Asia. The territory of Britain's empire equaled in extent that of the empire the Russian czars, but its colonies were scattered all over the globe and were not contiguous to one another. (The second-largest, contiguous empire in history centered in Europe was that governed from Rome.) The population of 210 million that the Soviet Union claimed to have at the end of World War II made it the fourth-largest population in the world. The current 142.4 million inhabitants of the Russian Federation, which has replaced the Union of Soviet Socialist Republics, is sixth in size among the world's populations.

The Soviet rulers of the former Russian Empire retained one of the most deeply engrained cultural behaviors of the czars: the addition of adjacent territory to their empire. (The USSR was the only European imperialist power to gain rather than lose territory as a result of participating in World War II.) Indeed, the Soviet Union formally allied itself with the National Socialist government of Germany (the Nazis) in August 1939 for the explicit purpose of adding eastern Poland to its empire. That coordinate invasion of Poland by the international totalitarian socialist Stalin and the national totalitarian socialist Hitler started World War II in Europe in September 1939. The next year, Stalin on his own invaded the adjacent Baltic nations of Latvia, Lithuania, and Estonia and parts of Finland and added them to the Soviet empire.

When World War II ended in May of 1945, Stalin by prearrangement with his Western allies Winston Churchill and Franklin Roosevelt (the USSR was also the only major combatant in World War II to switch sides during the war), the Red Army occupied all of Poland, the eastern part of Germany, Czechoslovakia (today's Slovakia and the Czech Republic), and Hungary with the intent of incorporating them into its empire, which it did in 1945–1947. These areas which comprised half of the territory and one-third of the population of Central Europe remained part of the Soviet Empire until shortly before the collapse of the USSR in 1991.

But these Soviet colonies — Czechoslovakia, East Germany, Hungary, and Poland — were not called colonies, of course, because that diction would have branded the Soviet Union an imperialist power; and according to Marxist theory, only capitalist nations are imperialists. Therefore, Soviet propaganda called these Central European colonies of the USSR (Poland, East Germany, Czechoslovakia, and Hungary) "satellites," a brilliant propaganda designation because it suggested the Soviet Union had an irresistible political attractiveness analogous to the gravity of the sun which brought smaller bodies in its vicinity into its orbit and held them there. For the same reason, Soviet propaganda called Central Europe "Eastern Europe" to make it seem that the Red Army had a legitimate reason for occupying and controlling half of Central Europe since "Eastern Europe" was the part of Europe where Russian dominance had historically prevailed. But the truth of the matter was that Soviet imperialism did add half of Central Europe to its empire after World War II, which is readily apparent in the geographical fact that the border separating East and West Germany marking the Red Army's fartherest west line of occupation in Europe was 1,150 miles from Moscow but only 420 miles from London. So successful was Soviet propaganda in masking Soviet colonization of half of Central Europe that even today, a quarter-century after the fall of the Soviet Union, one still finds in Western publications numerous references to Hungary, the Czech Republic, Slovakia, and Poland as "Eastern Europe" when in truth these European nations are *west of Europe's central longitude.* Marxist revolutionaries use agitprop to redefine reality, and they are quite good at it which is why there was a bureau of agitation and propaganda in the Soviet government.

The government of the United States had no cultural compulsion like the desire of the Russian and Soviet czars to conquer and incorporated into their empire as much adjacent territory as opportunity permitted. Had it felt such a cultural compulsion, it could have brought, in the middle of the nineteenth century, the entire continent of North America from the Arctic Circle to the Isthmus of Panama under American rule. Certainly, the opportunity to do so was there, and had the United States acted on it, it would have become one of the biggest empires the world has ever seen. The empire of the Russian czars before its takeover by Marxists encompassed roughly a sixth of the planet's land area. Britain at the height of its empire in the late nineteenth and early twentieth centuries had worldwide possessions encompassing perhaps a quarter of the world's inhabited area and people.

Having in the early 1840s offered to buy Mexico's northern territories and been rebuffed, the United States government in 1846–1848 invaded and occupied that territory militarily, along with the rest of Mexico, including its capital in the southern part of Mexico. After conquering all of Mexico, the U.S. government ordered its military forces to withdraw from present-day Mexico south of the Rio Grande, retaining only the northern territories it had offered to purchase. *Then the United States paid Mexico for the territories it retained.* The

United States could have kept the whole country without making any payment whatsoever. But the United States did not have a culture like Europe's whose imperial powers always expanded their territory to the maximum extent possible without paying for the lands they seized. Which is what the European imperialists expected the U.S. to do in 1848 with regard to conquered Mexico, because it is what they would have done. But the U.S. paid for the land it forced Mexico to surrender.

Similarly, seventeen years later, at the end of the Civil War in 1865, the U.S. government would have been justified in dispatching a sufficient portion of the million men it had under arms to take Canada in reparation for the military aid Britain had given the Confederate States of America during the war, which had prolonged it at an incalculable loss of American lives and treasure, and Britain could not have projected a large enough army into North America to prevent the conquest. Again to the surprise of Europe's imperial powers, America did not seize Canada in 1865.

Had America's culture been like that of imperial Britain, France, Russia, Spain, and the rest of Europe's imperial and former imperial powers in the nineteenth century, the United States was in a position in the middle decades of that century to have militarily established its rule over North America's entire 6.88 million square miles of territory, a territory of grand imperial proportions not unlike the extent of the empires Queen Victoria ruled before World War I and Chairman Stalin ruled after World War II. But America's territorial expansion was culturally self-limiting. Indeed, the world's four largest authentic nations (as distinct from the "Russian Federation" which in truth is the remains of Europe's final great empire) have a natural size of between 3.29 and 3.85 million square miles compared to the Russian Federation's 6.6 square miles. (The Russian Federation's recent military conquests in southern and eastern Ukraine represent the last gasps of an imperial power trying to regain lost territory.) Canada's 3.85 million square miles, America's 3.79, China's 3.7, and Brazil's 3.29

average 3.66 million square miles. The continent of Europe is slightly smaller than Canada.

During the eight generations from 1610 to 1770 in the immense wilderness of the Atlantic Coastal Plain of North America, Americans created a non-European culture, and after winning their independence from British rule in 1783 rapidly settled the much larger Stone Age wilderness to the west of that immense coastal plain between the latitudes of the Great Lakes and the Gulf of Mexico, all the way to the Mississippi; and then, after the accessions of territory between those latitudes in 1803 and 1848, all the way to the Pacific Ocean and, after 1867, Alaska. Title to these immense mostly contiguous land areas was acquired from Mexico and Europe's imperial powers through treaty and purchase. (It is an interesting fact that three of the world's four largest authentic nations: Canada, the United States, and Brazil are in the Western Hemisphere, an indication of how sparsely populated this Hemisphere was when it became known to Europe's imperial powers and they colonized it.) As sections of the North America wilderness after 1783 were civilized and populated by Americans, thirty-seven new American States were added to the original thirteen under the authority of the U.S. Constitution, to create something the world had never seen before: a rapidly growing republic of self-determined States of different sizes but equal sovereignty sharing by consent the same self-determined constitution.

Unlike the French Revolution in the eighteenth century and the communist revolutions of the twentieth century, the so-called American Revolution did not attempt the creation a new culture by force. It was a war for independence, not a revolution, because the defining purpose of a revolution is to force into being a new culture, which naturally provokes a counter-revolution to preserve the culture that existed when the revolution occurred, if it is a sudden change of regime. The so-called American Revolution was an expression of America's set of non-European cultural beliefs which formed slowly and naturally between 1610 and 1770 on the huge Atlantic Coastal

Plain of North America. The formation of that new set of cultural belief-behaviors, which included behaviors based on the belief that "all Men are created equal" in having the same God-given birthright to "Life, Liberty, and the Pursuit of Happiness" and to government by "Consent of the Governed" was the true American revolution, not the war with Britain in 1775–1783.

The chief factor in slowly bringing about the formation of this culture was the concentration in a vast, opportunity-rich geography of millions of ambitious, self-selected immigrants from many nations and Christian denominations of Europe and their American-born offspring. The beliefs which these immigrants to the Atlantic Coastal Plain of North America enculturated through their behavior in the eight generations between 1610 and 1770 emphasized self-determination (see Appendix A). The culture they created rejected the aristocratic cultures of Europe based on belief in ruling classes constituted by "noble" and "royal" blood and the acceptance by the lower classes in Europe of the proposition that some people have superior bloodlines and are entitled to govern persons of inferior birth. As America's non-aristocratic culture formed in the seventeenth and eighteenth centuries, Americans found it increasingly difficult to continue their political deference to a culture based on ruling classes who monopolized arable land and governed because they claimed superior birth, and who maintained their monopoly of arable land and of governmental authority through the practice of primogeniture.

Of the four major areas of European colonization on the two continents of the Western Hemisphere after Columbus's world-changing, transatlantic voyage of 1492–1493 — Brazil, Spanish America, Canada, and the colonies that became the United States — only the latter received a European immigrant population which was self-selected rather than screened for a particular European nationality and Christian religion. As Thomas Paine truly wrote in his essay "Common Sense," published in Philadelphia the same year Americans declared independence from Britain: "Europe, and not England, is the parent country of America." The kings of Spain allowed only Spanish Catholics into their New World colonies. Only Portuguese Catholics could go to Brazil. The monarchs of France permitted only French Catholics to live in Canada during their century and a half of rule which preceded Britain's conquest of that part of North America and its incorporation into the British empire.

In order to build up as large a population as possible in the shortest possible time, the British monarchs, unlike any of Europe's other imperialists, allowed immigrants from any European nationality or religion into their thirteen colonies on the North American mainland. The only restriction put on immigration was that immigrants who were not already subjects of the English crown had to take an oath of allegiance. Besides this unique demographic feature of immigration to colonial America, the future United States had two unique geographical features. It was adjacent to the only territory in the Western Hemisphere of continental dimensions that had a predominately temperate climate and a comparatively high proportion of arable land.

Immigrants to Canada, Brazil, and Spanish America from Europe in the sixteenth, seventeenth, and eighteenth century were joining colonial societies which had the same language as they spoke, the same religious establishment as their European homeland, and the same aristocratic social and political class structure they were culturally accustomed to in Europe. Only the self-selected immigrants to the future United States were entering a truly "new world" where non-European geographical, social, religious, economic, and political conditions existed. This new ambience of novelty with its emphasis on self-determination rather than obedience to a high-born ruling class and established state-church naturally led to the formation of a set of non-European cultural belief-behaviors. (See the chart "Comparative Synopsis of Conditions for Cultural Formation in Spanish America, Brazil, Canada, and the United States" in my *American Beliefs*, p. 35.) The unique combination of conditions that characterized colonial life on the Atlantic Coastal Plain of North America in the 1600s and 1700s compared to Europe and other parts of the Western Hemisphere in those centuries produced by the mid-eighteenth century a culture whose belief-behaviors favored and encouraged freedom of movement, upward social mobility, and the creation of as much property as possible from wilderness in as short a time as possible. This culture also believed in the respectability of manual labor. The central belief of America's new, non-European culture was that all men are created equal in having from God the same birthright, a cultural belief quite unlike the cultural belief in class privileges based on birth that characterized European culture. The self-selected immigrants to America and their American-born descendants who mainly populated the future United States freely associated with one another generation after generation and, if they were not already English speakers, voluntary adopted that language so they would share one language in their common pursuit of their various individual ambitions. The Negro slaves in this society were its great anomaly.

Naturally, America's non-European culture obtained independence from Europe much sooner in its history than any other part of the Western Hemisphere. Everyone knows the United States was the first place in the Western Hemisphere to become independent of Europe. No one, it seems, has considered the far more culturally important fact that Americans gained their independence from European authority much sooner in their history than any other colonial population in the Western Hemisphere. It took the United States just 169 years from the time of the first permanent English-speaking settlement on the Atlantic Coastal Plain to become independent (1607–1776). It took Canada 374 years to become independent of European rule (1608–1982). Brazil required 290 years (1532–1822). The mainland nations of Spanish America, 303 years (1521–1824). Ruling classes of titled noblemen developed in colonial Brazil, colonial Canada, and colonial Spanish America which undoubtedly slowed their attainment of independence from Europe.

Russia like the rest of Europe had an aristocratic culture based on the supposed superiority of one's biological lineage, which the communist revolution of 1917 smashed and replaced with a ruling class based on the purity of one's ideological "line." The role of government in Marxist Russia after 1917 was to create the correct environment to assure the correct ideological outcome ("social" justice) and socio-economico-political behaviors because man, according to Marxist dogma, is, like every other animal species, the result of reactions to the environment.

Because they were primarily looked upon as chattel, or live property, the slaves imported into the future United States from Africa in the late seventeenth and the eighteenth centuries, and the first eight years of the nineteenth century, were denied the cultural birthright the Declaration of Independence proclaimed for "all men," since they were not regarded as men. Their status as chattel took precedence over their human being. Had they been looked upon as human beings having the same God-given human birthright to liberty as their masters, they could not have been held in bondage or bought and sold as property. Nor could their offspring have inherited their slave status and been bought and sold as property. At the sacrifice of perhaps as many as 700,000 American lives, the Civil War of 1861–1865 settled once and for all the cultural question of whether Negroes were endowed with the same God-given birthright as other Americans.

The defeat of the eleven Confederate States that seceded from the Union over the issue of slavery occasioned the ratification of three post-Civil War amendments to the Constitution of the United States. The Thirteenth abolishing slavery in America. The Fourteenth conferring on every freeborn, naturalized, and emancipated Negro American the same freedoms, rights, privileges, and immunities under the Bill of Rights that white freeborn and naturalized Americans enjoyed under the Constitution of the United States. And the Fifteenth granting Negro Americans the essential right of American citizenship to vote, which had to be granted them as American citizens. In each of these amendments to the Constitution, Congress was given power to protect the personal liberties of Negro Americans from infringement by any State. However, in the hundred years following ratification of the XIII, XIV, and XV Amendments, the Fourteenth and the Fifteenth Amendments conferring personal liberties and the right to vote on Negro Americans *were not enforced by the U.S. government* as they should have been. Not until Negro Americans, unified under the non-violent leadership of a Christian minister, the Rev. Martin Luther King, Jr., demanded federal protection and enforcement of their personal liberties, as Americans, did Congress, the president, and the federal courts begin to behave as the Fourteenth and Fifteen Amendments stipulated they were to behave.

In regard to America's relations with other countries after its independence from Europe, the first president elected under the authority of the Constitution of the United States, George Washington, set forth the essentials of American culture in regard to foreign policy. Washington's "Farewell Address" (1796) urged Americans to seek commerce and trade with all nations but advised them to avoid entanglement in their political affairs. Because American culture lacked the Soviet ambition to "liberate" other nations by deliberately imposing American beliefs on them, Washington's culturally congenial recommendation that Americans reject "entangling [political] alliances" with other nations guided U.S. foreign relations for the next 120 years. Then, in 1917, America was bamboozled into participating in a European war. A generation later, in 1941, the United States was attacked by the fascist government of Japan and had to fight a full-fledged war in the Pacific with that country while at the same time leading a coalition of nations in Europe against fascist Germany which had declared war on the United States in fulfillment of its treaty obligation with its ally Japan.

Following U.S. involvement in that global war in 1942–1945, the United States entered into an alliance of free nations on both sides of the North Atlantic to protect Western Europe from Soviet dominance (the North Atlantic Treaty Organization, 1949). Ever since then, the United States has been widely and continually entangled in the political affairs of other nations, usually not to its advantage.

❧

As emphasized earlier, "Political Correctness" is the uninterrupted continuation of the movement to install Cultural Marxism in the United States that began in the 1960s under the name "the Counter Culture." The value American culture gives freedom of speech and association allowed the agitprop of the Counter Culture/Political Correctness Movement to flourish in America. But no equivalent domestic front for anti-Soviet agitation and propaganda could be created by the United States inside the Soviet Union during the Cold War. To be sure, the Constitution of the USSR guaranteed freedom of speech, press, association, and assembly, the same as the U.S. Constitution, but with a tremendous caveat: the exercise of those rights and freedoms had to strengthen Marxism. "In accordance with the interests of the people and in order to strengthen and develop the socialist system, citizens of the USSR are guaranteed freedom of speech, of the press and of assembly, meetings, street processions and demonstrations" (Chapter 7, Article 50, *The Constitution of the Union of Soviet Socialist Republics*). In the same part of the Soviet Constitution, we find that "Citizens of the USSR, in accordance with the aims of building communism, are guaranteed freedom of scientific, technical, and artistic work" (Article 47, Chapter 7).

Other guarantees in Chapter 7 of the Soviet Constitution declared that, "Citizens' exercise of their rights and freedoms is inseparable from the performance of their duties and obligations. Citizens of the USSR are obliged to obey the Constitution of the USSR and Soviet laws, comply with the standards of socialist conduct, and uphold the honor and dignity of Soviet citizenship" (Article 59). Soviet citizens were also obliged by the Constitution of the USSR to "safeguard the interests of the Soviet state, and to enhance its power and prestige"

(Article 62); to be "uncompromising towards anti-social behavior" (Article 65); and to "promote friendship and cooperation with peoples of other lands and help maintain and strengthen world peace" (Article 69). The "world peace" referred to in Article 69 had reference to establishing communist regimes worldwide. Only after that had been accomplished could there be "world peace," according to Marxist theory.

Political Correctness in the United States manifests its Marxist origin partly by its uncompromising dogmatism. This characteristic is a necessity of revolutionary Marxism because, as Lenin pointed out in his book *State and Revolution* (1917), any compromise with or modification of Marxist dogmas would weaken the worldwide Marxist revolution. Maintaining the purity and uniformity of Marxist doctrine was an absolute necessity for the success of the worldwide revolution. Even slight departures from Marxist dogma (referred to in Marxist jargon as "deviationism") would be intolerable. Marxists had to be undeviating in their commitment to the international revolution. Any departure from Marxist dogma and "Party discipline" was a sign of political immaturity, "bourgeois sentimentality," and "defeatism." It could even be considered a symptom of mental derangement requiring treatment in a psychiatric clinic.

For a doctrinaire Marxist, the refusal to "build communism" could easily be viewed as a kind of irrational, anti-science behavior. It is crucial to the understanding of Marxism to note that Marxism for its adherents is not just another political theory. *It's science.* (You may have noticed the tendency of Marxists and their sympathizers in the United States to denounce political opponents as "anti-science" and label them "science deniers.") Whoever opposes the doctrines and dogmas of Karl Marx is manifesting a willful preference for the "superstition" of religion. To a Marxist, science and religion are irreconcilable. Political Correctness as a type of Marxism regards its opponents as mentally deficient and morally corrupt. Under no circumstances should the unscientific views of the opponents of Marxism ever be taken into consideration in making political decisions since their views are entirely worthless and deplorable. Hence in 2010, President Obama's politically correct party (the Democrats) did not consult any Republican member of Congress, as they ought to have done, in drawing up their socialist healthcare bill known as the Patient Protection and Affordable Care Act ("Obamacare").

Another way Political Correctness manifests its Marxist origin is in its intrinsic deceptiveness. Political Correctness represents itself as a champion of fundamental American values. That brazen pretense, that Marxism is identical to American liberalism and progressivism, is why the Counter Culture/Political Correctness Movement has had so much success in the United States.

Political Correctness also shows its Marxist pedigree by provoking its opponents into reacting and then denouncing them as "reactionaries," as if no one has a right to disagree with any aspect of "scientific" Marxism. This is standard Marxist rhetoric.

Yet another reflection of the Marxist origin of Political Correctness is its tendency to provoke a crisis in order to propose a Marxist solution to it; thus increasing the authority and power of the PC movement. Politically correct solutions invariably require the expenditure of enormous sums of money by the U.S. government which of course necessitates an ever-larger bureaucracy to administer the government's "social" justice programs. To Marxists every human problem is material in nature and its amelioration requires only material solutions.

The American Marxist Saul Alinsky (1909–1972) identified himself in the Prologue to his handbook for mounting a Marxist revolution in the United States as a survivor of "the Joe McCarthy holocaust of the early 1950s." *Rules For Radicals: A Pragmatic Primer for Realistic Radicals*, which Alinsky published in 1971 at the outset of the decade in which the Counter Culture/Political Correctness Movement began gaining momentum, typically equates the hearings in the 1950s of U.S. Senator Joseph McCarthy (R-WI) on Soviet spy rings in Washington,

D.C. to Hitler's "holocaust" against the Jews. That assertion illustrates the degree to which Marxists distort truth for political ends.

In reading *Rules for Radicals*, one discovers Alinsky is saying the same thing over and over in different ways, namely that to acquire political power in the United States one must give Americans the impression of sincerely believing in American cultural values. Alinsky's handbook explains that a "radical" must appear to respect "equality, justice, freedom, peace" and to have "a deep concern for the preciousness of human life, and all those rights and values propounded by Judeo-Christianity and the democratic political tradition" (*Rules for Radicals*, Vintage Books, 1989; p. 12). All of this is sham. Saul Alinsky was an atheist. He cared nothing about Judeo-Christianity and its values or "the preciousness of human life." But he knew middle-class Americans did, and taught his followers how to project the appearance of a liberal reverence for those values in order to curry favor with middle-class American voters. One remembers in this regard Barack Obama's Star-Spangled-Banner speech on American patriotism and unity at the 2004 Democrat National Convention which led to his rapid rise in the Democrat Party as its candidate for the U.S. presidency in 2007 and his election to that office.

Saul Alinsky established a center for teaching his rules for Marxist revolution in his hometown of Chicago. He set up the training center under the nondescript name of the Industrial Areas Foundation and used the innocuous term "community organizing" for what was taught there. He called those he trained in subversion, deception, and provocation "community organizers." Alinsky in his handbook for Marxist revolution expresses pride in the tactics he had so astutely and meticulously tailored to play upon the beliefs of American culture. His training center in Chicago has outlived him and continues to this day its work of teaching "community organizing." Alinsky's Political Correctness is designed to give an impression of community improvement, something inherent to America's cultural history. Had

Alinsky been honest, he would have called his training facility in Chicago "The Foundation for Marxist Class Struggle."

Barack Obama got his start in politics after Alinsky's death, by being hired and trained as an instructor in Alinsky's center for teaching "community organizing" (David Freddom, *The Case against Barack Obama*, Regnery, 2008; pp. 139–143). His election as president of the United States in 2007 after his rapid rise from community organizer in Chicago to the Illinois legislature, to the U.S. Senate, and then presidential nominee was made possible by decades of agitprop in America harping on racism and applying Alinsky's rule of pretending to revere American cultural beliefs while manipulating them for purposes of Marxist revolution.

The Soviet Union disappeared from the world's political map the last week of December 1991 (some authorities give December 26 as the precise date; others, December 31). But the agitprop front established inside the United States in the 1960s did not vanish with the collapse of the USSR. It is still going strong today. And the strategies for deceiving the American middle class that Alinsky taught and published in his *Rules for Radicals* are still being employed to bring about the fundamental "transformation" of the United States that Obama promised his presidency would establish. Where Political Correctness holds sway, the persons who promote its dogmas regard themselves as above the law. Their correct politics is the law as far as they are concerned. Where Political Correctness prevails, only its opponents are liable to prosecution under the law.

But how should we identify the anti-America Americans who have been working so hard for such a long time to "transform" the United States? They want to be called "progressives." But that is a ruse. Theodore Roosevelt was a progressive, and I don't think his old-fashioned America-first patriotism or his profound respect for Judeo-Christian morality would have inclined him to associate with the likes of Bill Ayers, Joe Biden, Noam Chomsky, William Jefferson and Hillary Rodham Clinton, Raul Grijalva, the late Ted Kennedy,

John Kerry, Loretta Lynch, Barack and Michele Obama, Nancy Pelosi, Harry Reid, Bernie Sanders, Maxine Waters, or any other American having politically correct views. Even less should the Americans who have been working nonstop for decades to impose Cultural Marxism on the United States be called "liberals" as Alinsky taught his "community organizers" to call themselves to make it seem that they were true-blue Americans who believed in American cultural values. Using the term "liberal" to label these agitators is part of their disguise to conceal their anti-Americanism.

Anti-America Americans do not deserve to be called liberals because they don't believe in equal civil and criminal justice for all, the sanctity of human life, free speech, freedom of religion, majority rule, political compromise, or tolerance — all of which are highly valued by liberals. One has only to recall the tactics Democrat President Obama, Democrat Speaker Nancy Pelosi, and Democrat Senate Majority Leader Harry Reid employed in 2010 to ram the Patient Protection and Affordable Care Act through Congress to see that such persons and their sympathizers do not deserve to be called liberals. The mistake of applying the term liberal to Americans who promote "social" justice and government by elites (Political Correctness) is easily made, however, since most recruits to the Counter Culture/Political Correctness Movement have come, it seems, from the ranks of American liberals who apparently do not perceive the nature and purpose of Political Correctness. Liberals who embrace Political Correctness cease, of course, to be liberals the moment they become politically correct.

Perhaps we should just categorize these anti-America Americans as "Leftists" and let it go at that. I don't think so. That classification for the self-righteous zealots who have been assaulting American culture for half a century is too namby-pamby. These agitators and propagandists ought to bear a name appropriate to the grave damage they have done to American cultural beliefs, a name which identifies their status as agents of subversion in America, whether knowingly or as dupes.

Well, then, what should they be called? They should, I think, be called PC Marxists and their politics should be identified as PC Marxism.

PC Marxists in America want what Marxists in the Soviet Union wanted. They want Cultural Marxism, one-party government, total dependence on Big Government, government regulation of every aspect of life, "social" justice and government "entitlements" for those who obey their dictates. PC Marxists manipulate fear of losing government "entitlements" to increase their power and control. PC Marxists lack an America First outlook. PC Marxists put loyalty to Political Correctness above the national interest. PC Marxists claim only their views are worth respecting. PC Marxists are uncompromisingly partisan. PC Marxists regard their opponents as wrong on every issue because they're stupid.

The elitist mentality of PC Marxists readily embraces "crony capitalism" and sees nothing wrong with using government officeholding for personal profit and plunder, the same as Soviet apparatchiks did. They regard the U.S. Constitution as meaning whatever they need it to mean to advance their political agenda, and equate being in federal office with being "in power," a term they enjoy using and getting others to use, even though the only people in power under the U.S. Constitution are the people of the States. (The persons the people of the States put in office to serve them are just "in office.") PC Marxists think they alone are capable of compassion and know what other people need.

Perhaps the most damaging of the PC dogmas is the idea of "Separation of Church and State" which PC Marxists are using with great effectiveness to destroy Christianity in America. This destruction is the most important long-range item on their agenda as revolutionaries because belief in God is the cornerstone of American culture while atheism is the cornerstone of Marxism.

PC Marxists go about in the guise of respectable, middle-class Americans, scoff at the belief that there is a God-given birthright of life, liberty, and the pursuit of happiness, and reject belief in America's Judeo-Christian morality. They do not believe in the ideal of equal justice for all that American school kids used to pledge allegiance to at the beginning of each school day, before PC Marxists (in the name of freedom, of course) made reciting the Pledge of Allegiance optional. Instead of believing in equal justice for all, PC Marxists and their sympathizers relentlessly insist on "social" justice.

PC Marxists and their sympathizers characterize life in America as "unfair" and demand that the slightest wrinkle of unfairness in the social fabric of America be ironed out, no matter how much money must be borrowed to fund the ironing—vast sums of money which future generations of Americans will have to pay interest on without ever benefiting from them. Is that "fair"?

Hypocrisy is inherent to PC Marxism, and running a close second to it as PC Marxism's identifying attitudinal marker is paranoia, the sense of being conspired against by their "enemies" whom they regard as everyone who refuses to accept their dogmas.

The middle-class Americans who've been persuaded to sympathize with PC Marxism have been duped into believing that Political Correctness represents a more genuine form of democracy, equality, and freedom than American culture. This pretense accounts for much of the hideous strength of Political Correctness, or PC Marxism, in America.

PC Marxists are not grateful to be Americans. They are grateful they're not bigots, homophobes, misogynists, racists, and xenophobes full of greed and hate like everyone who disagrees with them.

# A 1970 Interview with Three Counter Culture Agitators

FTER GETTING MY PHD in 1966, I took a teaching job as an Assistant Professor at the University of Wisconsin-Madison. Without knowing it, I was going to one of the two epicenters of the Counter Culture Movement in the Midwest, the other being the University of Michigan. On the West Coast the University of California-Berkeley served that purpose and on the East Coast, Columbia University. I do not believe this evenly spaced distribution of well-known liberal universities for spreading agitprop in the east, the middle, and the west of a big country was mere coincidence, any more than the counter culture's use across the entire breadth of the world's third-largest nation of identical slogans and chants was a coincidence. "Question authority!" "Don't trust anyone over thirty!" "Do your own thing!" "Make love not war!" "One, two, three, four, we don't want your f***** war!" "Hey, hey, LBJ, how many babies you killed today?" The use of these chants and slogans from one end to the other of the United States, in conjunction with the even-spacing of four major centers for agitprop, suggest planning for a nationwide campaign of agitation and propaganda against U.S. military involvement in Vietnam and against America's cultural beliefs to undermine the anti-communist foreign policy of the United States.

Where that planning took place and who the planners were, is impossible to say. But whoever orchestrated the Counter Culture Movement on the campuses of American colleges and universities in the 1960s evidently was experienced in the techniques of agitprop and how to employ them. And whoever did the planning for the Counter Culture campaign in America in the 1960s had a vested interest in undermining America's culture not only because it was the basis of support for the war in Vietnam but for America's whole post-World War II policy of worldwide opposition to communist expansion. The immediate traction that the Counter Culture had among middle-class American college students in the 60s indicates that the movement's tactics represented years of high-level professional analysis of the dynamics of America's culture. American culture has been under persistent assault ever since the 1960s. And the attacks have been amazingly successful. Ten years ago, few Americans would have believed that "same-sex marriage" (note how deftly this term finesses the phrase "homosexual marriage") would ever be considered a constitutional right in America. Five years ago, no one would have predicted a day would come in America when it would be possible for biological males to claim to have a constitutional right to use toilets, dressing rooms, and showers belonging to biological females just because they said they had the sensibilities of a female, and get away with it.

Normal minds of course find it difficult to believe in a "culture war" that has gone on for half a century and that aims to transform the world's oldest, most successful republic into a center for Cultural Marxism. Because the project is so audacious, it has taken many middle-class Americans a long time to believe such a movement exists; and many middle-class Americans apparently still refuse to believe a systematic assault is underway on American culture and has been going on in America for fifty years. But whether you believe it or not, a culture war is in progress in America, as evidenced by the fact that many Americans now prefer the dogmas of Marxism to the beliefs of America's culture (cf. Appendix A and Appendix B).

Marxian disdain for the concept of American exceptionalism now typifies classroom instruction in American colleges and universities and public schools. Half a century of incessant agitprop has likewise diminished belief in God in America and knowledge of the Constitution of the United States. The understanding of free markets and the desire to lead a self-determined life independent of Big Government have also been noticeably diminished in the last five decades. As these vital aspects of America's culture have been undergoing "change" under incessant ideological pummeling by agitprop, the government of the United States has acquired habits and attitudes reminiscent of the regulatory totalitarianism of Soviet "democracy." And in recent decades, there have been too many instances of federal officials in Washington using the information they have as members of the government for personal profit, which was a commonplace trait of the one-party Soviet state. The increasing dependence of American citizens on Big Government "entitlements" also smacks of life in the former Soviet Union. Perhaps only Americans old enough to have lived part of their adult lives before the 1960s are in a position to be aware of these changes to the American way of life.

Saddest of all, I think, the forgiveness for the slavery in U.S. history — forgiveness which the Rev. Martin Luther King, Jr., by his example and oratory in the 1950s and 1960s, persuaded both white Americans and Negro Americans to recognize the need for — has been replaced by an accusation that the lives of Negro Americans do not matter to white Americans. Agitprop accusations today about racism are so strident it's as if Martin Luther King, Jr. had never lived and the old Jim Crow laws that once existed in the South and demeaned Negro Americans had never been repealed and racism today is the same as it was during the days of Jim Crow. Americans are being told by PC agitprop not to believe what they can see with their own eyes in workplaces and schools: the manifestations of friendship, respect, and courtesy between Negro and white Americans that now exist.

In a 1990 poll, 63% of non-black Americans said they would be very or somewhat opposed to a close relative marrying a Negro American; in 2016, when that same question was asked in a poll, only 14% of non-black Americans said they would be opposed to such a marriage. In 1967 in the United States, interracial nuptials accounted for just 3% of new marriages; now they account for 17%, a more than fivefold increase (*Wall Street Journal*, May 19, 2017, p. A3). Despite all of this, PC Marxists insist there has been little change in the degree or extent of racism in America compared to what it was sixty years ago and that the federal government must adopt more thorough draconian measures to curb it. (PC Marxists say that the only real change in racism in America is that it has become more subtle.) Whatever their skin color, Americans ought to remember it was not the federal government that organized and manned the movement Martin Luther King, Jr. led in the 1950s and 1960s. That movement was of, by, and for the Americans most afflicted by racism: Negro Americans. It was *their* non-violent, Christian solution to a deeply rooted, historic problem in the United States; and white, middle-class American Christians eventually supported the justice of their cause and came to admire King's non-violent method of pursuing it. That eventual support was essential to the great success of the Civil Rights Movement which Negro Americans conducted in their country in the 1950s and 60s.

In regard to the question of whether a culture war has been going in the United States since the 1960s, I understand why so many Americans refuse to believe it. When I first heard in 1970 that a revolution was underway in America, I did not believe it. The first time I heard this said was in Madison, Wisconsin, one morning in 1970 as I and my Cuban wife were driving into work and I picked up a hitchhiker. He was the purveyor of the news as he boasted that he and his fellow rioters on the campus of the University of Wisconsin were "starting a revolution." As my wife and I listened to him — as I recall his boasts were quite matter of fact — neither she nor I believed him. A revolution in America? Be serious. We had lived through the Cuban

Revolution from a distance (we were living in Hawaii in 1958–1960) by experiencing vicariously what was happening to Ony's family in Cuba. We knew how fundamentally different the political, economic, and social situation in the United States was compared to Cuba's. The United States was eighty times bigger than Cuba and had the world's most prosperous national economy, a widely revered constitution, and many stable social, political, and economic institutions. We both thought it was surreal that this young hitchhiker would call the rioting on the University of Wisconsin campus, though it had gone on for weeks, a "revolution."

But as events have unfolded in the United States since 1970, and I've observed them from the perspective of the cultural historian I've become, I have to agree with that boastful young hitchhiker. A revolution was underway in America when he said it was. Not a shoot-'em-up revolution such as people usually think of when they hear that word but a slow-motion upheaval involving many forms of coercion and powered by indefatigable agitation and propaganda: a revolution relentlessly focused on slowly but surely changing America's cultural beliefs, the set of convictions Americans have historically lived by and acted on. I was unable to conceive of such a revolution in 1970. In my mid-thirties then, I had not yet become a cultural historian or read Lenin's 1902 book *What Is To Be Done?* advocating "agitprop" as the way to prepare for the communist takeover of czarist Russian which occurred in 1917 (the first syllables of the words for agitation and propaganda are the same in Russian and English). Nor had I read the American Marxist Saul Alinsky's handbook for incremental revolution, *Rules for Radicals,* which was not yet published in 1970.

I had, however, by 1970 acquired some knowledge of Marxism in action from living in post-revolutionary Cuba the summer of 1960, a year and a half after Cuban Marxists came into power there. I had learned that summer, which Ony and I spent visiting her family in Havana whom she had not seen for two years, how shamelessly deceptive Marxist propaganda can be, and therefore had a sort of intuition in 1970 that the rioting I was witnessing in Madison, Wisconsin, and then "protesting" I was hearing of on other U.S. campuses were not altogether spontaneous events but might be the results of some sort of coordinated planning.

A few days after Ony and I spoke with the self-proclaimed revolutionary hitchhiker, the principal newspaper in the Wisconsin capital, *The Capital Times*, published a lengthy taped interview with three of the Madison rioters. I have preserved my copy of that interview, which appeared on May 7, 1970, starting at the top of the newspaper's front page, and I am going to summarize it here, in this book, because I think it still offers a revealing insight into the nature of agitprop in America.

To get the three rioters to speak frankly with him, Jim Hougan, *The Capital Times* reporter who conducted the interview, promised them anonymity and assigned them pseudonyms. He characterized "Bonnie," the daughter of a big-city cop, as "long, blonde, and lovely." "Jeff" was the name he gave a Californian active in the Weathermen, the violent wing of Students for a Democratic Society, and Black Liberation, another radical organization known for violence. "Charlie" was the son of wealthy parents who had, he said, "dragged" him all over the United States and the world, facts which suggest that "Charlie" was very likely the son of an executive in an American corporation with international interests who moved around a lot. Though all three of the interviewees were of college age and lived in a neighborhood in Madison where many university students rented rooms ("the Mifflin Street ghetto," as it was called), none of them was enrolled as a student at the University of Wisconsin.

They identified themselves as "street people" and "druggies," and joked with the reporter that taking drugs was part of their "revolution." They obviously had rejected the work ethic of American culture in favor of another "life style." (In 1970, this now-ubiquitous, agitprop term lifestyle had just been invented and was not yet spelled as one word.) Jeff scorned the Young Socialist Alliance, he said, because its members "read Marx and Lenin from an historical standpoint instead of how to use it [for] what they're doing." Charlie said liberals made him "sick to my stomach" and called them "our enemies as much as the rest of the pigs." Charlie's contempt for liberals is noteworthy as indicative of the mindset of PC Marxists before Saul Alinsky taught them the usefulness of pretending to be liberals.

It is also important to note, I think, that these three college-age agitators said they did not want to be referred to as rioters in the newspaper piece *The Capital Times* would publish. They told Hougan to call them "trashers" and to refer to what they were doing as "trashing." These terms are politically significant for two reasons. First, they show how agitprop invents new language to create new perceptions; second, the terms trashing and trashers are loaded with Marxist theory. "Trashing" implies that burning cars and smashing the plate glass windows of banks and stores with lengths of heavy chain — the kind of violence going on in Madison in 1970 — was justified because private property in the U.S. represented the ill-gotten gains of "capitalism" and "American imperialism." From the perspective of Marxist theory, private property was "trash" because it represented the spoils of an immoral, "exploitive" economic system. Hence, destroying property should be referred to as "trashing," and those who did such useful work should be called "trashers." Bonnie, Jeff, and Charlie saw themselves as Marxist revolutionaries "doing their thing": the needful job of taking out the trash. This sort of diction put their violence in the righteous political context of Marxism without using any reference to Marx or Marxism.

When *The Capital Times* reporter asked Charlie, "Are you a Marxist?" he replied, "I think most of us are anarcho-communists ... we believe in a communistic sort of life style, but we're anarchists at heart, too." He elaborated on this idea by saying, "We're into as little government as possible. Just enough to supply people with their needs: for free." Bonnie agreed. "Yeah, it's a thing of just being free, you know, anyway you can. And whatever you have to do to get your freedom, that's what you got to do." Jeff added: "The idea is to keep opening new battle fronts. We're in the heart of the motherland [of capitalism] and that's where — you know Che Guevara said he wished he could come back here, man, because you could do a helluva lot of damage here."

Marxist agitprop had persuaded this trio of young Americans that their country was not the land of freedom and opportunity Americans said it was, and that it was their duty to free the United States from the chains of capitalism, not just for the sake of their own liberty but for the sake of everyone in the world that "American imperialism" was "exploiting." Capitalism, they had been persuaded, was the great exploiter while Marxism was the great liberator. Marxism if it were given a chance would provide free stuff for everyone, everywhere. "From each according to his ability, to each according to his needs" was a promise Marx and Engels made in their 1848 *Communist Manifesto* about life in a communist future. These three young Americans apparently thought of themselves as fighters in a revolutionary struggle to establish the ideas of Marxism in America.

When the reporter asked Bonnie, Jeff, and Charlie whether the rioting in Madison, Wisconsin, was the result of a conspiracy, they indignantly denied that possibility. "There ain't no such thing," Jeff declared. "I don't know where [the cops] got that idea." Charlie said, "There's no ******* conspiracy, man." Bonnie made the most telling point. She said there wasn't any *need* to conspire. "People just know [what to do]. They just know." Charlie concurred. "The way it's been going the last few months, people know to bring their chain and their nightstick with them under their coat and their mask. Nobody has to talk about [it] — we go. People can sense it. There's no talk. There was no plan for that last action, no plan for trashing." The riot on April 18, 1970 in Madison that Charlie was referring to destroyed an estimated hundred thousand dollars worth of property; and one of the biggest arsons in Wisconsin's capital that spring was a million-dollar blaze that burned down a supermarket in the Mifflin Street "ghetto" that radical students said was "ripping them off." Charlie rounded off his comments backing Bonnie's point by saying, "We don't hold meetings or anything... there's no conspiracy or pre-planning."

It should be pointed out here that in the sixteen months from January 1969 through April 1970 some 5,000 bombings occurred in the United States, according to Kenneth J. Heineman (*Put Your Bodies Upon the Wheels: Student Revolt in the 1960s*, Ivan R. Dee, 2001; p. 170), an average of around ten bombings a day across the United States for most of a year and a half. Violence was an integral part of the Counter Culture in its early days before the movement — having gained the momentous victory of forcing U.S. troops to withdraw from Vietnam — switched to social and governmental coercion of the sort Kimberley Strassel describes in her recently published *The Intimidation Game* (Twelve, 2016; see especially Chapter 19 which features events in Wisconsin in the last few years).

Further questioning of the three "trashers" by *The Capital Times* reporter revealed that although there might not be a single command center directing the destruction of property in Madison in 1970, there were "affinity groups" of three or four persons who knew and trusted each other which made them invulnerable to police infiltration. And these "affinity groups" (Lenin would have called them "revolutionary cells") did communicate with each other and did coordinate their actions. Again, Marxist revolutionary ideas were being expressed in novel language.

Once agitprop convinced enough young Americans like this trio that the United States was guilty of "imperialism" and that action was needed to eliminate American capitalism and imperialism, everyone in the Counter Culture Movement knew what they were supposed to do, which was Bonnie's point which Charlie elaborated. They had to attack U.S. capitalism and imperialism by destroying private property in America. The conviction that America was guilty of "imperialism" determined and justified their conduct. Similarly, in recent years, once the idea spreads among militant young Muslims that infidels have to be killed in the name of Allah, the killing of infidels in the name of Allah follows without any direct orders for particular murders. The same is true of the recent agitprop that American police are murdering young Negro American males which has led to the slaying of policemen.

When asked whether "the role of the police" in Madison — the attempt to suppress the rioting and arsons through arrests and calling in the Wisconsin National Guard — had contributed to the success of the "trashings," Charlie said: "Oh, absolutely. I mean they deserve an academy award for making the revolution. After the war we'll give them all big gold caps to wear. Without them we couldn't do it. They should be commended. The media, too, deserves an Oscar. I mean they built it." Jeff chimed in, saying: "Like, man, when we push this city up so far that they have to call in the National Guard, that's it, man, because there they go — in the national press. And you just build it out of proportion. It's the stupidest thing Mayor Dyke, I mean [Governor] Knowles, can do is call in the National Guard because it just makes us look all the better. And you get all the liberals to say 'Ah, police brutality, and all that stuff,' you know, which really helps us." Charlie added: "What can they do? If they don't call them [the National Guard] then we'll do our job — even better. They're losing. They can't win. We've got them coming and going." (This is the Alinsky tactic of provoking your enemy to react and making his reaction the issue.)

Charlie said: "Right now people are trashing out windows, next week they may be trashing pigs" (i.e. killing policemen and guardsmen). He explained: "Trashing, for one thing, gives people … confidence. And then they can do bigger and better things." "The job of revolutionaries in the mother country is to bring it down, to create pandemonium and chaos." "The empire is falling here. Everything is falling. And if we don't win, we'll at least bring this country down. We'll destroy it, and everybody can cry on the ashes because it's not going to be here any more."

Jim Hougan asked his three informants what they thought would be "an effective deterrent to trashing." Charlie's answer was simple and emphatic: "Total surrender."

The United States did totally surrender by pulling its troops out of South Vietnam after years of intense agitprop and widespread violence on the home front. Once this important agitprop victory had been obtained, the Counter Culture turned its attention to taking over American institutions, especially U.S. public schools, and condemning the history and culture of America.

Agitprop in the last fifty years by relentlessly "trashing" America's history and culture, by creating an all-encompassing biological class consciousness in America, and by making it seem that Marx's credo of materialistic determinism, "secularism," and "social" justice represents a superior set of convictions compared to American culture's belief in God, Judeo-Christian morality, and justice for all has made the Counter Culture/Political Correctness Movement a greater threat today to America than it was in the 1960s. By slowly replacing American cultural beliefs with Marxist dogmas, agitprop is destroying America's culture and rebuilding it as Cultural Marxism.

$$*$$

Following World War II, Soviet propaganda developed three enormous lies addressed to three distinct audiences.

To the inhabitants of the Soviet Union, the Big Lie was, "You never had it so good." That populace was not permitted to speak publicly about the ideological nature of justice in the Soviet Union or the tens of millions of Soviet citizens who had been executed or sent to forced labor camps because their political views did not conform to Marxist dogmas. Nor were they permitted to openly discuss the disaster of applying Marxist dogmas regarding how farmland had to be owned and worked which transformed the Ukraine from Europe's breadbasket (its largest producer and exporter of wheat) into a region of dire famine where millions of emaciated, unburied corpses littered the rural roadsides: the bumper crop of starvation produced by sowing Marxist theory. Applied Marxism in the Soviet Union caused more deaths than Nazi armies.

To the free nations of the world, the propaganda line was, "You are no better than we are." You, too, only pretend to be democracies when in reality you are run by greedy capitalist profiteers, war-mongering imperialists, and power-hungry politicians. You, too, are materialists. We, at least, have a high, humanitarian goal in mind — eventual world peace and social justice — a noble end to the unavoidably sordid means we must use to accomplish that end. You have no noble goal. You're the moral equivalent to us.

The Big Lie to the world's poor — the so-called Third World — was, "Only by following the example of the Marxist countries can you obtain freedom and prosperity." Your conversion to Marxism will make it possible for peace to reign in the world and the exploitation and oppression of the poor by the rich to cease forever. Only through the global triumph of Marxism will a new day for humanity dawn. You should hasten the coming of that day by becoming dedicated, disciplined Marxists or tolerating those in your midst who do become active Marxists.

Projecting such Big Lies as these and promising a new world order based on them were the distinguishing features of the agitprop which took over the empire of the Russian czars in 1917 and established the USSR in 1922, a regime, which collapsed in 1991. Such Big Lies have also been the distinguishing features of the agitprop which has been undermining the culture of the United States for the last fifty years and replacing it with the dogmas of Cultural Marxism. Grandiose appeals to human idealism, in the guise of "scientific" truth, is the hallmark of Marxism. But, of course, it is Marxism's disregard for truth and reality that is also its main weakness. For sooner or later human beings grow weary of living a lie and having to hate fellow human beings as enemies of humanity because their politics differs from that of Marxism. In the long run, human beings require something more than hatred of "capitalists" and "imperialists" as the way to salvation. They require the spiritual nourishment and forgiveness which comes through the Word from on high, the Word deriving from the Creator of the Universe who tells us we are his creations whom he has endowed with a semblance of his own capacity for choosing to do good.

Political Correctness in the last half-century has infiltrated and co-opted institution after institution in the United States and has influenced the thought and feeling of countless Americans like "Charlie," "Bonnie," and "Jeff." In the early years of the present century, the influence of agitprop managed to put an ultra-suave, second-generation PC Marxist in the White House (Barack Obama, b. 1961).

Nonetheless, multiparty elections continue to be held in the United States of America, and the result of the 2016 presidential election shows that county by county, State by State, American voters still find the beliefs of American culture more endearing than the dogmas of Cultural Marxism. Ultimate power is still vested where it has always been by America's culture, in the people of the States and the U.S. Constitution. Though badly battered in recent decades, the Constitution of the United States is still intact. By far the most significant fact to bear in mind, however, in contemplating America's future, is that the main citadel of orthodox Marxist power in the world, the Union of Soviet Socialist Republics, is no more. It has disintegrated. The government of the USSR collapsed more than a generation ago despite its totalitarian control of the Soviet Union and its one-party system of governing.

But American Marxists and their collaborators in America deny the failure of Marxism in the USSR. Yes, they do. They even deny that Political Correctness is a Marxist movement traceable to the 1960s.

Americans on the PC Marxist end of the political spectrum told me not long after the collapse of the USSR in December 1991 that it wasn't communism which had failed in the Soviet Union. Communism has yet to be tried there, you see. What failed in the Soviet Union was "*Stalinism*"!

Fellow professors of mine at the University of Arizona in Tucson, Arizona who were Marxist sympathizers actually told me shortly after the dissolution of the USSR, "*Communism has yet to be tried in Russia.*" It took only a few weeks for that preposterous line of propaganda to be formulated (somewhere) and transmitted (somehow) to the University of Arizona campus to be repeated to anyone who would listen to it.

The refusal to admit defeat typifies the mentality of hardcore PC Marxists.

PART II

# THE LEXICON

# Commentary on Politically Correct Language as a Means of Revolution

AGITATION in combination with propaganda (agitprop) is essential to Political Correctness, which can also be referred to as PC Marxism. Both of these terms refer to the dogmatic use of "correct" language to control perceptions, and thus behavior. Without the manipulation of language to produce a desired perception, communist regimes could never get established or last very long once established. Language has an influence on human perceptions, feelings, thoughts, and behavior as fundamental as physical conditions. American culture, which like all cultures is a set of historical beliefs continuously expressed in and transmitted through *behavior* generation after generation, has been changed fundamentally by agitprop since the 1960s without being destroyed by it.

From the 1960s down to the present, politically correct language, dogmatically insisted on and strictly enforced, has moved Americans in the direction of Cultural Marxism. PC Marxism has gained influence by altering American speech, a process that will continue until Americans come to understand that Political Correctness is not a harmless, transient phenomenon but rather a deeply dangerous movement dedicated to destroying America's culture and rebuilding it as Cultural Marxism, no matter how long that may take. Until Americans understand what's happening inside their nation, the transformation of American culture will continue until nothing but a memory of it is left among the oldest Americans, and with their deaths even that will vanish. Because of agitprop's success in America, the U.S. could be the last place where Marxist dogmas are actually believed and acted on. In the former Soviet empire, Marxism has certainly been rejected.

PC Marxists have used, and still use, three techniques to change American speech. (1) The invention of new words. (2) The redefinition of fundamental words like freedom, marriage, equality, gender, patriotism, religion, etc. (3) Censorship.

To illustrate (1), the invention of new vocabulary, let me call to your attention these examples. Before the Counter Culture/Political Correctness Movement became firmly entrenched in America in the 1970s, no major Negro American leader ever used the term "African American." Not Frederick Douglass (1817?–1895); not Booker T. Washington (1856–1915) — both of these men had slave mothers and thus were also slaves (servile status inherited at birth is the special curse of chattel slavery); not W. E. B. Du Bois (1868–1963), a founder of the National Association for the Advancement of Colored People; not the eminent Negro American scholar John Hope Franklin (1915–2009), author of *From Slavery to Freedom: A History of Negro Americans* which during his life had six editions before the term African American was substituted for the term Negro American in its title; not Martin Luther King, Jr. (1929–1968), the principal leader of the Negro American civil rights movement of the 1950s and 60s.

"African American" is the agitprop substitute for "Negro American." PC Marxists and their sympathizers have insisted on the substitution because it keeps both white and Negro Americans constantly aware that most Negro Americans have remote ancestors brought to America from Africa in chains as slaves. "Negro" and "Negro American" are, respectively, merely terms of racial and national identification, but "African American" is a term of alienation loaded with overtones of "victimization." It implies that Negro

Americans are not really Americans but persons from Africa forced to live in America, almost as if the slave trade between Africa and the American continents was still going on.

It should be noted in this regard that there was no big exodus of Negro Americans from the United States to Africa after the Thirteenth Amendment to the Constitution abolished chattel slavery in the United States. Nor was there any mass exodus to Africa prior to that abolition when only some 17,000 of the approximately 100,000 freeborn Negro Americans then living in the United States availed themselves of the American Colonization Society's offer to pay for resettling freeborn Negro Americans in Africa. If a person's nationality is judged by the percentage of their ancestry born in the nation where they choose to reside, then Negro Americans are more American than most white Americans because African slaves were no longer imported into the United States after 1808 (Article I, Section 9, U.S. Constitution) whereas the massive immigrations of Europeans to the United States occurred generations after 1808.

In making the switch from the use of "Negro American" to the usage "African American," the term black, as in Black Power and Black Panthers, and then the term Afro-American were briefly used. But the aim from the beginning in making this change to American speech appears to have been to replace the customary designation Negro American with "African American." And that goal has been thoroughly achieved. Anyone today who dares (as I do) to continue using the respectful, truthful, traditional term Negro American, as Martin Luther King, Jr., John Hope Franklin, W. E. B. Du Bois, Booker T. Washington, and Frederick Douglass all did, is immediately labeled "a racist" which is absurd unless one is prepared to categorize the Rev. Martin Luther King, Jr. as a "racist."

Another noteworthy example of deliberately altering American speech for political purposes is the substitution of "migrant" for "illegal alien." A wholly factual designation, "illegal alien" identifies a non-American (an alien) who is in the United States in violation of

U.S. immigration laws. But that factual term is unsuitable to the revolution being conducted in America by PC Marxists. Consequently, the term illegal alien has been transformed, first by substituting "undocumented immigrant" for the term illegal alien and then changing the term undocumented immigrant to "immigrant" by dropping the adjective undocumented; and then clipping the first syllable of the word immigrant to produce "migrant" which has absolutely no connotation of anything illegal and is now the standard term of reference among American academics, bureaucrats, commentators, journalists, and politicians in regard to an illegal alien. A further alteration of language in reference to illegal aliens is in progress: the replacement of "migrant" with the term "entrant." An American tourist returning home from Europe could be designated as an "entrant," and that term is now being applied to an illegal alien walking into Arizona across the Sonora Desert from Mexico.

Yet another example of this sort of deceptive language is the replacement of the pejorative term homosexuality with the scientific-sounding phrase "sexual orientation," something everybody may be presumed to have. The phrase sexual orientation entirely changes the tenor of discourse about a homosexual person or act. Use of the term "sexual orientation" in reference to homosexuality eliminates every hint of deviant behavior because all human beings may be thought to have a "sexual orientation." This phrase completely transforms the term homosexuality and removes it from any overtone of disapproval.

(2) In the category of redefining words, we find that bureaucrats in the executive branch of the federal government making regulations having the weight and force of law are calling themselves "regulators," a term which conceals the fact that Congress has created an illicit "Administrative State" that is performing the legislative function which the Constitution in Article I, Section 1 assigns exclusively to the Congress the people of the States elect. Congress has delegated, without the consent of the people of the States, their duty to make the nation's laws. Without constitutional warrant, Congress has

made unelected "regulators" into legislators, in violation of the Constitution's first requirement. "All legislative Powers herein granted shall be vested in a Congress of the United States, which shall consist of a Senate and House of Representatives." American speech has been fundamentally perverted by calling legislators "regulators." The "Administrative State" is a constitutional abomination because it is the spawn of illicit amendments to the Constitution. Not only that but the "Administrative State" executes the laws it illicitly makes and judges and punishes the violations of its laws. Thus the "Administrative State" combines in itself all three functions of government — legislative, executive, judicial — a concentration of power the framers of the Constitution of the United States consistently forbade because it promotes tyranny. Our Constitution was written to keep the legislative, executive, and judicial powers of government separate in order to protect the God-given rights and liberties of Americans.

We now have within the constitutional government the people of the States have authorized an unconstitutional government which the elected Congress and president and the appointed federal judges have created in defiance of the Constitution. Agitprop has been influential in bringing about this perversion of constitutional government in America, a development that much resembles the authoritarian, one-party government of the former Soviet Union. Today, hundreds of thousands of unelected bureaucrats in Washington (the "Administrative State") have a legislative authority akin to Congress, a judicial authority like that of the federal courts, and an executive ability that exceeds the president's, because the "Administrative State" makes the laws it executes and adjudicates them, something no president has done because doing that would make him an un-reelectable dictator. The "Administrative State" is an illegitimate parallel government. The noble term lawmaker has been redefined by Congress, the president, and the federal courts as "regulator."

The American cultural belief that all human beings have from God, their creator, the same birthright to life, liberty, the pursuit of

happiness, and government by consent of the governed is being redefined by the PC Marxists who want Americans to be beholden to government for their rights. Politically correct dogma makes American
rights the gift of government.

Political Correctness is redefining liberty to mean liberation from
the Ten Commandments which God conveyed to mankind through
revelation to be a guide for human freedom.

Likewise, the sense of being "entitled" to receive government benefits is replacing the American belief that human beings are responsible
for making their own way in the world, though Jews and Christians
are obligated by the moral teachings of their religions to help persons
incapable of helping themselves. "Entitled" is an old lawyer's word
used in regard to the technicalities of having title to property, which
PC Marxist have appropriated to give their welfare practices a tone of
constitutional legality.

The word "patriotism" has been redefined as the right to show
gross disrespect for the American flag, the symbol of the United States
of America and its history, in such hateful acts as burning the flag at
political rallies while screaming hate-America slogans. Such behavior
is the clearest proof that America's culture is under attack with the
intent to destroy it. PC Marxists justify these attacks as just "free
speech."

PC Marxists have given the word "discrimination," which once had
the meaning of making careful distinctions and judgments, the meaning of expressing prejudice and bigotry. Making distinctions is now
discouraged because Political Correctness could not flourish in an
atmosphere of making careful distinctions. To augment their redefinition of discrimination as bigotry and prejudice, PC Marxists have
coined the word judgmentalism. Anyone who still judges behavior according to the discriminating moral standards of the Judeo-Christian
moral tradition is guilty of "judgmentalism."

(3) Censorship has also accompanied the rise of agitprop in the
United States. For example, applying such words as "chairman" and

"congressman" to a female director of an entity or a female member of Congress is now forbidden because those words contain the suffix man, a word-construction commonly found in English because one of the meanings of "man" is a human being regardless of sex or age, a meaning which PC Marxism has censored as insulting to women. Both of the meanings of the word man — an adult male and human beings regardless of sex or age — are found in the earliest examples of written English going back more than a thousand years. Agitprop has outlawed that sense of the word as a suffix in words referring to females and insists that the only meaning *man* has is adult male; hence the word must never be used as a suffix in reference to females as, for instance, calling the female head of an organization its "chairman." Agitprop insists on referring to a female head of an organization as a "chairwoman" or as the "chair." The same censorship is evident in substituting the PC word "congresswoman" for "congressman" in reference to a female member of Congress. Many words containing the suffix "man" have been censored this way. For example, the use of "flagman" and "freshman" in reference to women is prohibited by PC Marxism. The PC language police require that a woman using a flag or other signaling devised to control traffic at a road construction site be referred to as "a flagperson" and a first-year female student in high school or college be called "a freshperson." The political purpose of such censorship is to create a consciousness among American women of belonging to an aggrieved class of society. Anyone who refuses to go along with such censorship is labeled a "sexist" by the PC language police. (Believe it or not, PC Marxists go so far as to insist that "snowperson" be used to refer to a snow sculpture with breasts! This insistence can only be attributed to the PC love of uniformity since inanimate objects cannot be insulted.)

One thing, however, must be noted. If this theory of offensive language was correct, then the censorship of words containing the suffix "man" ought to begin with the word "woman" which contains the (supposedly) insulting suffix "man." And what about that word "female"? Shouldn't it be banned by the PC language police? After all, its second syllable is unequivocally masculine. There is no double meaning in the case of the word male which has only an unequivocally masculine meaning. PC language police have failed, however, in all their efforts to censor the words wo*man* and fe*male*.

The words "homemaker" and "housewife" have, however, been successfully eradicated because, according to the PC language police, they refer to an allegedly slave-like oppression of women. "Homemaker" and "housewife," terms which once referred to honored vocations, are seldom heard in American speech these days and almost never seen in print except in the obituaries of elderly American women to identify the hard work they did during their lives. (It must be pointed out here that censoring a word describing some vocation is, in effect, a ban on that vocation.)

The alteration of American speech in the past fifty years by (1) inventing new words and phrases, (2) radically redefining the meaning of important existing terms, and (3) prohibiting terms PC Marxists find offensive has changed the perceptions of innumerable Americans and has thereby altered their fundamental belief-behaviors, which is the ultimate goal of Political Correctness in its ongoing campaign to replace American culture with Cultural Marxism.

Perhaps the most consequential PC redefinition of a word is "minority." Since 1946, women have comprised the majority of the U.S. population (*Historical Statistics of the United States: Colonial Times to 1970*, Bureau of the Census, Part 1, Series A 23–28, p. 9). The revolutionary goals of PC agitators and propagandists, however, require that women be perceived as a "minority." Decades of agitprop have, therefore, been devoted to redefining American women as a minority. This deceit has been necessary because in making a revolution no one sympathizes with the majority. The PC revolution in America requires that the majority of Americans (women) feel that they are an aggrieved "minority" so they will join the war on American culture. A systematic deception regarding women in America — that they are a minority — has therefore been one of the principal goals of agitprop. The allegation that a "war against women" is being waged in America has credibility only if American women are seen as a minority. Unless American women feel themselves to be an oppressed, aggrieved *minority*, they cannot have a class consciousness strong enough to move them to engage in class struggle to throw off the shackles of "victimization" forged by their fathers, husbands, sons, lovers, and men generally. This deceit exemplifies how agitprop manipulates truth for political ends.

Language, of course, is always changing. But it changes in piecemeal, spontaneous, undirected ways. The language changes I'm describing are deliberate, systematic, and coordinated alterations of American speech for long-range political purposes. An important piece of evidence in support of that judgment is the fact that anyone who does not conform to PC speech dictates will be stigmatized and punished. They will be called unpleasant names (bigot, fascist, homophobe, racist, sexist, etc.) for not conforming to the usages and meanings the PC language police want to put in place. They can be demoted, fined, fired, or excluded from benefits they would otherwise receive. And they are liable to be forced to undergo what in communist regimes is called "re-education" but in the United States is known by the dainty term of "sensitivity training": an unprecedented kind of political bullying and indoctrination never before seen in American life. "Sensitivity training" is a central feature of PC language policing today. In short, Americans, especially American opinion makers, are being made to fear speaking in ways that do not conform to politically correct language.

In the decades since the Counter Culture/Political Correctness campaign was launched in America in the 1960s, Americans have been told countless times that their country's history is essentially a story of bigotry, genocide, greed, homophobia, imperialism, insensitivity, intolerance, misogyny, oppression, racism, "raping" the environment, religious persecution, slavery, and xenophobia. So extreme and so relentless has the condemnation of America's history been that many Americans no longer believe as their forebears did that the United States is a great nation. Certainly, there seem to be far fewer Americans today than there were two generations ago who feel grateful to be Americans. (It is a simple but revealing gauge of patriotism to ask a person, "Are you grateful to be an American?" Try it, and see what sort of response you get.)

Because PC agitprop condemns America's history and culture and because agitprop has been a feature of American life for the last half-century, fewer Americans today have the faith in the future of the United States that moved Americans in the 1950s and earlier to marry and have children, which gave them a concrete interest in America's future. Fewer young Americans today seem to care whether they marry and have kids. The anti-American agitation and propaganda that has been so damaging to American patriotism has made many Americans indifferent toward their country's future. PC agitprop has especially weakened the patriotism of Americans who came of age in the 1960s, the 1980s, and the turn of the last century (the so-called "millennials" who attained their majority around the year 2000), and that has noticeably weakened America's cultural unity.

However, the love which an overwhelming majority of Americans still naturally feel for their homeland has by no means been exterminated. The good things about life in America are too numerous and too real to permit the lies, half truths, deceits, and distortions of agitprop to eradicate the truth of them. And patriotism is too natural a feeling to be easily eliminated, as the history of Poland in the nineteenth and twentieth centuries clearly demonstrates. What has been most severely damaged by agitprop in America since the 1960s is an understanding of why America should be regarded as an exceptional nation and why Americans ought to be grateful for its history (for instance, there's never been a religious war in U.S. history). Many public school students today do not seem to be getting a proper understanding of why they should be grateful to be Americans.

# Terms Related to and Used by the Counter Culture/Political Correctness Movement

GITPROP SPEECH began to be systematically introduced in the United States on college campuses half a century ago. When this new speech is analyzed, its goals of destroying America's culture and building Cultural Marxism are clear, as are the reasons for starting a campaign to change American speech on college campuses. Foremost among these reasons, of course, was the likelihood that college-educated persons would be the future opinonmolders of America. Also, college-age Americans were in their most idealistic years and thus most susceptible to the deceit that Marxism stands for true freedom and equality, compassion for the poor, and world peace.

Born during and soon after World War II, the Americans who went to college in the 1960s and 70s came of age during an economic boom time. An unusually large, pampered generation, the "Baby Boomers" presented an ideal "cadre" for Marxists agitators and propagandists to "transform" by getting them to use new words that would inculcate new perceptions, by redefining for them the meanings of existing words to change existing perceptions of theirs, and by prohibiting the use of words which expressed perceptions that PC Marxists did not want them to have. For instance, agitprop has taught successive generations of young Americans to think of the family in terms which "liberate" them from Judeo-Christian morality. Terms like: Abortion redefined as simply a woman's right to choose, No-Fault Divorce, Pornography as only a matter of free speech, Same-Sex Marriage, Single Parenting, and having a "Relationship" rather than a marriage (see the commentaries on these six terms in the following Lexicon). At the same time, agitprop has attacked and eliminated from use the words "housewife" and "homemaker" because of the slave-like subservience which agitprop claims they signify.

Agitprop has also accomplished changes of perception in regard to the government of the United States (see in the Lexicon, for example, the entry War on Poverty), religion (see entry on Christianity), American justice (see Social Justice), and human nature (see Animal Rights). Deliberate alterations to American speech since the 1960s in these and other fundamental areas of American thought have produced pronounced divisions between Americans who have embraced the new agitprop perceptions and Americans who have continued to live in accordance with the belief-behaviors of America's historic culture. This destructive, deliberately created antagonism has been achieved by the unceasing agitprop of PC Marxists and their sympathizers in America during the last fifty years.

The 234 terms commented on in the following Lexicon are not, of course, the entire vocabulary used by agitprop in America in the last fifty years to deconstruct America's culture while constructing Cultural Marxism. They merely illustrate the kind of speech changes which have been prosecuted in implementing those coordinate goals. Many PC terms ("cisgender," "fatshaming," "heteronormative," "intersectionality," "rape culture," and "woke," for instance) are not in this sample.

Ableism
Abortion Rights
Academic Freedom
Activist
Addiction
Affirmative Action
African American
Alienate/Alienation
Alt-Right, the
America/American
Anecdotal
Animal Rights
Arrogant/Arrogance
Art
Atheism
Bias-Free
Bible, the
Big Bang, the
Biocentrism
Bioethics
Biological Class Consciousness
Black English
Bourgeois/Bourgeoisie
Budget Cut
Bully/Bullying
Capitalism
Censorship
Change
Character Assassination
Chauvinism
Choice
Christianity
Class Consciousness
Class Struggle
Climate Change, Man-Made
Cold War, the
Collude, to
Colonialism
Communism

Community Organizing
Compassion
Conformity
Consciousness Raising
Consenting Adults
Conservative
Conspiracy
Constitution of the United States, the
Controversial
Co-opt, to
Counter Culture Movement
Crime
Crisis
Critical Theory
Culture
Culture War
Czars (slang)
Deadnaming
Death with Dignity
Deconstructionism
Democracy
Dependence
Dialogue
Discrimination
Diversity
Double Standards
Empower, to
Entitled/Entitlement
Entrant
Environmentalism
Environmental Racism
Equality
Establishment, the
Euro-American
Eurocentric
Evil
Evolution
Exceptionalism
Existential Threat

Exploit/Exploitation
Extremist/Extremism
Fairness
Fake News
Family, the
Fascist
Fear Monger
Feminism
Flash Mob
Frankfurt School, the
Freedom
Freedom of Religion
Free Market, the
Free Speech
Gloating
Globalism
Graffiti
Greed
Hardwired
Hate Speech
Hedonism
Hispanic
Homelessness
Homophobia
Humanitarian
Hypocrisy
Illegal Alien
Imperialism
Impose, to
Inappropriate
Inclusive/Inclusiveness
Individualism
Indoctrination
In Power
Intelligent Design
Internationalism
Investing in the Future
Islamophobia
-ism (suffix)

Jesus of Nazareth
Judgmentalism
Liberal
Liberal Education
Liberation
Liberation Theology
Lifestyle
Living Constitution, the
Lookism
Mainstream
Majority Rule
Male Chauvinism
Man
Marginalize, to
Materialistic Determinism
McCarthyism
Mean-Spirited
Microaggression
Minority
Mistake
Moral Autonomy
Move On
Multiculturalism
Myth
Name Calling
Nationalism
Native American
Negro American
Neo- (prefix)
Neoteny
9/11
No-Fault Divorce
Nonjudgmental
Obscene
Offensive
Open-Minded
Oppression/Oppressor
Oreo (slang)
Overreach

Overseas Contingency Operations
Paranoia
Partisan (adj.)
Patriotism
People of Color
Person of Size
Personal Responsibility
Pluralism
Pop Culture
Pornography
Post-Truth
Power
Preemptive Accusation
Prejudice
Privacy
Progressivism
Race Norming
Racial Profiling
Racism
Reactionary
Relationship
Religion
Revisionism
Revolution
Right-Wing Extremism
Safe Space
Same-Sex Marriage
Sanctuary Cities
Scenario
Science
Scientism
Secular/Secularism
Self-Esteem
Sensitivity
Sensitivity Training
Sexual Orientation
Sex Worker
Single Parenting
Situational Ethics

Sizeism
Snowflake (slang)
Social Engineering
Socialism
Social Justice
Sophistication
Special Interests
Speciesism
Speech Code
Status Quo
Supernatural, the
Superstition
Supreme Court, the U.S.
Taboo
Tax Correction
Ten Commandments, the
Theory
Transformation
Transparency
Trans Person
Tribalism
Triumphalism
Truth
Underprivileged
Unfair
Unilateralism
Urban Renewal
Useful Idiot
Victimless Crime
War on Poverty
Weaponize, to
Wedge Issue
Welfare
White
White Privilege
White Supremacy
Witch Hunt
Xenophobia
Zoological Thesis, the

## Ableism

A faux bias cooked up by PC agitprop, ableism is an alleged prejudice against a person with a disability as, for instance, refusing to hire someone with a stutter or substandard comprehension of spoken English as an office receptionist. Not hiring a person with a patently disqualifying deficiency constitutes the prejudice of "ableism," according to PC Marxists.

See entry on Sizeism.

## Abortion Rights

These are rights that are supposedly bestowed by the Constitution of the United States on every American female biologically capable of conceiving human life within her body but which were not recognized in constitutional law before 1973. Under the influence of agitprop, the U.S. Supreme Court began with *Roe v. Wade*, 410 U.S. 113 (1973) a decades-long redefinition of abortion which has climaxed in the current PC dogma that a pregnant woman in the United States has an absolute and comprehensive right to choose to terminate her child's prenatal life at any stage of development, including the moment the baby emerges from the mother's body at the conclusion of a full-term, normal gestation. The U.S. Supreme Court's redefinition of abortion as "a woman's right to choose" confers on a pregnant woman the right to have an abortion for whatever reason she deems sufficient because only she can say whether allowing her pregnancy to result in a live baby outside her body would be "an undue burden" for her (*Planned Parenthood of Southeastern Pennsylvania v. Casey*, 505 U.S. 833, 1992). In not a few instances, *abortion as choice* has resulted in the prenatal extermination of a human life for no better reason than the pregnant woman's discovery that the child developing within her body has a gender different from that which she prefers her baby to have. Such abortions, which might be thought of as boutique or chichi abortions, can hardly be justified by the "undue burden" argument because gender has no bearing on whether the child whose life is snuffed out would have been an "undue burden" since the woman making the decision to abort would have given birth to the child developing within her body had the developing baby been of the preferred gender.

From 1791 to 1973, that is to say from the ratification of the Tenth Amendment to the Supreme Court's decision in *Roe v. Wade*, State legislatures and courts in the United States under the authority granted them in the Tenth Amendment ("The powers not delegated to the United States by the Constitution, nor prohibited by it to the States, are reserved to the States respectively, or to the people") exercised sole jurisdiction over matters of abortion and regarded the procedure as the taking of a human life in development. The States therefore either prohibited or restricted abortion. In *Roe v. Wade*, the Supreme Court, under color of interpreting the Constitution, amended the Constitution by usurping the States' constitutional jurisdiction in matters of abortion under the Tenth Amendment and thus also violated the Fifth Article of the Constitution, which confers on the people of the States acting through their representatives in their States sole authority to amend the Constitution of the United States.

Post-1973 abortion rulings by federal judges have denied the developing child in a woman's body any God-given right to life, and have put the extirpation of a human zygote, human embryo, human fetus, or fully formed human baby emerging from the mother's body in the same category of medical procedures as the elimination of a tumor whether life-threatening or not. *Abortion as choice* makes a woman's choice the only consideration to the exclusion of what she chooses. But if that reasoning were valid, then premeditated murder which is also a choice might be condoned when the killing rid the murderer of a "burden." In America's culture, humans are regarded as made in "the image of God." *Abortion as choice* denies life in the womb any sanctity whatsoever.

Of the millions of abortions performed annually in the United States since 1973, *approximately 50% of them have been done to Negro women* though Negro Americans make up less than 15% of the whole U.S. population. Thus, providers and promoters of *abortion as choice* such as Planned Parenthood are having an undue effect on the Negro American population, an effect that certainly has an appearance of being genocidal.

See entries on Animal Rights, Choice, the Family, War on Poverty.

## Academic Freedom

Academic freedom is the contention that unless college and university professors can say in their classrooms and their publications whatever they want to say with impunity, the discovery and transmission of knowledge, which are the coordinate missions of institutions of higher learning, will be inhibited or thwarted. There is truth in that contention. The problem is that American institutions of higher learning today have faculties comprised overwhelmingly of politically correct dogmatists who feel that only politically correct ideas are worthy of expression and contrary views ought to be suppressed. PC Marxists invoke the idea of academic freedom to propound the ideology of Political Correctness while suppressing the academic freedom of anyone who criticizes that ideology.

See entries on Censorship, Free Speech, Hate Speech, Safe Space, Speech Code.

## Activist

A term used to avoid use of the term "agitator" with its strong associations with the rise of communism. Lenin in his book *What Is To Be Done?* (1902) recommended a combination of two kinds of extreme advocacy, agitation and propaganda, which he termed "agitprop," to rouse the Russian masses to revolutionary action. He designated agitation as the province of orators and propaganda the province of writers. Lenin had a formidable talent in both areas.

# Addiction

Addiction is slow-motion suicide, day after day. It is living without care for tomorrow. Addiction obliterates all sense of social responsibility. It makes the addict a slave to his addiction and renders him incapable of normal human social relations.

Nonetheless, the Counter Culture Movement of the 1960s actively encouraged addictive behavior of all kinds among American college students, particularly addiction to drugs but also to alcohol ("binge drinking") and sexual promiscuity ("the sexual revolution"). Such behavior was promoted as "liberation" from the allegedly oppressive values of America's Judeo-Christian, middle-class morality which emphasizes self-control. Never before had a political movement in the United States promoted addiction because never before had there been a political movement whose ultimate goal was the destruction and replacement of America's culture. Only political operatives who desire the destruction of the United States would deliberately encourage addiction.

See entries on Deconstruction/Deconstructionism, Hedonism.

# Affirmative Action

The federal Affirmative Action laws enacted by Congress in the 1960s and 70s, and upheld in federal courts, "entitled" certain biological classes of Americans to exclusive privileges which other biological classes of Americans were not to receive. Preferential, set-aside quotas for jobs and college admissions were the result. Affirmative Action is a concept of advancement as a member of a biological class of persons. It makes "society" responsible for identifying which sorts of persons have the right to succeed in life. It is perhaps best described as a form of racism in the name of fighting racism.

See entries on Diversity and Race Norming, and the commentary Biological Class Consciousness in Part III below.

# African American

A term not found in the writings or speeches of such major pre-1970s American Negro leaders as Frederick Douglass, Booker T. Washington, W. E. B. Du Bois, Martin Luther King, Jr., or John Hope Franklin (see his magisterial *From Slavery to Freedom: A History of Negro Americans*, Sixth Edition, 1989). "African American" is a term invented by Marxists for political purposes. Its use is now dogmatically insisted on by all PC agitators and propagandists and their supporters. Anyone who dares to use the term Negro American is instantly labeled a racist.

Why was this change in American speech required? The usage "African American" has become mandatory because everyone who uses the term in speech, hears it being used, or reads it in print becomes conscious that ancestors of Negro Americans were forced to come to America from Africa as slaves. The term implies that Negro Americans are not genuinely American because ancestors of theirs did not come to America as free immigrants. Such consciousness undermines the ideal of integrating Negro Americans into American society which the Rev. Martin Luther King, Jr. described in his speech "I Have a Dream," delivered at the Lincoln Memorial in Washington, D.C. in 1963 on the 100th anniversary of Lincoln's Emancipation Proclamation. "African American" is a term that promotes permanent alienation from what PC propaganda terms "Euro-American" society.

Atrocities every bit as horrific as the history of chattel slavery in the United States and worse (e.g. Stalin's mass genocide of Ukrainian peasants by starvation and Hitler's genocide against European Jewry and other nationalities) are allowed to fade with time and the passing of the generations which perpetrated the atrocities. But PC Marxists want to keep alive and fresh in the mind and feelings of every American, white and black, the memory of the chattel slavery that existed in America from the 1660s to 1865; hence they have substituted the term African American for the term Negro American. The PC term, African American, declares that Negro Americans are really

Africans living in America, whereas "Negro American" merely refers to Americans whose skin is to some degree black.

See entries on Euro-American, Native American, and Racism and the commentary Biological Class Consciousness in Part III below.

## Alienate/Alienation

Standard Marxist diction, these terms are used to describe the existence or promotion of strong discontent with a culture, a government, a ruling class, or an economic system which is supposedly exploiting a particular class of persons, all of which "social" injustice Political Correctness promises to remedy. Marxist agitprop promotes alienation because it is conducive to revolution.

See entry on Exploit/Exploitation and the summary of the 1970 interview with the three Counter Culture agitators in Part I above.

## Alt-Right

The agitprop synonym for fascists (when used with a definite article) and fascism.

## America/American

In the 1970s, Marxist agitprop in the U.S. went so far as to say that Americans in naming their country the United States of America in 1776 arrogantly appropriated for their exclusive use the words America and Americans which belong to every nation and people in the Western Hemisphere. The exaggerated silliness of this criticism failed to catch on outside of academia, and since the 1980s has fallen into disuse even there. Nonetheless the argument that Americans had no right to use the word America in naming their country (the same as any people in the Western Hemisphere would have, had they been the first to win independence from Europe) is worth mentioning as an indication of how extremely anti-American and intemperate agitprop has been.

## Anecdotal

A label used to invalidate any testimony on the deficiencies of applied Marxism based on personal experience. By employing this term, criticism of Marxism deriving from personal experience becomes something merely idiosyncratic and therefore insignificant: just an "anecdote." To discredit empirical studies such as scientific critiques of the PC dogma "Man-Made Climate Change," for instance, a different tactic is used. In that case, the credentials of the authors of such criticism are attacked or they are said to be in the pay of capitalists and not credible for that reason.

See entries on Climate Change and Myth.

## Animal Rights

This momentous PC term puts the rights of animals on a par with the rights of human beings, thus abolishing the distinction between them. The doctrine that all animals, including "the human animal," are on the same ethical level would seem to be an upgrading of animal rights. But putting animal and human rights on the same level is actually *a degradation of human rights* which makes human beings vulnerable to the kind of treatment a domesticated animal may be subjected to: "putting them down" when they are old, crippled, incurably ill, or otherwise incapable of performing some useful function. According to PC Marxism, the human animal has no special sanctity conferred by God but only those rights which pertain to any animal. If that proposition is accepted, nothing would prevent human beings from becoming candidates for such procedures as scientific experiments or mandatory euthanasia.

The PC dogma that man is just another animal having the same ethical status as other animals is a variant of Charles Darwin's unscientific assertion in 1871 that man's "mental faculties" differ from those of other animals only "in degree," not "in kind" (*The Descent of Man*, Part I, Chapter VI). Darwin's assertion might be taken seriously if it could be shown that some other species of animal besides man had written a book, composed a symphony, launched an earth-orbiting satellite, performed brain surgery, or formed a society for the prevention of cruelty to another species of animal. The belief that human beings have no motives which differentiate them from other forms of life is absurd on the face of it. Yet this ridiculous PC dogma has been seriously asserted by one of its foremost advocates, Peter Singer, a "bioethics" professor at Princeton University, in the following PC terms in his 1985 book *In Defense of Animals*: "There is no ethical basis for elevating membership in one particular species into a morally crucial characteristic. From an ethical point of view, we all stand on an equal footing — whether we stand on two feet, or four, or none at all" (p. 6).

See entries on Biocentrism, Bioethics, Death with Dignity, the Zoological Thesis.

## Arrogant/Arrogance

General terms of reproach in vogue among PC Marxists in America. But these words, as is so often the case with politically correct diction, apply with special relevance to the PC Marxists who use them to denigrate their opponents. Indeed, it seems to me that in faulting others, PC Marxists often describe themselves, especially when they accuse others of hate and intolerance.

See entry on Preemptive Accusation.

## Art

No matter how iconoclastic, inartistic, obscene, silly, ugly, or vulgar a song, a movie, a play, a painting, a sculpture, an "art performance," a piece of music, or a literary work may be, if it purports to be "art" *and* ridicules middle-class American values, PC Marxists will laud it as "avant-garde," "creative," "cutting edge," "experimental," "original," or praiseworthy in some other way. By the same token, PC Marxists use negative terms like "dull," "old-fashioned," or "outdated" to describe works of art that express the values of middle-class, Christian Americans.

See entry on Graffiti.

## Atheism

PC Marxists promote the dogma that there is no omnipotent, intelligent designer of the universe (God) who created not only Nature but the laws which have no physical existence that govern Nature, as well as moral ordinances to guide human beings in the use of their unique freedom (Exodus 20:1–17). Judeo-Christianity teaches that man is the only being God created "in his own image" which may mean that only human beings have a semblance of God's perception of good and evil and his freedom of will to decide to do what is good (Genesis 1:3–31). But, of course, man's capacity for goodness is limited and intermittent compared to God's infinite, unerring, constant goodness and justice. Every human being ought to be grateful for the capacity to do good which their Creator has bestowed on him, even though it be limited.

Perhaps more thoroughly than any other people on earth, Americans have incorporated into their culture the belief President John F. Kennedy alluded to in his Inaugural Address (1961) when he said "the rights of man come not from the generosity of the state but from the hand of God." PC Marxists want to replace that American cultural conviction with "secularism" (as they euphemistically call atheism) and the Marxist belief in government-bestowed rights. Belief in the existence of God is a political imperative in American culture because the civil rights of Americans are based on it. Cultural Marxism will not, and cannot, come to pass in the United States as long as the great majority of Americans believe that the right to life, liberty, the pursuit of happiness, and government by consent of the governed has been bestowed on mankind by the creator of the universe.

See entry on Secular.

## Bias-Free

A not-much-used but highly significant coinage of PC Marxists, this phrase was designed to praise persons and behaviors which exhibit absolutely no traces of such "biases" as Christian respect for life and a strict interpretation of the U.S. Constitution.

See entries on Judgmentalism, Nonjudgmental.

## Bible, the

The Bible has an authority of the highest importance to Western civilization because it is widely believed to be the revealed word of God, the truth human beings can only comprehend if they live through faith in its teachings. According to the Bible, God revealed himself to Moses as the "I AM" and as "holy," a term signifying his absolute difference from his creations (Exodus 3:1–14). Jews and Christians believe the heavens and the earth and all they contain manifest the infinite glory of God the Creator. Marxists regard the Bible as a collection of myths, oral and historical traditions, and superstitions of entirely human origin and ridicule the biblical account of the origin of the cosmos. They scorn Judeo-Christian belief in God, saying that if such a powerful entity existed he, she, or it would be immeasurable, and Marxism does not accept the possibility of any such realities, despite the fact that the Laws of Nature which Marxists claim to revere and on which science is based are definitely immaterial, transcendent, and powerful. Marxists reject the Creator that the harmony, order, and pervasiveness of the Laws of Nature suggest.

PC Marxists ridicule the Bible as just a compendium of folklore, myth, and superstition of purely human origin with no transcendent authority and say it contradicts the operative assumption of strict materialists who contend that only measurable material entities and forces can be real, whereas God (if he, she, or it existed) would be something immeasurable. PC Marxists will not concede even the possible existence of an immaterial reality (agnosticism), despite the facts

that the science they revere is based on laws having no material existence and that the presence of these laws is necessary to the material
world's orderly operation. Strict materialists refuse to acknowledge
the significance of the willful harmony and fearful constancy of the
great laws of existence.

See entries on the Big Bang, Jesus of Nazareth, the Supernatural.

## Big Bang, the

The trouble with the politically correct, materialist attacks on the authority of the Bible is that science's own account of how the cosmos
came into being ("the Big Bang") contradicts all measurable, material
causality and should, therefore, be regarded as unscientific. The Big
Bang, which scientists have reason to believe happened in a single
instant some fourteen billion years ago, could not have been caused
by any known force or normal condition. Scientist have had to admit
that the Big Bang which instantly created and structured the cosmos,
as inferred by its observable effects, exceeded all known physical
conditions and forces and cannot be explained by them, which is the
definition of a miracle. But scientists refuse to use the term miracle to
categorize the event. Instead, they refer to the Big Bang as "a singular-
ity" which is a distinction without a difference.

Likewise, scientists have no scientific explanation for the origin of
life. Charles Darwin's theory of the origin of animal and plant species starts with the supposition of a living cell's existence. No scientific explanation of that cell, consistent with the protocols of scientific
reasoning and proof, has ever been proposed and demonstrated. Life,
whose ability to reproduce itself differentiates it from all other kinds
of matter, could not have derived from non-living matter as Darwin
theorized since the reproductive capacity which defines life is not only
tremendously complicated but strictly sequential. This set of sequential intricacies had to be intact and coeval with the existence of life.
Otherwise, Darwin's hypothesis could not be considered functional.
Though aware of the complicated sequence of biological processes

that constitutes reproduction, Darwin and his followers nonetheless claimed and still claim that the sequence "must have" come into existence by chance from non-living matter. (Readers of Darwin's 1859 book-length exposition of his theory, *On the Origin of Species*, will be familiar with the phrase "must have" which appears with disconcertingly unscientific regularity in his argument.)

Then, too, one ought to inquire, did electricity "evolve," since the pumping action of the heart in animals with blood systems depends for its control on precisely timed electrical signals. How about light? What about gravity? Did they "evolve"? Did water, the chief component of living organisms, "evolve"? The initial nineteen verses of the first book in the Bible reveals that a grand sequence of creations preceded the creation of various organisms, culminating in God creating man "in His own image; in the image of God He created him: male and female He created them" (Genesis 1:20–27, New King James Translation). More "must haves" or assumptions are needed to assert that the cosmos created itself accidently than are needed to believe in the Grand Sequence of Acts by a Creator which the first verses in the Bible report. Jews and Christians attribute the harmony of such things as light, electricity, gravity, water, and life to God, the never-completely-comprehensible, holy, and omnipotent source of all being, the "I AM" they worship with praise and thanksgiving. "The Big Bang" is science's drab reference to God's ineffable power of omnipresent creativity.

Scientists don't ask questions to which they don't expect to find answers. Science's commitment is to the discovery of as many of the Laws of Nature as possible. Darwinian scientists, for instance, declare that no intelligent design is evident in living organisms because they don't want to believe in the implications of admitting to seeing it, and instead want to believe chance can explain everything. Yet answerable questions (the ones that can be subjected to experimental investigation) are not the most significant. Why is there such unity among the

Laws of Nature? That's the sort of question that would reveal the most if it could be probed by science.

Believers in God ask, how did the things that are said to "evolve" come to be, and how did the Laws of Nature which scientists are so busy discovering come to be? Could a cosmos replete with lawfulness have created itself by chance, as materialistic determinists insist actually happened?

## Biocentrism

This agitprop coinage criticizes human beings for valuing their own species more than any other animal species. PC Marxists in their effort to deconstruct the existing culture of the United States insist that the planet earth exists for every species equally, not for humans especially. Neither assumption is more presumptuous than the other.

At the core of America's culture is the belief that human beings have a unique relationship with the Creator (Genesis 1:20–28) in having been uniquely endowed by God with a semblance of his being. Political Correctness says man is just another species of animal, having no characteristic that is unique to the animal kingdom, a dogma which — it cannot be pointed out too often — is refuted by every book written in formulating this inept thesis. For only mankind writes and reads books. One might just as well claim that there's no difference in kind between porpoises and human swimmers since both can propel themselves through water. Despite Darwin's assertion that man's mental capacities and those of other species differ only in degree, not kind, I would say some differences of degree are so great as to constitute a difference in kind.

See entries on Animal Rights, Evolution, Intelligent Design.

## Bioethics

An academic field dating from the 1970s, bioethics applies to human beings the ethical reasoning formerly applied only to animals.

It denies the Judeo-Christian belief that God has endowed human beings with characteristics which set them apart from the rest of the animal kingdom as an essentially different kind of creature.

See entry on Animal Rights.

## Biological Class Consciousness

This is the class consciousness agitprop has been creating in the United States since the 1960s through agitprop to make Marxian class struggle possible in America. Sometimes inadequately referred to as "identity politics."

See entry on Class Consciousness and the commentary Biological Class Consciousness in Part III below.

## Black English

This term asserts the right of a small segment of Negro Americans to express themselves in a patois (Black English) that other Americans, including other Negro Americans, find incomprehensible. Those who use Black English find it impossible to communicate with or assimilate into the society that exists beyond their communities. This so-called Black English is a sort of justified apartheid which serves to advance the PC agenda of disunifying American society.

See entries on African American, Bilingual Education, Multiculturalism.

## Bourgeois/Bourgeoisie

Borrowings from the French, the equivalent terms in English are middle-class (adj.) and middle class (n.). Marx and Lenin used "bourgeois" and "bourgeoisie" to identify everything they loathed and wanted to sweep into the "dust bin" (trash barrel) of history. Belief in God. Judeo-Christian morality. The family. Patriotism. Private property. Consumerism. Personal responsibility. Private charity. Profit making. Self-determination. Marxists feel only contempt for these cultural values and beliefs and want to replace them with Marxism's allegedly more humane, rational, "scientific" values.

## Brainwashing

Intense conditioning and indoctrination for the purpose of controlling behavior.

See entry on Open-Minded.

## Budget Cut

A budget cut in PC newspeak is a failure to increase funding for a government program by the same *percentage* of increase as the previous year's budget; so, if the previous year's increase was, say, 4% but the next budget calls for an increase in funding of only 3%, that is *a budget cut*. This attitude toward the federal budget, that no item in it should ever be funded at a lesser percentage of increase has produced a national debt as large as the U.S. Gross Domestic Product (GDP) and an executive branch of the U.S. government which now employs millions of persons.

## Bully/Bullying

An immensely old (one might say archetypal) human persona and behavior, *bully* and *bullying* have in the last few years acquired national prominence because of their use by PC Marxists to explain the poor performance of students in America's politicized public schools (there have been a series of such explanations). Agitprop about bullies and bullying deflects attention from the true causes of the decline in public schooling in America which are: the federalization, politicization, and unionization of the schools.

See the commentary on U.S. public schools in Part IV below.

## Capitalism

Capitalism is a necessary component of the free-market economic system which exists in all of the world's wealthiest nations, including a semblance of it in present-day communist China which practices a highly regulated "state capitalism." Capitalism — the accumulation of money and acquisition of credit to use in for-profit investment — has emancipated more human beings from poverty than all the Marxist revolutions in history combined. Indeed, the body count between 1917 and the present for putting Marxist regimes in power in Cambodia, China, countries in Central and Eastern Europe, Cuba, Nicaragua, North Korea, the USSR, Venezuela, and Vietnam is around one hundred million. For country-by-country estimates, see *The Black Book of Communism*, first published in French in 1997 and in English translation in 1999.

The benefits of capitalism compared to applied Marxism are clear in the comparison of capitalist South Korea where the infant mortality rate per one thousand births is 8 and Marxist North Korea where it is 88. In South Korea, the average lifespan of men is twenty years longer than the lifespan of men in North Korea. Such disparities were also seen when there were two Germanies, a capitalist West Germany and a Marxist East Germany. One prosperous and the other economically depressed; one bustling and free and the other listless and restrained; West Germans generally had more of everything that makes life good while East Germans lived in gloom and fear.

See entry on the Free Market.

## Censorship

A practice invariably found wherever Marxists govern or a Marxist revolutionary movement exists. PC Marxists in America accuse "right-wing extremists" and "Christian fundamentalists" of censorship, saying they are trying to impose their values on America. But despite this accusation, it is really PC Marxists in America who are hostile to free speech, who are imposing their views, and who routinely practice censorship.

See entries on Academic Freedom, Free Speech, Preemptive Accusation and the commentary "Correct" Free Speech in Part III below.

## Change

Middle-class Americans are not much bothered, it seems, by this non-threatening Marxist euphemism for revolution, whereas if Marxists were to use the word "revolution" instead of the word "change" for what they're engaged in, it would cause opposition among middle-class Americans, whose acquiescence PC Marxists want. "Change" is one of the most seemingly harmless, most truly sinister terms in the lexicon of Political Correctness.

See entries on Revolution and Transformation.

## Character Assassination

One of the customary ways PC Marxists eliminate political opponents is to accuse them of immoral behavior, even though they themselves do not consider moral conduct essential in their leaders. Name-calling (bigot, fascist, homophobe, racist, sexist, xenophobe, etc.) is another way they have of eliminating or reducing the influence of a political opponent. Both techniques — character assassination and name-calling — are used whenever any politically correct leader is exposed as a wrongdoer. In that case, the exposed person's PC supporters make an all-out, sustained assault on the character of the witness or witnesses to their leader's wrongdoing. (PC insiders having information on the misbehavior of a prominent PC leader when their willingness to remain silent is in doubt have actually been known to turn up dead.) It is an iron rule among PC Marxists never to admit wrongdoing. When they do something wrong, they call it a "mistake."

See entries on Controversial, Mistake, Name-Calling, and Preemptive Accusation and the commentary A Standard of Double Standards in Part III below.

## Chauvinism

To American Marxists, gratitude for being an American is the same as chauvinism, a term which means to them militant nationalism. Putting America's national interests first is to a Marxist the equivalent of xenophobia or fear of foreigners. It is typical of PC Marxists to condemn the patriotism most Americans feel for their country, because Marxists regard nationalism as the main cause of wars. Nationalism and patriotism for them are signs of "bourgeois values" and political immaturity.

See entries on Globalism, Internationalism, Nationalism, Patriotism, Xenophobia.

## Choice

When it suits their purpose, PC Marxists adamantly favor choice, as their dogmatism on the matter of abortion shows. But they just as adamantly oppose choice whenever such opposition advances their agenda, as in their rejection of allowing parents to choose the school they would like their children to attend.

See entries on Abortion Rights and Freedom, and the commentary A Standard of Double Standards in Part III below.

## Christianity

Christianity is the principal obstacle to the establishment of Cultural Marxism because Christianity teaches that God created the universe, including the laws that govern his creations and the free will that is inherent to human nature. PC Marxists denounce such beliefs because they are antithetical to the Marxist dogmas that nothing but the material universe exists; that man is an unexceptional animal species among the millions of species which have "evolved" on this planet without design or purpose; that man like other animals has no free will and is the product of his environment. Marxists claim to know "scientifically" what is best for the human species. To them, anyone who says man has been created by God to know and enjoy him forever is an enemy of human beings.

See entries on Atheism, the Bible, Secular, and in Part III below the commentary A Culture without God.

## Class Consciousness

The principal goal of agitprop in America has been to create class consciousness because without class consciousness there can be no class struggle, the indispensable element in Marxist revolutions. PC Marxists in America for decades have been creating biological class consciousness based on birth (i.e. biology) among Negro Americans, women, and other groups as a prerequisite for class struggle. Class struggle is the opposite of individual striving to improve one's life. The concept of individuals improving their lives through their own decisions and efforts is a deeply embedded belief-behavior of American culture.

See entries on Class Struggle and Consciousness Raising and the commentary on Biological Class Consciousness in Part III below.

## Class Struggle

The primary mechanism for Marxist revolution is "class struggle." Marxist revolution is, essentially, the idea of oppressed classes struggling to liberate themselves from an oppressive ruling class. But to have class struggle, there must first be class consciousness and a keen sense of class grievances or "alienation" from the existing society and its culture. Agitprop in America in the last fifty years has been creating that class consciousness and sense of class grievances.

See entries on Class Consciousness and Consciousness Raising and the commentary Biological Class Consciousness in Part III below.

## Climate Change, Man-Made

Man-made climate change is a political, not a scientific theorem. It claims the human race is producing atmospheric pollutants in sufficient quantities to alter earth's climate; therefore, governments must league together to control industrial activities and auto emissions worldwide to "save the planet." There has never been, however, a scientific calculation of the amount of man-made pollutants it would take to change Earth's climate. Furthermore, the Earth's geological history prior to the advent of large-scale auto and industrial emissions shows sharp climactic variations. For example, a lowering of global temperatures tens of thousands of years ago caused a *miles-thick icecap* to form across northern Europe, Asia, and North America; then a warming trend reversed that frigid climate and melted that stupendous icecap. Those episodes of cooling and warming cannot be attributed to human activities since they occurred thousands of years prior to the Industrial Revolution. (Fluctuating outputs of the sun's energy are the most probable cause.) Until scientists can agree on how to separate the effects on climate of human activities and the sun's uncontrollable variations in energy output, the tempting Marxist proposal to regulate human activities to protect Earth's climate must be resisted in the interest of sanity, even though PC Marxists want to implement such control without delay to advance their agenda of creating a world government having comprehensive regulatory powers.

The flimsiness of PC thinking in regard to "man-made climate change" is seen in its fickleness. In the 1970s, PC Marxists claimed human pollution was causing "global winter" or *cooling*. When that thesis didn't pan out, they switched to global *warming* propaganda. Finally, in the last twenty years, they have come up with a surefire thesis: "manmade climate change." In pursuing this thesis, no matter what happens, whether the planet's climate warms or cools, the agitators and propagandists for Political Correctness can claim they "scientifically" predicted it. Such shiftiness is ridiculous.

Former U.S. Vice President Al Gore, the Democrat Party's candidate for president in 2000, is the most prominent American propagandist for "manmade climate change."

See entries on Power, Truth, Science, and Scientism.

## Cold War, the

The forty-four-year struggle between the USA and the USSR (1947–1991) called the Cold War ended with the disintegration of the USSR. The political movement which began in the 1960s in the United States under the name the Counter Culture Movement was a Marxist front in that Cold War. It was opened to (1) get U.S. military forces out of South Vietnam; (2) replace American culture with Cultural Marxism. The first of these goals was accomplished in the early 1970s; the second has yet to be reached.

See entries Culture War and Useful Idiot.

## Collude, to

This verb, meaning *to conspire*, became in the first year of Donald Trump's presidency the obsessive harangue of PC Marxists in explanation of why their candidate Hillary Clinton (an early devotee of Saul Alinsky) had been defeated in the 2016 election by Donald Trump, the America-First candidate. According to this "scenario," Trump "colluded with the Russians" who in some way never specified, demonstrated, or proven had an ability to change electoral results in States of the United States, and it was only through this supposed Russian prowess that Trump won the election.

This accusation is decidedly ironic since Barack Obama, the PC Marxist candidate for U.S. president four years before, was caught on a live mic saying to a high official of the Russian government, "Tell Vladimir [Putin] I'll have more flexibility after I'm elected." Moreover,

Hillary Clinton in 2009 as U.S. Secretary of State made a big to-do about "resetting" relations with the former Soviet Union. She certainly colluded with the Russians in making a deal to sell them strategic supplies of U.S. uranium.

Deriding the "conspiracy theories" of opponents and ridiculing them as "conspiracy nuts" is typical of the rhetoric of PC Marxists who of course (as Marxists) believe with all their being in Marx's theory of history as the conspiracy of the rich against the poor. Such is the monumental hypocrisy of Political Correctness.

See entries on Conspiracy, Double Standards, Fake News, Hypocrisy, Paranoia, and in Part III below the commentary on A Standard of Double Standards.

## Colonialism

Colonialism, or imperialism, is the practice of establishing colonies for the economic benefit of the imperial power which establishes them. The Roman Empire, the Spanish Empire, the British Empire, and the Russian Empire — which the Communist Party of the Soviet Union seized, reorganized, and in 1922 renamed the Union of Soviet Socialist Republics — have been the largest colonial empires centered in Europe. The Spanish and British empires were maintained by maritime and naval power; the Roman and Russian empires were land empires contiguous with their European centers, Rome and Moscow. (Some naval power was needed to maintain the Roman Empire which surrounded the Mediterranean Sea, but the Roman army was the mainstay of that imperium.) The USSR was the final one of these European-centered mega-empires to collapse. But its remnant, the Russian Federation, remains the world's largest political entity, having a territory three million square miles larger than the average size of Canada, the United States, China, and Brazil: the world's four largest nations. The Marxists who ruled the USSR said they were enemies of imperialism while governing the final gigantic empire in European history. This is perhaps the most glaring hypocrisy in the Soviet Union's history of hypocrisy.

See entries on Collude, Hypocrisy, Imperialism, and the commentary A Standard of Double Standards in Part III below.

## Communism

Theoretically, a humane and just form of government administered by an elite or "vanguard" of supposed scientific experts, aimed at achieving universal human happiness through Marxism. The end result of applied Marxism, communism, was defined in *The Communist Manifesto* as: "From each according to his abilities, to each according to his needs." In practice, communism is not beneficial but a ruthless form of one-party tyranny which governs through dogma and terror. The essential deficiency of Marxism is stated in the observation, "In theory there is no difference between theory and practice. In practice, there is."

## Community Organizing

PC Marxists in America use the term community organizing as a synonym for what was called "building communism" in the USSR. The innocuous sound of "community organizing" lulls persons who would oppose the idea of "building communism" were that term used. The American Marxist Saul Alinsky in his *Rules for Radicals* outlined how to organize communities for "change," i.e. Marxist revolution, and popularized the terms community organizing and community organizer. Barack Obama, the 44th U.S. president, got his political start in Chicago through his appointment as an instructor in Saul Alinsky's school for community organizers.

See entry on Social Justice and the commentary "Social" Justice in Part III below.

## Compassion

PC Marxists consider that only they are capable of compassion, and regard private charity as insufficient to serve the needs of mass societies, which, they think, require immense, centralized government bureaucracies. The ultimate goal of Marxism is to set up a world government which conforms to Marxist theories. George W. Bush's slogan "compassionate conservatism" in his first run for the U.S. presidency was an attempt to recapture the idea of compassion for Republican Party use. Of course, to demonstrate his compassion, he had to do as PC Marxists do and create more government "entitlement" programs, and immense bureaucracies to administer them.

See entry on Mean-Spirited.

## Conformity

The idea that American culture requires a stifling conformity is one of the main talking points of Political Correctness. It would have Americans believe their culture is hostile to freedom, whereas the historical record shows that Marxism requires rigid conformity to the Party "line" and that American culture has stood for freedom.

## Consciousness Raising

One of the foremost goals of agitprop is "consciousness raising." In the U.S. this takes the form of creating a strong class consciousness among biological groups (women, Negro Americans, ethnic groups, homosexuals) and endowing each of them with a sense of "victimization" and the need to remedy their class grievances through class struggle.

See entry on Social Justice, and the commentaries Biological Class Consciousness and "Social" Justice in Part III below.

## Consenting Adults

In freeing or liberating Americans from Judeo-Christian morality which is one of the goals of agitprop, the idea of consenting adults has great importance. By convincing middle-class Americans that conduct in private between "consenting adults," no matter what it may be or whom it may affect, is OK, the foundation of Judeo-Christian morality is shattered because that foundation is the belief that some conduct is inherently wrong in the sight of God and other conduct is inherently right in the nature of things as God has created the world and man in it. When the rightness or wrongness of an act becomes merely a matter of who knows about it and whether it is done with the consent of its participants, right and wrong cease to be relevant moral considerations.

See entries on Abortion Rights, No-Fault Divorce, Victimless Crime.

## Conservative

A conservative, as the term indicates, wants to preserve, or conserve, what has been handed down from the past that he considers good; conservatives, therefore, have a disposition generally opposed to change. Conservatism can only be considered completely and always right, however, if one assumes that whatever has been handed down from the past is in every instance and in all respects right and there is never any room for improvement. And that is not a prudent position to take, since human beings must be regarded on the evidence of both history and personal experience as lacking God's infallibility. But the opposite proposition is likewise flawed: "change" is not in and of itself always good because the same evidence of fallibility also applies to many proposals to improve society by changing it. It may further be said, on the evidence of history and personal experience, that conduct which has generally been felt to be good for a long time by most people in a society probably does have some merit or it would not have been believed over a long period of time to be good. Though human beings are often foolish, they generally have a healthy sense of what is in their best interest (hence, the general presence in human cultures of belief in a higher Being). Unlike conservatives, revolutionaries want (as their name suggests) to turn the world upside down and start over. That is not a policy for wholesome living. More often than not, revolutions are a waste of spirit in a blood bath of self-righteousness.

## Conspiracy

Marxism is a conspiracy theory. It sees history as a conspiracy of the rich and powerful (in modern times, capitalists and imperialists) against the weak and the poor. It claims this view of history is based on science and is in no way a matter of opinion but of hard, scientific data. This claim allows PC Marxists to avoid the charge of paranoia, of being conspiracy nuts who think capitalists-imperialists are lurking under every bed. Marxists attribute conspiracy theories and paranoia exclusively to their opponents. They never see themselves in those terms, though they would if they were honest with themselves. Marxists promise to overthrow the conspiracy of the rich ("the haves," as Marx called them) against the poor ("the have-nots") and to dispel the "superstitions" of religion which they see as part of the conspiracy of the rich against the poor.

Marxist "liberators" who regard history from the perspective of their conspiracy theory naturally feel themselves surrounded by "enemies." They believe plots against Marxism are ubiquitous and must be guarded against, and that deviationists within their own ranks must be ferreted out and eliminated. The discovery of "deviationists" and "enemies of the people" are ever-present concerns of Political Correctness. These attitudes are part and parcel of the Marxist concept of history as conspiracy. The PC presidential candidate Hillary Clinton and her supporters explain her debacle in 2016 by saying her opponent "colluded" with a foreign government to defeat her. To "collude" means to conspire, but they don't used the word conspire because it would make them seem like "conspiracy nuts," something they accuse their "enemies" of being.

See entries on Paranoia and Witch Hunt.

## Constitution of the United States, the

Without obedience to this supreme law which has been made supreme by its ratification by the people of every one of the fifty U.S. States when they joined the Union, there is no United States of America. To be an American is to revere the Constitution of the United States as the fundamental, unifying law of the land. Therefore, PC Marxists as part of their desire to destroy American culture want to subvert and nullify as many of the principles, procedures, prohibitions, and provisions of the Constitution as possible.

See entry on the Living Constitution.

## Controversial

When a PC Marxist wants to call into question an idea, person, policy, or proposal he has targeted for elimination, he labels it "controversial." This labeling suggests that many persons object to the idea, proposal, person, or policy without having to specify their number or the nature of their objections, if there actually are any. Constant repetition that something or someone is "controversial" will erode support for it or him, no matter how much support he or it may have had before the label was affixed.

See entries on Anecdotal and Myth.

## Co-opt, to

To infiltrate and take control of (co-opt) as many existing institutions and organizations in the United States as possible has been an objective of agitprop from the start of the Counter Culture/Political Correctness Movement.

## Counter Culture Movement

The anti-American movement which went by this name in the 1960s began on American campuses where young, idealistic, middle-class Americans were vulnerable to being misled into believing they were building a more humane, freer culture in America, when in fact they were being recruited to destroy America (see the interview with the three young American agitators in Part I above). The Counter Culture Movement, as its name indicated, opposed everything pertaining to American culture, not just some, specific aspects of it. The movement was the Soviet Union's front inside the United States in its Cold War with the U.S. In the 1970s, the Counter Culture began to be called by some Americans "Political Correctness" because they noticed its similarities to the "culture war" of Mao Zedong's in communist China. Though the name "Counter Culture" became "Political Correctness" in the 1970s, the movement's long-term objective remained constant: to destroy America's culture and rebuild it as Cultural Marxism, thus eliminating America as the main impediment to the global expansion of Marxism. The movement's immediate goal, of course, was to get U.S. military forces out of South Vietnam so North Vietnamese communist forces from could take over the entire country.

By the 1970s, because of violent agitation and highly effective propaganda inside the United States, American troops were ordered home from South Vietnam by the U.S. government, turning that country over to communist rule. After American withdrawal from South Vietnam, less physical forms of intimidation began replacing the violence which had characterized the initial phase of agitprop in America. Physical violence remains, however, congenial to PC Marxists.

See entries on the Cold War, Community Organizing, the Establishment.

# Crime

Crime to a PC Marxist is a relative matter. Any behavior connected with redressing an historical grievance by a member of a "victimized" biological class, even though it is a crime, is not considered a crime by PC Marxists. They say it is "understandable" when weighed against historical wrongs (racism, for instance). Robbery, kidnapping, arson, assault with a deadly weapon, breaking and entering, rioting, mugging, rape, shoplifting, and so on — even murder — are "understandable" in a context of historical "social" injustice against "victimized" biological classes.

To a Marxist, crime and wrongdoing are always a matter of the environment. No criminal is personally accountable for his actions. His environment is responsible. Of course, if a person opposes Marxism, that's different. Any behavior of that sort is prosecutable and punishable, however that can be arranged.

See entries on Environmentalism and Personal Responsibility and the commentary A Standard of Double Standards in Part III below.

# Crisis

PC Marxists foster crises which allow them to propose solutions to increase the scope of their power and control.

# Critical Theory

This is the name that was given by German Marxists in the 1930s to criticism and condemnation of major elements of Western culture: capitalism, Christianity, consumerism, nationalism, etc. The Marxist intellectuals in the Frankfort School who began this work in Germany continued it as refugees at universities in the United States when Nazis in Germany began rounding up, imprisoning, and executing Marxists. It is fashionable at prestigious U.S. law schools today to offer courses in "Critical Theory."

See entry on the Frankfort School.

## Culture

Culture in the sense it is used in this book is a set of right beliefs which are right because they have been acted on in a society for more than four generations, which is to say the beliefs have been acted on for so many generations (four is the minimum) they have acquired a compelling *historical* authority. Cultures are a set of beliefs expressed in behavior which is not coerced. It is not possible to "build" an authentic culture according to a blueprint, as Marxists think can be done. The reason it takes four generations for a set of beliefs to acquire an historical character and become a culture is not difficult to see. The second and third generations who act on the beliefs of an incipient culture as they come of age are imitating the behaviors of their parents and grandparents which express the beliefs. But as the fourth generation comes of age which did not know their great-grandparents (the initial generation of the incipient culture), they acquire a sense of belonging to an *historic* way of life that existed before they were born. They perceive their parents and grandparents expressing reverence for a deceased generation. It is this sense, in the fourth generation and subsequent generations, of sharing a set of belief-behaviors which existed before these generations did that gives a set of belief-behaviors the historical authority it must have if it is to be a culture.

PC Marxists are interrupting in various ways the behaviors which express American culture and thus interrupting the transmission of America's culture, thereby weakening and diminishing it. The process of such interruption naturally focuses on young adults and adolescents, the generation that has not yet fully internalized the culture's beliefs by habitually acting on them. Marxist agitprop in the United States has been attacking American culture with ever greater ferocity and comprehensiveness since the 1960s. The attacks have weakened the transmission of American cultural beliefs in the last three generations.

See entries on Culture War, Neoteny, Open-Minded, Pop Culture.

# Culture War

To wage a culture war is to attack an existing culture's historical beliefs by ceaselessly deploying intense agitprop against them. The purpose of culture war is to destroy the historical authority of an existing set of belief-behaviors by finding fault with all aspects of it, especially by denouncing its history. Culture war is relentless condemnation of a culture motivated by hatred of it and a revolutionary desire to replace it with a different set of belief-behaviors.

# Czars (slang)

The executive branch of the U.S. government has for a long time now been assigning excessive power to individuals to solve problems, a practice which the Constitution does not authorize. The first of these executive-branch "czars" (though the nickname wasn't used then) was President Woodrow Wilson's personal emissary Colonel E. M. House before, during, and after the First World War. Franklin Roosevelt had many such envoys during his twelve-year presidency (1933–1945), e.g. Harry Hopkins, a clandestine Soviet agent who lived with FDR in the White House (see Diana West's *American Betrayal*, pp. 129–148, 180–191; also Tim Tzouliadis's *The Forsaken*, p. 284–285). Such emissaries have been nicknamed czars because of the extraordinary power they wield as surrogate presidents. President Obama employed over a score of them. The empowerment of such persons is one of the signs that America's form of constitutional, republican government is unraveling. It is past the time when the people of the States should exert their "reserved" powers to restore America's constitutional, republican form of government.

# Deadnaming

This recent PC coinage refers to continuing to call a person by the name he or she was given at birth before they changed their gender.

Anyone who persists in using the old name instead of the name indicating the new gender is guilty of "deadnaming."

## Death with Dignity

A more attractive expression than the term euthanasia but standing for the same thing, "death with dignity" reflects the PC dogma that man is only another species of animal whose life has no special value. Just as we speak of "putting down" a pet, so agitprop has invented the term "death with dignity" for euthanizing human beings.

See the entry on Animal Rights.

## Deconstructionism

Deconstructionism is a theory of language that originated in France in the 1960s, with roots in the postwar period of the late 1940s and 50s. It was avidly embraced by U.S. academics in the 1970s (perhaps because it represented a vast new field for academic publications). In any case, deconstructionism deeply influenced academic thought in America in the later twentieth century. According to the theory, language has no fixed, coherent meaning, and any text can be "unpacked" to take from it whatever meaning one wants and has predetermined is "appropriate." All language is "problematic" (even the meaning of the word *is*). By applying this concept of language to the documents which underlie the institutions of Western civilization, they have been made to a high degree malleable and contingent. In other words, their stability is being undermined and destroyed ("deconstructed") which is extremely useful to the campaign of PC Marxists to demolish America's culture and reconstruct it as Cultural Marxism. But if language is infinitely malleable (as this theory claims), deconstructionism itself has no objectivity or authority unless it is viewed as an exception to its own theory. PC Marxists have absolutely no trouble with making that exception. Double standards are part of the Marxian modus operandi.

See commentary A Standard of Double Standards in Part III below.

## Democracy

The American understanding of democracy may be stated as majority rule under a written constitution with protection for the personal
liberties of individuals, a process in which the practical, immediate
interests of the people are formulated by diverse political parties
independent of the government. PC Marxists think that only one
political party is needed, the party of Marxism, because the Marxian
view of history as "class struggle" for "social" justice is "scientific." In
fact, the Prologue to the Constitution of the Union of Soviet Socialist
Republics in effect when the Soviet Union fell, described the Soviet
government as based on science.

## Dependence

The opposite of the creativity, freedom, independence, and self-
determination of individuals, dependence on Big Government is the
essence and common denominator of every kind of socialism, from
the most benign to the most ruthless. In the milder forms of socialism — those that use the qualifier "Christian" to characterize themselves — actual persons may receive a modicum of benefit if the size
of the country is not too large, it's prosperous, and multiple political
parties are allowed. But dependence on one-party socialism in a large
country like the United States (the world's third-largest in size and
inhabitants) would replicate the disaster of one-party socialism in the
USSR. Agitprop has been steadily moving America in that disastrous
direction.

In a one-party socialist system where truth is whatever the Party
says it is, which is why the newspaper of the Communist Party of
the Soviet Union was called "Pravda" (Truth), it is extremely difficult to get a full-blown socialist system to stop once it's operating.
And the results will be to some degree disagreeable because once the

bureaucratic structures of a socialist state are functioning, whatever they determine you need is what you get. In a thoroughly socialist regime, government experts make the decisions which most affect the lives of people rather than the people themselves. Individuals decide very little. The scale of human suffering and political executions which resulted from the attempt to make Marxism work in the USSR offers ample proof of the evils of a one-party, socialist dictatorship having a mania for Political Correctness.

Marxists want uniform government for the world. Such global uniformity, they claim, is imperative because politically incorrect people do not know what's "scientifically" good for them and will sabotage the "scientific" efforts of those who do. To a Marxist, opponents of Political Correctness are enemies of humanity, and must be crushed to clear the way "forward."

## Dialogue

PC Marxists want "dialogue" whenever their doctrines have been effectively opposed. The purpose of dialogue for Marxists is to reestablish ascendancy whenever that is weakened.

## Discrimination

Discrimination once had the meaning of making careful distinctions based on evidence. Agitprop has given this term a wholly different meaning. Discrimination is now a synonym for prejudice. This is an enormous change. It makes any judgment not predicated on and in accord with PC Marxism a matter of "racism," "sexism," "xenophobia," etc. Only judgments in accord with the dogmas of Political Correctness are objective, just, and acceptable to PC Marxists.

See entries on Bias-Free, Double Standards, and the commentary A Standard of Double Standards in Part III below.

## Diversity

In the lexicon of redefinitions devised by agitprop, "diversity" is among the most consequential terms, if not the most consequential. Political Correctness has made mandatory "diversity" the Marxist counterpart of American culture's belief in self-determination. Every American institution of higher learning of any consequence today has a diversity office to set and administer student admission quotas and quotas for hiring and promoting faculty in accordance with the membership of students and faculty in "diverse" biological classes. Likewise, U.S. corporations of any consequence today employ an estimated 15,000 persons nationwide whose sole task is to explain and implement "diversity." This "diversity" is nothing more or less than a requirement that certain biological classes in American society be compensated through making their biology the primary qualification for hiring and promoting them. The responsibility of individuals for their lives, one of the central beliefs of American culture, is being supplanted by privileges tied to Marxian class struggle defined by biology. Mandatory "diversity" is a Marxist concept with tremendous ideological ramifications in the agitprop war against America's culture.

See commentaries Biological Class Consciousness, Mandatory "Diversity," and "Social" Justice in Part III below.

## Double Standards

The replacement of existing perceptions and standards of judgment with new perceptions and standards of judgment is essential to the revolution now taking place in America. The existing perceptions and standards are the beliefs of America's culture; the new perceptions and standards are the dogmas of Cultural Marxism. PC Marxists refuse to allow their behavior to be judged by any other standard than Cultural Marxism, and according to that standard, the beliefs of American culture are contemptible. Adherents of America's existing culture of course disagree with that view and want the historic beliefs of

American culture to be the standard for judging behavior. The conflict over which standard should apply, Marxist or American, is the main cause of the polarization now dividing and distressing America.

See the commentary A Standard of Double Standards in Part III below.

## Empower, to

The verb empower is used today by PC Marxists to indicate a distribution of privileges and benefits to "victimized" biological classes. But when a PC Marxist speaks of empowering biological classes, he is really speaking of making the movement he is part of more powerful, which is done through creating more government programs to (supposedly) benefit the "victimized" classes, which PC Marxists are (supposedly) helping. The destruction of the Negro American family under the so-called War on Poverty, however, shows what can happen when PC Marxists "empower" those in need by defining and controlling what they receive from government. PC Marxists are not really as concerned about the human needs of "victimized" biological classes as they are with gaining more political power. Political Correctness grows ever stronger by making Americans more dependent on "entitlements."

See entries on Victimize/Victimization and War on Poverty, and the commentary Biological Class Consciousness in Part III below.

## Entitled/Entitlement

PC Marxists use these terms, which were once used only by lawyers in regard to legal technicalities regarding property ownership, to give their redistribution of wealth in the United States an aura of constitutional lawfulness, as if programmatic wealth redistribution had some basis in the Constitution of the United States. In truth, of course, the federal government has no constitutional warrant to redistribute wealth in the U.S.

See entries on Dependence and Empower.

## Entrant

PC Marxists use this term to describe the tens of millions of illegal aliens (no one can say how many) whose presence in the United States they favor and are principally responsible for. *Entrant* is the result of deliberate modifications to the term "illegal alien." First, the phrase "illegal alien" was changed to "undocumented immigrant"; then that term was simplified to "immigrant" by dropping the adjective undocumented and further changed to "migrant" by clipping off the first syllable of "immigrant." *Migrant* is now the most commonly used term of reference for someone who ought truthfully to be called "an illegal alien." George Soros in his op-ed piece in the *Wall Street Journal* for Sept. 20, 2016 refers to illegal aliens eleven times as *migrant*s and never once uses the term illegal alien. But as deceitful as the word migrant is, the process of linguistic transformation has continued. *Entrant* is now replacing *migrant*. This newest euphemism, "entrant," for "illegal alien" not only has no connection even in a roundabout way to any behavior that could be associated with an illegal act but no connection at all with immigration. *Entrant* refers simply to a person who has entered. It is connected especially with entering a contest to win a prize. For the aliens swarming across the southern border of the United States illegally or overstaying their visas in violation of U.S. immigration statutes, that is appropriate. Every illegal alien wants to win the prize of living in the United States which includes nowadays so many "entitlements."

## Environmentalism

A crucially important PC term, this invented word is an essential part of the lexicon of agitprop. Every time the term environmentalism is seen or heard, the idea it stands for becomes more deeply engrained in the American consciousness, namely that the environment determines human behavior which is a foundational idea of Marxism.

The Russian scientist I. P. Pavlov (1849–1936) demonstrated that the behavior of dogs could be conditioned by stimuli from their environment, and the Marxists who took over Russia in 1917 embraced Pavlov's finding wholeheartedly because what he discovered refuted the contention of the Russian czars and nobility that their right to rule was established by their superior biological lineage or blood. Marxists wanted rule based on the purity of one's political "line" (such "scientific" propositions as the idea that a superior human environment will produce superior human behavior). The determinant relation of the environment to human conduct was perhaps the most fundamental flaw in the Marxian theories on history and human nature.

America's culture is based on belief in self-determination, the conviction that human beings can improve their lives through their own efforts as stewards of the life God has given them. Political Correctness scorns the idea of man's unique, God-endowed nature. In Christian cultures, man determines the quality of his environment rather than the quality of the environment determining his behavior.

Environmentalism is now being taught at every level of American education from kindergarten though graduate school, and various academic specialties have been created in the field (e.g. environmental anthropology, environmental engineering, environmental biology, environmental law). Environmentalism is inherent to the philosophy of materialistic determinism which lies at the center of Marxian politics.

## Environmental Racism

A combination of two PC dogmas, environmentalism and racism, "environmental racism" teaches that American capitalists locate their most hazardous manufacturing operations in American communities and foreign countries populated by dark-skinned persons rather than in communities inhabited by white Americans.

## Equality

Equality in American culture is the belief the Declaration of Independence expresses in saying human beings have from God the same rights to life, liberty, and the pursuit of happiness which is to say the freedom to improve their lives. To a PC Marxist, however, equality means government-planned sameness of outcomes by controlled distribution of wealth. Deciding which social classes get what is the Marxian concept of equality.

## Establishment, the

A term used by the Counter Culture Movement in the 1960s in referring to anyone who supported the "status quo" in America. The movement's favorite epithet for the establishment then was "the pigs" (see interview with the three young American agitators in Part I above). Because those who were on the outside of the "establishment" in the 1960s and 70s trying to take power have now become the establishment, the derogatory label pigs has been dropped. But the term establishment continues to be used.

## Euro-American

A word invented like the term African American to prevent an unequivocal American identity. "Euro-American" implies that Americans are a sort of transatlantic European. It is a way of suggesting Americans are Europeans living in America, just as "African American" suggests Negro Americans are Africans living in America.

See entry on African American.

## Eurocentric

A descriptive term for anything pertaining to the Marxist designation Euro-American, "Eurocentric" suggests that the way of life of Americans (their culture) derives from Europe and its history, which is not the case. America's culture derives from the behaviors of a certain kind of person (self-selected ambitious immigrants) living in a resource-rich environment for four consecutive centuries. The set of cultural beliefs which generation upon generation of Americans developed from a dynamic of unique demographic, political, social, economic, and geographic factors produced America's distinctive way of life known as American culture.

See entry on Culture.

## Evil

This word refers to something in human nature quite apart from the influence of environment and beyond the power of either government or science to control. Therefore, the word evil is never used by Marxists. Its use would contradict their philosophy of materialistic determinism, as can be seen in the great hullabaloo President Ronald Reagan caused in 1983 in calling the Soviet Union "an evil empire" which violated rule number one among Marxist intellectuals: Marxism must never be judged by Judeo-Christian standards. Not only was the reaction to Reagan's pronouncement enormous in the Soviet Union, but also among PC Marxists and their sympathizers in the United States who were likewise appalled. The Soviets reacted vehemently to the effrontery of Reagan bluntly calling their empire what it was, an empire, and condemning their project of "building communism" as evil. The same seems to have also been true among U.S. Marxists.

## Evolution

One of the big ideas of the modern world popularized by the followers of Charles Darwin (1809–1882), evolution refers to Darwin's theory of biological developments on earth after the first single-cell living organism began reproducing. In his study titled *On the Origin of Species* (1859), Darwin said that what animal breeders had been doing for thousands of years: modifying domesticated species of animals through deliberate selective breeding for desired traits, random biological variations had been achieving in nature since the beginning of life on Earth. The environment had been doing the selecting. Because randomly generated traits which enhanced survival would be more likely to be passed on, those traits were constantly accumulating and producing new species better adapted to survival and reproduction. It was a closed loop which enhanced survival, but it had not been designed. The loop operated randomly though it had a purpose which could be described as survival of the fittest. Darwin's chief postulate was that new plant and animal species better able to survive were being produced. He called his theory "Natural Selection" and said that over the course of millions of generations Natural Selection had slowly but inexorably produced every one of the millions of plant and animal species that had ever existed on the planet.

For many scientifically minded persons, Darwin's theory of Natural Selection replaced the biblical account of creation in Genesis because it was touted as "science."

Darwin thought corroborating evidence for his theory would be discovered in the fossil record of ancient life forms as knowledge of those life forms (paleontology) became more complete. But that did not happen. The unearthing and classifying of innumerable fossil life forms in the century following Darwin's death in 1882 did not reveal the immense number of transitional life forms from one species to another which he postulated. Such evidence ought to have been abundant, since Natural Selection was supposed to be a universal, constant process. Despite the absence of scientific evidence, however, Darwin's explanation of how new species of animals and plants are generated (Natural Selection, popularly known as "evolution") is now regarded as proven science by Marxists and other materialistic determinists because of its political attractiveness, regardless of the fact that the fossil record has not corroborated the theory. Indeed, whoever questions the scientific validity of Natural Selection will instantly bring down on themselves the wrath of agitprop. Promising young scientists with good records in research have been denied tenure for raising questions about Darwin's theory.

More important than the failure of the now plentiful record of ancient life forms preserved as fossils (paleontology) to validate Natural Selection as science, advances in cellular biology, a field of science which didn't exist in Darwin's day, are demonstrating that the highly complex biological functions of living cells require enormous amounts of sequentially and lawfully delivered information to perform their specialized functions. Cellular processes, it turns out, are governed by precise laws. How could such complex laws have "evolved" rather than come into existence as designed sets? Take for instance the ability to reproduce which distinguishes living matter from non-living matter. That process (reproduction) which is essential to the theory of Natural Selection could not itself have "evolved." It had to be coeval with life for life to exist since it defines what it means to be alive. The modern stumbling block for Darwinian theory is how to reconcile the theory with the fact that such vital cellular processes as reproduction and the coagulation of blood to staunch a wound (then shutting down coagulation before the whole blood supply solidifies) are impossible to explain by means of Darwin's theory.

Darwin's doctrine that all living things in response to their environments are constantly and inexorably producing new species of plants and animals better adapted to survival has become the world's most influential unproven idea. In that respect, it is not unlike the never-demonstrated, common belief among medieval alchemists that base metals can be transformed into gold through the use of "the Philosopher's Stone." Like Natural Selection, that idea too had a highly attractive theoretical potential.

See entries on the Bible, the Big Bang, Intelligent Design.

## Exceptionalism

A Marxist coinage of the 1920s, the term exceptionalism expresses the scorn Marxists feel for the American conviction that the history of the

United States contradicts Marx's theory of history as class struggle. The belief that America's history differs from that of other nations, which was once nearly universal among Americans, offends Marxian historicism, according to which there can be no exceptions to history as "science." To a Marxist, class struggle is universal, and any claim that some country's history could deviate from that universality is intolerable because the study of history is "science."

## Existential Threat

A danger that imperils the existence of whatever is said to be under such a threat, this term is used by PC Marxists to frighten people into accepting Marxist doctrines as offering the only viable solution to a dire problem.

## Exploit/Exploitation

According to PC Marxists, capitalism exploits workers. It does not benefit workers in any way. Marxism promises to stop the exploitation forever once it is globally implemented. It would be folly, however, to consider the history of labor in the USSR or Poland when Marxists ruled those countries or in Cuba today as proof that workers are better off under Marxism than they are under a free market economy.

See entries on Capitalism and the Free Market.

## Extremist/Extremism

Terms which PC Marxists use to characterize their opponents, as in the phrases "right-wing extremists" and "Christian extremists," the words extremist and extremism more accurately characterize Marxist thinking and practices.

## Fairness

This broad term is crucial to PC Marxism's promise to create a new society in which capitalism's *unfairness* will be replaced by the planned *fairness* of "social" justice.

See entry on Social Justice and the commentary "Social" Justice in Part III below.

## Fake News

A lie deliberately placed in the media to influence public opinion, as, for example, the false account President Obama, Secretary of State Clinton, and various spokesmen for the Obama administration gave the media about the nature of the attack on the American diplomatic compound at Benghazi, Libya in 2012 by a heavily armed group of men who killed the U.S. ambassador to Libya and three other Americans. The attack, the Obama administration said, was a spontaneous mob reaction to a vile anti-Muslim video produced in the United States. The media's acceptance and publication of that fake story without verifying it made Obama's re-election possible. Had American voters known the truth of how deceitful the Obama administration's account of what happened at Benghazi was, they might well have refused to keep Obama in the White House another four years.

## Family, the

As the means by which procreating, nurturing, and rearing children in a stable, safe home, the one-man-one-woman family is the essential social institution of Western civilization, including America's Christian culture. Marx and Engels, however, considered the "bourgeois" family a serious obstacle to the restructuring of human life they desired because near the end of section III of their *Communist Manifesto* (1848) they declared that "abolition of the family" would be one of the changes to "existing society" that communism would effect. The politically correct implementation of belief in rearing children by one parent ("single parenting"), out of wedlock births, unlimited abortions, "no-fault divorce," and homosexual "marriage" are indications that that Marxist aim, the destruction of the Judeo-Christian family, is being accomplished in the United States.

See entries on Abortion Rights, Single Parenting, Same-Sex Marriage.

## Fascist

Fascism or totalitarian socialism of the nationalist kind (e.g. the German National Socialist Workers Party or "Nazis") was a formidable rival to Marxism in the 1930s. To this day, "fascist" and "fascism" are the strongest pejoratives in the PC Marxist lexicon.

## Fear Monger

Though perhaps a bit outdated, this accusatory term is still a standard epithet of agitprop. It alleges that opponents of Marxism make invalid accusations against it to create fear of Marxist doctrines. However, it must be remembered that it is PC Marxists not their opponents who every election cycle in the United States instigated rumors that Republican candidates intend to abolish social security if elected.

See entries on McCarthyism and Witch Hunt.

## Feminism

Feminism is the name given the "mystique" of female sensibilities pumped up by agitprop as part of its rhetoric that American women are an oppressed "minority."

## Flash Mob

A "flash mob" is a spur of the moment, improvised counter-demonstration by Marxist agitators in response to a demonstration by opponents of which they had no prior notice.

# Frankfurt School, the

Founded in Frankfurt, Germany in 1923 by a group of Marxist intellectuals, the Institute for Social Research (the Frankfurt School) was the leading center for research in Europe outside of Russia during the 1920s and early 30s on philosophy, political and economic theory, and the arts from a Marxist perspective. In 1930, the Institute inaugurated a critique of Western civilization called "Critical Theory" which denounced key elements of Western civilization (capitalism, Christianity, the family, Judeo-Christian morality, consumerism, nationalism, etc.) as instances of oppression.

When the Nazi regime began persecuting Marxists and Jews, members of the Frankfurt School (many of whom were both) fled to the United States where they found jobs at liberal universities such as Berkeley, Brandeis, Columbia, and Princeton and through their academic positions at these prestigious American institutions of higher learning continued the work they had been doing in Germany. Former members of the Frankfort School in exile in America exerted significant influence on the Counter Culture Movement on American campuses in the 1960s. (Members of the Frankfort School may have been under orders from Moscow to seek asylum in the U.S. rather than the USSR.)

Herbert Marcuse (1898–1979) is a particularly noteworthy example of the effect of this Marxist Diaspora. His U.S. publications provided the rationale for a great deal of the "protesting" against American culture on American university and college campuses in the 1960s and had a general formative influence on the thinking and behavior of young Americans in college in the 60s and 70s. His works with the most impact among American academics and college students were *Eros and Civilization* (1955) and *One-Dimensional Man* (1964). The former contributed to the change known as "the sexual revolution" and everything that it involved. (The idea of "free love" has always been part of Marxist anti-family rhetoric.) Marcuse's *Eros and Civilization* provided a high-sounding justification for sexual promiscuity. *One-Dimensional Man* argued for "liberating tolerance," which is to say adamant intolerance for proposals from conservatives and absolute tolerance for any proposal emanating from the Left.

Among other members of the Frankfort School whose writings and teaching had a notable influence in America in the 1960s and 70s were the sociologist Wilhelm Reich and the psychologist Erich Fromm.

## Freedom

Agitation and propaganda for Political Correctness have redefined freedom to mean liberation from belief in God and Judeo-Christian morality and emancipation from capitalism. To destroy America's culture, as the necessary precondition for establishing Cultural Marxism in the United States and, therefore, around the world, the PC definition of freedom is used as a wrecking ball to smash American cultural beliefs. Freedom in America's culture is essentially the freedom which comes from accepting God's Ten Commandments and the teachings of Jesus as moral guides, and Jesus as a personal savior.

See entries on Consenting Adults, Freedom of Religion, Liberation, Lifestyle, Victimless Crime, and in Part III below A Culture without Belief in God.

## Freedom of Religion

Belief in a God-given birthright to "Life, Liberty, and the Pursuit of Happiness" is the foundational belief of America's culture, and from it stems the belief that governments derive "their just Powers from Consent of the Governed" (second paragraph Declaration of Independence, 1776). Freedom of religion is necessary to preserving that birthright, because no meaningful belief in God is possible without freedom of religion, which is to say freedom of conscience. Freedom of religion has, therefore, been a special target of agitprop which has been doing everything in its power for decades to diminish the influence of Christianity in America. Agitprop's most impressive accomplishment in this regard has been establishing the Separation of Church and State dogma and using it to suppress public expressions of belief in God. Separation of Church and State argues that because public religious expressions are offensive to atheists and to believers in God who are intolerant of religions that differ from their own, all public expressions of religious belief should be banned, even though the Constitution guarantees freedom of religious expression. This is a surefire argument for suppressing religious expressions in public places because there are no religious views which will not offend someone.

PC agitprop is now making this same argument regarding freedom of speech, that speech which is offensive to someone ought not to be allowed. To PC Marxists, only the expression of politically correct dogmas is permissible.

The perverse argument *that freedom of religion requires suppression of religion* began with the false definitions of religious establishment put forth in 1947 in *Everson v. Board of Education* (330 U.S. 1, 1947) by the late U.S. Supreme Court Justice Hugo Black who epitomizes the meaning of Lenin's concept of "useful idiot." In articulating the dogma of Separation of Church and State in that decision, Hugo Black gave the world four definitions of "a religious establishment," not one of which was grounded in history, reason, or constitutional law. For example, he proclaimed that a law that promoted "all religions" is a religious establishment, whereas a religious establishment law invariably favors *a single religion* (which the law names) and never "all religions." But Black's nonsensical definitions of religious establishments in *Everson*, because they appeared in a write up of a Supreme Court verdict, have provided the rationale for the federal judiciary's numerous suppressions of religious freedom in the last half-century.

See entry on Useful Idiot and the commentary "Social" Justice in Part III below.

## Free Market, the

The economic system in the world's most prosperous nations, the free market developed in Europe during the Enlightenment (the 17th and 18th centuries) and has spread throughout the world. Sometimes called free enterprise, the free market has particularly flourished in America's individualistic, freedom-loving, hard-working, capitalistic culture. Such free market institutions as freedom of contract, rule of law, and representative government favor individual enterprise and promote the formation of private property. Freedom of assembly, association, press, religion, and speech and multiparty politics are also conducive to free market activities. The one-man-one-woman family which has tended to foster the virtues of diligence, honesty, and personal responsibility has also played a major role in developing the free market, which has brought material improvements and general prosperity to every society where it exists.

Marxism with its ideological hostility to the family as an institution, belief in unlimited government regulation, animosity toward private property, and ideological dedication to state-owned property and state monopolies is strongly opposed to everything associated with the free market.

## Free Speech

PC Marxists absolutely believe in free speech for themselves, but no one else. Language for them is not a means for discovering and communicating truth or expressing love and devotion, but rather a means of political propaganda, agitation, and indoctrination. For a Marxist, language serves nothing but partisan interests.

See entry Academic Freedom and the commentary Correct "Free" Speech in Part III below.

# Gloating

A commonplace word used with special significance by PC agitators and propagandists in the United States in connection with the collapse of the Soviet Union the last week of December 1991. Americans were advised not to "gloat" over that event by celebrating it. To "gloat" over the demise of the Soviet Union, they were told, would add insult to injury for the Soviet leaders and be downright insensitive. Consequently in 1992, there were no nationwide celebrations of the total, unconditional triumph of the United States in its Cold War with the Soviet Union.

See entries on the Cold War and Triumphalism.

# Globalism

Globalism is an act, doctrine, or institution of international significance showing global awareness. Globalism has been a prominent feature of Marxist theory. The call Marx made, for instance, in *The Communist Manifesto* to overthrow capitalism was addressed to "workers of *the world*" (italics added). A series of numbered "Internationals," or international meetings of Marxists, form a conspicuous part of the history of Marxism. The first of them was organized by Marx himself, before Lenin founded the USSR. These "Internationals" were intended to support and facilitate the spread of communism to every part of the globe. The Third International, set up by Lenin in 1919, remained in existence and convened meetings in the Soviet Union until 1943. This international conspiratorial feature of Marxism became, through Lenin's genius, an inherent feature of Soviet foreign policy. The "liberation wars" instigated and sponsored by the Soviet Union in Africa in the 1960s reflect the global thinking of Lenin's successors. The inauguration in the 1960s of the Counter Culture Movement inside the United States was another major initiative of Marxian globalism. The chief manifestation of globalism in the twentieth century, however, was the founding of the United Nations in 1945 in which the Soviet Union played a leading role because globalism is intrinsic to Marxism.

See entry on Internationalism.

## Graffiti

PC Marxists insist that graffiti is art, something human beings value. The insistence that graffiti is art disguises what it really is: an assault on private property. Graffiti is a form of intimidation justified as art. It vividly demonstrates that no building, whether the property be a business, a church, a government workplace, a home, or even an entire neighborhood, is immune from attack. Graffiti either transforms property into a billboard for political propaganda or defaces it so it cannot properly serve its intended purpose decorously. Graffiti is an expropriation of property for revolutionary purposes.

See entry on Art.

## Greed

In the political speech agitprop is creating in the United States, greed is a synonym for capitalism.

## Hardwired

A behavior Marxists want to change but are finding it difficult to alter, because it is probably genetically determined, is designated in PC newspeak as "hardwired." This usage suggests the importance environmentalism has for Marxists in contrast to genetics.

## Hate Speech

In 2010 at the University of Illinois, Ken Howell was fired for having engaged in "hate speech." What did he say that merited being labeled "hate speech" and cost him his job? He explained the Catholic Church's teachings on extramarital sex and homosexuality. "Hate speech" is any speech PC Marxists regard as intolerable because it does not accord with and support politically correct dogmas. Creating rules defining "hate speech" and designating punishments for their violation is one of the ways PC Marxists have of controlling language; hence perceptions and behavior. The concept of "hate speech" is a highly effective tool for controlling speech. PC "speech codes" make it impossible to freely discuss topics PC Marxists do not want discussed, such as the Catholic church's teachings on extramarital sex and homosexuality.

See entries on Microaggression, Safe Space, Speech Codes.

## Hedonism

A kind of behavior encouraged by agitprop as part of its agenda to demolish America's middle-class, Judeo-Christian morality, hedonism includes adultery, alcoholism, "recreational" drugs, "recreational" sex, pornography, and all other forms of self-indulgence. Because self-control is crucial to America's Christian culture, Political Correctness promotes hedonism, which is the opposite of self-control.

See entry on Addiction.

## Hispanic

An ethnic consciousness created by PC agitprop which has contributed to dividing American society into classes defined by birth.

See entries on Class Consciousness and Multiculturalism and the commentary Biological Class Consciousness in Part III below.

## Homeless, the

The persons with no fixed abode designated by this term are typically single men who've lost their jobs and been unable to find new ones, single men and women who prefer a vagabond life, persons (including parents with children) who've experienced a sudden and devastating financial reversal, persons who've been totally alienated from American culture by agitprop but are too listless to become agitators for "change," or persons suffering some mild, nonviolent form of mental illness. An agitprop campaign was mounted in the 1970s to have mentally ill persons deinstitutionalized, if they were not "a danger to themselves or others," to increase the number of homeless persons and thus contribute to destabilizing American society. Homelessness is a significant source of social disorder. Promoting and supporting it through privately organized or governmental aid damages one of the essential principles of America's culture — self-determination — and fosters a crude form of dependence, the *sine qua non* of socialism.

See entries on Alienate/Alienation and Dependence.

## Homophobia

A brilliant propaganda invention, the agitprop term "homophobia" refers to the fear and loathing of homosexuals which supposedly (according to Political Correctness) all Americans feel more or less and which moves them to want to oppress the lesbian, gay, bisexual, transgender, questioning (LGBTQ) community and to tolerate violence against it.

See entries on Islamophobia and Sexual Orientation.

## Humanitarian

A term in the PC lexicon which gives compassion priority over obedience to the law, as in such PC yard signs regarding illegal aliens as "Humanitarian Aid Is Never a Crime" and "No Human Being Is Illegal." The idea that humanitarianism justifies aiding and abetting illegal immigration into the United States appeals to the charitable sentiments which are part of the Christian nature of America's culture.

See entry on Compassion, and the commentary "Sensitivity" Above All Else in Part III.

## Hypocrisy

Hypocrisy is a leading characteristic of Marxism, along with its regressive orientation to the past, conspiratorial theory of history, and disregard of truth. Hypocrisy is an accurate description of the dispar-ity between the righteous claims of Political Correctness and its often-sordid results; between its pretentious dogmas and their disastrous results.

## Illegal Alien

The accurate designation for a person from another country in the United States in violation of U.S. immigration law, "illegal alien" is the matter-of-fact term PC Marxists never use and criticize others for using. Rather, they disseminate language to obscure the fact that tens of millions of aliens are present in the United States illegally. PC Marxists and their supporters prefer not to think in terms of legal and illegal entry into the United States which is why they so adamantly oppose building a physical barrier across America's southern border to keep illegal aliens out of the United States and any proposal by a State of the United States to require proof of U.S. citizenship to vote in U.S. elections. They want millions of illegal aliens to vote in U.S. elections to increase the power of PC Marxism in America.

## Imperialism

This is what Marxists in the 1960s and 70s in the United States and elsewhere vehemently accused the United States of practicing, par-ticularly in its defense of South Vietnam from communist invaders from North Vietnam.

See summary of 1970 interview with Marxist agitators in Part I above.

## Impose, to

This verb is in frequent use by PC Marxists in their anti-Christian propaganda, one of the themes of which is that Christians are "im-posing" their beliefs on American society. In point of fact, of course, Christianity was widespread in the United States before the Counter

Culture/Political Correctness Movement began in the 1960s. Despite what PC Marxists say, Christians have no need to "impose" their religion on America. Christianity has from the outset of European settlement in America been the prevalent religion of Americans. In truth, it is Political Correctness which has been *imposing* itself on America through agitprop in the late twentieth century.

It is characteristic of PC Marxists to accuse others of doing what they are doing.

See entry on Preemptive Accusation.

## Inappropriate

PC activists consider the use of the words evil and sin "inappropriate" because they are Judeo-Christian terms. If a PC activist is caught doing evil or in a sin, his conduct is not referred to in those terms, but is called "inappropriate" or a "mistake," and everyone is advised to "take a deep breath and move on" — the advice Hillary Clinton gave regarding her husband's scandalous sexual behavior in the White House. No one, according to PC Marxists, ought to be upset by something that is only a "mistake" or "inappropriate."

See entry on Mistake.

## Inclusive/Inclusiveness

These terms have been imbued by PC agitprop with special virtue. In agitprop parlance, "inclusive" and "inclusiveness" indicate being without any prejudice that would exclude anyone from anything for any reason (except anti-Marxism). Example: San Domenico Catholic School in San Anselmo, California removed from its entryway in 2017 a statue of the Virgin Mary holding the baby Jesus so that the school would be "inclusive of other religions." This is like newscasters at ABC television studios in New York City being told on September 11, 2001 not to wear American-flag lapel pins while reporting the massacres of Americans by Islamic terrorists that day in Manhattan, Washington, and western Pennsylvania, lest wearing such patriotic emblems be regarded as "taking sides."

## Individualism

A fundamental difference between American culture and Cultural Marxism is that the former promotes individual aspirations and achievements as essential to social well-being. In America's culture, every person has primary responsibility for the outcome of his or her life. Marxism, on the other hand, makes "society" responsible for classes of persons "from the cradle to the grave."

## Indoctrination

PC Marxists are indoctrinating American public school students in the dogmas of Political Correctness instead of helping them get the skills and knowledge they need to lead independent, self-determined lives. There is a fundamental, immense difference between receiving indoctrination and getting an education.

See entries on Liberal Education, Sensitivity Training.

## In Power

The term in power is used by PC Marxists instead of the term being in office. The phrase is indicative of the degradation of constitutional republicanism in the United States under the influence of agitprop. In American culture, before its "deconstruction" by agitprop, the only persons "in power" were the people of the States. They periodically delegated — under the restrictions they created in the principles, procedures, prohibitions, and provisions of the Constitution of the United States — a portion of their authority to persons they elected to represent and serve their interest in liberty and limited government. But only under those constitutional requirements and conditions. The representatives they sent to Washington were their servants, not their overlords. They were merely "in office." The people of the States who put them in office were "in power."

Americans ought to reject the use of the phrase "in power" in reference to federal officeholders and rebuke those who use it, because it expresses an idea which will destroy the republic if it becomes widely accepted, namely the idea of a PC elite being the overlords of the people of the States. In the USSR, that politically correct elite was referred to as "the vanguard."

## Intelligent Design

The field of biology known as Intelligent Design undertakes to assess through the use of cellular biology the validity of Charles Darwin's theory of Natural Selection. Darwin, who was a pigeon breeder, extrapolated his theory from the modifications to species that animal breeders have been able to produce through selective breeding or design (e.g. the differences between a Great Dane and a Bulldog). In formulating his doctrine of Natural Selection, Darwin presumed that much greater modifications could be randomly obtained in nature over millions of years of time. (In the early nineteenth century, the new fields of geology and paleontology — the study of fossils — were providing an unprecedented sense of the Earth's age and the existence eons ago of species of plants and animals which no longer exist.) Random variations in individual plants and animals, Darwin said, would be "selected" in nature when they enhanced an organism's survival and ability to reproduce. Because of this selection, biological traits which aided survival would accumulate over time and new species of plants and animals better adapted to their environments would result. Indeed the process would create wholly new phyla or categories of animals.

Darwin contended in his *On the Origin of Species* (1859) that naturally occurring, advantageous variations would drive this process of creativity. Consequently, a creature which lived in ocean shallows might gradually develop through an accumulation of advantageous random variants into a land creature. Darwin asserted that all of the innumerable species of animals and plants that have existed during the history of the planet have been created in this way, through "natural selection." An inherent part of Darwin's thesis was his insistence that the process of Natural Selection had taken place ever so slowly from a single living cell, whose presence on Earth he did not explain. The existence of that living cell, capable of reproducing itself, was his theory's starting point.

Scientists now doing research on Intelligent Design believe too much *cellular information* would be required to produce even one new species thru "natural selection," let alone whole new phyla. (See Stephen C. Meyer, *Signature in the Cell: DNA and the Evidence for Intelligent Design*, HarperOne, 2009.) The multitude of information needed for the process of reproduction, which is essential to Natural Selection, must be present in living matter from the beginning of organic life on the planet for Darwin's theory of Natural Selection to be feasible. In other words, the biological laws governing reproduction had to be already present, in full, in the first living cell before it could "evolve," and the amount of information which reproduction requires, according to the findings of cellular biologists, could not be assembled randomly at the known rate of random cellular variations. Even the entire duration of the universe since the Big Bang (some twelve billion years) would be insufficient for that to occur randomly.

See entries on Big Bang and Evolution.

## Internationalism

The chief component of Marxist idealism, internationalism is the idea of a worldwide, benevolent government administering "social" justice. According to Marxist theory, a worldwide, humanitarian, atheistic culture is needed for the well-being of the human race.

See entry on Globalism and the commentary A Religion without God in Part III below.

## Investing in the Future

PC Marxists often refer to *deficit spending* by the U.S. government as "investing in the future." This investing in the future is nothing more or less than Congress increasing the federal debt limit so it can continue its now chronic habit of spending more money than it collects in revenues. The phrase "investing in the future" is an attempt to make the vice of deficit spending sound virtuous.

Words do have meanings, and investing in the future is not the same thing as running up tens, even hundreds, of *trillions* of dollars of national debt. (Roughly half of every dollar the government now spends is borrowed money.) If the government's vicious habit of unlimited borrowing and spending is not curbed, and soon, an unavoidable devastation of America's economy is assured. The national debt must be brought under control in fairness to future generations. Passing on to them an unmanageably large national debt is "investing" in catastrophe, not the future.

## Islamophobia

A spinoff of the term "homophobia" (fear of homosexuals), "Islamophobia" means fear of persons who practice Islam, the Moslem religion, an accusation which, like homophobia, is often made without corroborating evidence. The American people do not have an irrational fear of Islam but rather a justified apprehension of Moslem terrorists who call America "the Great Satan" and back up that declaration by murdering Americans in the United States and elsewhere. That has *not* produced a "phobia" on the part of Americans but a prudent concern over the killing of Americans by violent religious fanatics.

See entries on 9/11 and Racial Profiling.

## -ism (suffix)

PC Marxists use this suffix to coin new words for their agitprop. Any existing word can be made into a new, more important-sounding word by the suffix -ism (see entries on Ableism, Lookism, and Sizeism). Some of the most important terms in the PC lexicon have been formed in this way, both negative Marxist terms like *racism* and positive Marxist terms like *environmentalism*. Although persons besides PC Marxists use the suffix -ism, PC Marxists are more prone to use it because of their constant need to refresh the lexicon of their propaganda to keep it from getting stale.

See entry on the prefix neo-.

## Jesus of Nazareth

The belief that Jesus of Nazareth was both human in every way except sinfulness yet also one in being with his father in Heaven (consubstantial with God) is the defining tenet of Christianity (John 1:14; 3:16). Christians believe that Jesus in his sacrifice of himself on the Cross signified God's love for human beings by providing a way for them to redeem their sins through faith in Christ's sacrifice. That communication of divine love is complete, perfect, and eternally comprehensible because every human society, no matter where or when it exists, recognizes a person's willingness to sacrifice his life so another person might live as an expression of love. The significance of the death of Jesus of Nazareth is that he made such a sacrifice. His resurrection was the sign of his divine nature.

See commentary on A Culture without Belief in God in Part III below.

## Judgmentalism

A made-up word to condemn what PC Marxists view as the contemptible judgment of human conduct by the standards of the Judeo-Christian moral tradition.

See entries on Discrimination and Nonjudgmental.

# Liberal

PC Marxists encourage people to think of them as liberals, but that is a subterfuge. No one who knows from experience what liberals believe and how they behave would fall for this pretense. Liberals believe in and defend, as matters of principle and conviction, civil and criminal justice for all (as opposed to "social" justice for certain classes of people), freedom of conscience (also called freedom of religion), freedom of speech, majority rule with protection for the rights of individuals, tolerance, property rights, and multi-party politics. PC Marxists do not believe in any of these liberal virtues.

Falling for the deceitful claim of PC Marxists that they are "liberals" is easy to do, however, since most of the recruits to the Counter Culture/Political Correctness Movement in America in the last fifty years have come from the ranks of liberals, who cease to be liberals of course the moment they start acting in politically correct ways.

# Liberal Education

A liberal education is designed to enable individuals to reason from evidence and lead a more complete spiritual and intellectual life through an understanding of music and the arts and an understanding of freedom, logic, morality, and tolerance. Such an education helps humans to know their humanity and thus be more respectful of themselves and the humanity of others. Indoctrination in the dogmas of Marxism leads to mechanical, "correct" uniformity.

# Liberation

Liberation means to Marxists rejecting belief in God and Judeo-Christian morality. Jesus of Nazareth, the Christ, promised those who believe in him deliverance from their sins (John 8:31–32). Marxism delivers human beings from sin by abolishing the concepts of sin and evil and making adherence to Marxism the way to salvation for human beings.

See entries on Freedom and Moral Autonomy.

## Liberation Theology

Liberation theology claims Jesus of Nazareth, the Christ, or Messiah, was a socialist and that true followers of Christ must become socialists. The biblical evidence PC Marxists cite for this claim is Jesus' empathy for the poor and admonitions to minister to their needs. This view of Jesus denies his miraculous birth and resurrection and his divine mission to redeem human beings from death and sin through his willing sacrifice of himself on the Cross. Liberation theology permitted the Marxist dictator of Cuba, Fidel Castro, to refer to himself as "a Christian" while on a trip to Brazil, where the doctrine of liberation theology originated.

See entry on Jesus of Nazareth.

## Lifestyle

One of the earliest language inventions of agitprop in America, the word "lifestyle" has been a term of utmost importance in PC attacks on American culture because it is a substitute for Judeo-Christian morality. Instead of the Ten Commandments, a politically correct person has a lifestyle.

PC Marxists reject the authority of the Ten Commandments as the will of God because they reject the existence of God and believe human behavior is entirely determined by the socio-politico-economic influences of the environment. Decisions based on Judeo-Christian morality are detrimental to the pursuit of power by Marxists. There is nothing moral or immoral about a "lifestyle." Everyone can be said to have one, quite apart from any consideration of the authority of a culture. The moral neutrality of the concept of a "lifestyle" makes it the perfect instrument for destroying Judeo-Christian morality. The word, originally spelled as two words, life style, was coined at the outset of the Counter Culture Movement in America in the 1960s and has remained in constant use ever since. It "liberates" anyone who uses it from having to think in terms of Judeo-Christian right and wrong. So ubiquitous has the idea of "lifestyle" become that even devout Christians and Jews now use the word with no apparent understanding of how destructive it is to Judeo-Christian morality.

See entries on Choice, Moral Autonomy, Ten Commandments, Transparency.

## Living Constitution, the

This theory of interpreting the Constitution of the United States argues that the document belongs to living Americans to use as they please, to satisfy whatever political end they may have, without regard for the meaning inherent to the Constitution's language or respect for its authorization by the unanimous agreement of the people of the States. The doctrine of the Living Constitution sets aside Article V which makes the people of three-fourths of the States acting within their States the only power capable of amending the U.S. Constitution and makes the will of federal officeholders the supreme law of the United States.

The Constitution denies the federal courts, the president, and the Congress the authority to change the U.S. Constitution. The doctrine of the Living Constitution gives them that power. Under it, court decisions, executive orders, and congressional legislation can alter the Constitution of the United States without consent of the people in three-fourths of the States in the Union. That of course is a "high crime" (Article II, Section 4) worthy of impeachment, trial, and removal from office if proven.

The doctrine of the Living Constitution is the delight and darling of PC Marxists and an implicit accompaniment of all their agitprop. It is the despair of every American patriot who reveres the Constitution of the United States.

## Lookism

"Lookism" is a term related to women whose appearance does not embody the attributes (the look) of conventional female comeliness. It is a term of reproach directed at men who seek and praise such beauty. PC agitators use the term to make women who are not "good-looking" feel they are being "victimized." The term can also be used to make men feel guilty for preferring a certain female look.

See entries on Sizeism and Victim/Victimization.

## Mainstream

A highly versatile PC term, the word "mainstream" can be used as a synonym for the majority, in which case it carries a pleasant connotation of referring to a statistical majority without having to substantiate the inference. The word is used in this way by PC Marxists to declare their approval of something or someone "in the mainstream." The reverse is also the case. PC Marxists can use the term negatively by saying something or someone is "out of the mainstream," suggesting disapproval, again without having to furnish information on the implied lack of majority support.

See entry on Controversial.

## Majority Rule

Democracy is rule by and for a majority with protection for the rights of individuals. (A majority, for instance, could not cancel any of the twenty-five personal liberties enumerated in the Bill of Rights, the first eight amendments to the U.S. Constitution.) In contemplating the idea of majority rule, which Lincoln in his address at Gettysburg in 1863 referred to as "government of the people, by the people, for the people," we should keep in mind that the majority naturally is not always formed by *the same persons* on every issue. In free countries, the persons who comprise the majority vary. PC Marxists because they adhere to a "party line," "party discipline," and one-party rule can always count on the same majority on every issue. Majorities of the same persons characterize one-party communist tyrannies. Today in America, uniformity of thought and behavior is a goal of PC Marxism.

In a country where more than one political party is permitted to exist, but the parties hold pretty much the same view on every issue — that burning the national flag, say, is "free speech" — one may wonder whether personal liberties are going to be protected. In America today, the danger of such uniformity is quite real as the views of the two major political parties seem to be coalescing into monolithic Political Correctness.

See entry on Democracy.

## Male Chauvinism

This is the term PC Marxists invented to identify the attitude of superiority and insulting condescension which they claim all American males feel toward all American females.

See entries for Feminism, Sexism.

## Man

One of the earliest recorded words in the English language, being found in the oldest surviving manuscripts of written English, along with the word woman, the word man has always had two usages: human beings in general, and an adult male in particular. That is, until PC Marxism decreed, starting in the 1960s and 70s, that the word does not include women, that words with the suffix "man" in them are insulting to women when used in reference to them. This allegation overlooks the fact that the word wo*man* itself has the allegedly insulting suffix, undoubtedly used in the sense of human beings.

Americans who have conformed their thinking to the dogmas of Political Correctness accept the Marxian dictum that words having "man" in them must never be used in reference to women, despite the absurdity of it. Any American who persists in referring to a first-year female college student as a fresh*man* is castigated by PC Marxists as "a sexist" who enjoys insulting women. To be politically correct, we must refer to a first-year female college student as a *freshperson* (I kid you not). One fierce "feminist" of my acquaintance told me that even that usage (freshperson) is "sexist" because its final syllable (son) is "masculine." There's no satisfying some people.

## Marginalize, to

According to PC Marxists, to fail to give an "underprivileged" or "oppressed" class the benefits it deserves is to "marginalize" it (keep it on the margin of society).

## Materialistic Determinism

Materialistic determinism, the philosophy that pervades Marxism, claims that measurable reality is the only reality. From the point of view of materialistic determinism, free will and other features of the human spirit are illusions, and belief in them retards progress. But this view denies the world's manifest lawfulness — its fearful symmetry — and thus contradicts everything that makes the world livable. Besides which, the willfulness of Marxists contradicts their dogma that free will is a myth, unless one is willing to suppose (which I am not) that the beliefs and actions of Marxists are merely responses to their particular environments, since that would tend, in my judgment, to make their opinions completely mechanical and thus intellectually worthless.

## McCarthyism

PC Marxists regularly liken the government hearings conducted on communist espionage rings in Washington by U.S. Senator Joseph R. McCarthy (R-WI), who served in the Senate from 1947 until he died in 1957, to Hitler's genocidal campaign to exterminate Europe's Jews. Any endeavor to expose the presence, the influence, or the subversion of Marxism in America, is denounced by PC Marxists as "McCarthyism." Yet the book *Witness* (1952) by Whittaker Chambers, an American Quaker who committed acts of espionage for the Soviets and confessed his treason, substantiates in abundant detail Senator McCarthy's contention that Soviet spy rings made up of U.S. government officials were operating in Washington, D.C. when he said they were.

See entry on Witch Hunt.

## Mean-Spirited

PC Marxists when they've no argument to make to rebut a criticism of their doctrines often dismiss it as "mean-spirited" as if that were a substantial rebuttal.

See entries on Character Assassination and Name-Calling.

## Microaggression

A PC invention that has come into play in the last few years, a microaggression is an expression of an opinion or information that would allegedly offend persons of color, persons with disabilities, homosexuals, women, or some other "minority." The PC protocol on microaggression requires college professors to forewarn their students of any impending, possibly offensive remark so those who do not want to risk being offended can exit the classroom or lecture hall before they are forced to listen to it. The concept of a "microaggression" is an immense escalation of the PC sensitivity ploy to control the thinking of college professors and students. The PC Marxist protocol is as ridiculous as the one-party, one-nominee per office "elections" that Marxist regimes conduct and praise as "democracy."

See entry on Sensitivity Training and the commentary "Sensitivity" Above All in Part III below.

## Minority

In Russia prior to and during the Bolshevik Revolution of 1917, communist agitators used the slogan "All Power to the Soviets." In a quite similar way, agitprop speaks of "empowering minorities," i.e. biological classes such as "African Americans," homosexuals, "Mexican Americans," "Native Americans," "Asian Americans," but also women who comprise, by an estimated 1.6% margin, the majority of the U.S. population.

See entry on Class Struggle and the commentary Biological Class Consciousness in Part III below.

## Mistake

Is there a difference between making a *mistake* and committing a *crime*? Not necessarily for PC Marxists. A few years ago, Hillary Clinton, then U.S. Secretary of State, violated federal law by using an unsecured, non-government computer server to send and receive thousands of classified government documents, thus committing multiple felonies which endangered the lives of covert U.S. operatives overseas and gave foreign powers easy access to secret U.S. government information. When her crimes were exposed, she admitted to having made "a mistake" and was not indicted for her criminal behavior. James Comey, the head of the FBI, declared publicly that because she had not *intended* to do any harm, she should not be prosecuted. (It is necessary to note here that the head of the FBI has no authority to make recommendations regarding prosecutions: his statutory duty is to report the findings of FBI probes to the Attorney General who does have the statutory duty to decide if those findings constitute grounds for criminal indictment and prosecution.)

Similarly, in the 1990s in Tucson, Arizona, an eighteen-year-old male who grew up in the era of Political Correctness raped and set fire to a woman. When he was found guilty of these heinous assaults and was asked by the judge who was about to sentence him for his crimes

whether he had anything to say in his defense, this young man proclaimed in court that he'd had "a rough life" and had made a "mistake"
(*Arizona Daily Star*, August 15, 1995, p. B1). Personal responsibility
for criminal acts vanishes when one feels that one's environment is
responsible for one's actions.

See entries on Moral Autonomy and Situational Ethics.

## Moral Autonomy

One of the ways agitprop "deconstructs" Judeo-Christian morality
is by promoting the idea that persons are morally autonomous, that
no existing religious tradition has any relevance in judging human
conduct.

## Move On

A phrase in common use among PC Marxists, "move on" is what
PC Marxists recommend that everyone do when one of their own is
clearly implicated in a crime or has unequivocally been discovered to
have told a lie. The phrase is an admonition to regard the offense as if
it never occurred or is of little moment. "Move on" is a signal that what
was done was unimportant in the eyes of those who use the phrase.

See commentary on A Standard of Double Standards in Part III
below.

## Multiculturalism

A foremost goal of Marxist agitprop is to establish the idea that there is
no such thing as American culture. One of the primary ways of doing
that has been through the idea of multiculturalism, the proposition
that America has multiple cultures, languages, nationalities, races, and
religions, and that no national culture has ever unified America and
provided Americans a sense of common identity.

However, the fact of the assimilation of diverse immigrant eth-
nicities into one cultural identity was first commented on in 1782 in

the metaphor that they were being "melted into a new race of men [called] Americans" (Chapter 3, Paragraph 4 in Michel Guillaume de Crèvecoeur's *Letters from an American Farmer*). The PC Marxist dogma of multiculturalism regards Crèvecoeur and the Great Seal of the United States, with its motto *E Pluribus Unum* (Out of Many, One) which Congress created in 1782, as misrepresentations of America's history.

See entries on Culture and Pop Culture.

## Myth

This is a frequently used Marxist label for an event, fact, or discourse that they oppose. The term is congenial to them for this purpose because of its associations with the era before the rise of science. The history of communist regimes shows, however, that these regimes are anything but "scientific," which requires being objectively truthful in one's thinking. Marxist regimes make the people they rule live in fear of what the regime can and will do to them if they don't go along with their myth that applied Marxism is succeeding. Of the three myths of modern times that claim to be scientific, Marxism has inflicted the most deadly direct harm. The other two myths are Darwinism and Freudianism.

See entry on Scientism.

## Name-Calling

Without slander or name-calling, PC Marxism could probably not exist. Certainly, PC Marxist propaganda in the United States could not have acquired the influence it now has without calling its opponents unpleasant names. Only by slandering their opponents as "bigots," "chauvinists," "fascists," "homophobes," "racists," "sexists," "xenophobes," etc. (things middle-class Americans abhor) have PC Marxists been able to claim moral superiority and avert exposure of their consistent failures to make good their promises (for instance the pretenses of their "War on Poverty").

In using slander to forestall criticism, PC Marxists have proven that Hitler's chief of propaganda was right in saying the bigger the lie the easier it is to sell to people. A true racist regards being called a racist a badge of honor. He takes pride in the label. Only persons who are *not* racists dread being called that. Only they will change their behavior to avoid a repetition of the slur.

See entry on Preemptive Accusation.

## Nationalism

PC Marxists are hostile to nationalism. They frown on giving the interests of one's own nation priority over "humanity" as a whole. They are proud of being humanists and internationalists, lovers of mankind rather than of their own nation. When Nazi armies invaded the Soviet Union in June 1941, however, the communist dictator Stalin found it necessary to put aside his Marxist ideology and appeal to the patriotism of the Russian people, their love for Mother Russia, to repel the invader.

See entries on Globalism, Internationalism, Patriotism.

## Native American

A panel of Apache, Cherokee, Choctow, Hopi, Mescalero, Navajo, and other American Indians was once asked by someone in the audience that had gathered to hear them discuss matters of interest to them whether they preferred to be called "Native Americans" or "Indians." The chairman of the panel in reply asked for a show of hands of persons not born in the United States. Some hands went up in the audience but none from the panel. Everyone else, the chairman then said, must be a Native American and explained that Indians prefer to be called by their tribal names and use the term "Indian" when they don't know a person's tribal identity. The term "Native American" is a joke among American Indians (source: Tony Hillerman's autobiography *Seldom Disappointed*, pp. 273–274).

## Negro American

The term used by every Negro leader prior to the 1970s to identify Americans having evident Negro ancestry. The term "African American" is a PC Marxist invention for purposes of agitprop.

See entry on African American.

## Neo- (prefix)

This prefix gives new life to vocabulary worn out from overuse. Persons of political leanings other than PC Marxism also use this prefix, of course, but PC Marxists are under considerable pressure to come up with fresh terms and appear more inclined to use it and the suffix -ism as in neo-McCarthyism and neo-colonialism.

See entry on -ism.

## Neoteny

A little-known word, *neoteny* (pronounced ne-ot-e-ny with the accent on the second syllable) is a term which clinically describes a basic aim of Political Correctness in the United States, namely the retention of juvenile characteristics into adulthood that retard or prevent mature behavior. In the 1960s and 1970s, the Counter Culture/Political Correctness Movement encouraged young Americans to "drop out" of college, thus postponing and perhaps preventing the assumption of adult responsibilities and duties, such as becoming self-supporting. Interrupting the process of becoming an adult has weakened American society and pointed young Americans in the direction of Cultural Marxism with its dependence on Big Government.

"Snowflake," a recent slang term coined by opponents of PC Marxism, is a popular representation of what neoteny is: immature persons with little substance who melt at the first sign of opposition, criticism, or disagreement; who lack the ability to perform under trying circumstances; who are prone to whine and blame others for their deficiencies; physically mature persons whose behavior resembles that of a spoiled child. A symptom of the syndrome was evident in the Patient Protection and Affordable Care Act enacted in 2010 by Barack Obama and the 111th (Democrat) Congress which allowed young Americans to stay on their parents' health insurance as dependents until the age of twenty-six. The stereotypic image of neoteny is the unmarried, unemployed (or perhaps partly employed) thirty-year-old American male living in his parents' basement.

A lack of ambition, manliness, independence, and the urge to compete and "get ahead" has become evident among America's young men in recent years. This is no accident but rather the result of a deliberate "sissification" of America's public schools by PC Marxists who, to weaken America, discourage development of normal male traits. Sports ought not to be competitive; there ought not to be winners and losers in sports or in academics; everybody ought to be certified a winner. Keeping score and assigning grades ought to be discontinued. Everyone deserves and should be given a trophy or a certificate for having "participated." Identifying persons for their academic achievements ought to be discouraged because it injures the "self-esteem" of students who don't win such accolades. Grades where used ought to be inflated. "Social" promotion is a must. Boys must not be allowed to play with toy guns.

Neoteny is right up there with alcoholism, drug addiction, hardcore porn, skateboard riding by adult males, and the mania for video games as important symptoms of America's cultural destruction. The use of the term by psychologists evidently dates from the mid-1980s since the word neoteny is not found in the *American Heritage Dictionary,* second edition, copyrighted 1982, but does appear in *Webster's New World College Dictionary,* Third Edition, copyrighted in 1988.

See entry on Safe Space.

# 9/11

Why were the coordinated Islamic terrorist attacks on the United States of September 11, 2001, which killed as many Americans on American soil as the sneak attack by the Japanese Imperial Navy at Pearl Harbor on December 7, 1941, not given a name like the September 11th Massacre, or the Slaughter of 9/11, or the Islamic Terror Massacre, or the Twin Towers Jihad? Why has it become known simply as "9/11," the telephone number Americans use to call for emergency help? "9/11" conveys nothing of the horror of that day. It is a designation without substantive content. Was "9/11" deliberately chosen to drain these sneak air attacks on Manhattan and Washington and the killings in a field in western Pennsylvania of their true significance, and make them fade from the nation's memory as quickly as possible by giving them an inane designation? Who came up with that totally inappropriate name, "9/11"? Who made "9/11" the reference to a horrific jihadist slaughter?

Could whoever started using "9/11" for the worst day in the West's current war with Islamic terrorists have had in mind another September 11? The eleventh of September 1683, when a Moslem army besieging Vienna suffered one of the worst military defeats in Islamic history. Was "9/11" meant to suggest revenge for that event? The attacks on America in 2001 could have been carried out on any day or any month. They did not have to be carried out on September 11, and they did not have to be labeled "9/11."

# No-Fault Divorce

To facilitate granting a divorce, responsibility for it no longer has to be proven in a court of law. This change has weakened the institution of marriage, Western Civilization's basic social institution. Enemies of the family encouraged this development and devised the cutesy phrase "no-fault divorce" to proclaim that no one is responsible for the breakup of a marriage. It just happens. The idea of no-fault divorce is "liberation" from personal responsibility for the dissolution of a marriage.

See the entries on Liberation and Nonjudgmental.

## Nonjudgmental

This PC invention (and the related term nonjudgmental*ism*) makes the rejection of the Judeo-Christian moral tradition sound like a virtue. It suggests that refraining from making moral judgments is better than making them because being "non-judgmental" is the same as being tolerant and forgiving, avoiding conflict, and having an open mind.

See entries on Open-Minded, Value Free.

## Obscene

None of the pornography that agitprop promotes as "free speech" is considered obscene in the old sense of this word. Indeed, the word obscene is almost never used these days in the United States except to add emphasis to the condemnation of making profits ("obscene profits"). Nothing else seems to be considered obscene anymore. PC newspeak would like us to regard only American capitalism as obscene.

## Offensive

American mothers teach their children to be polite, to say please and thank you, and not to say anything if they can't say something nice. PC agitprop has taken advantage of this propensity of middle-class American manners and has used it to eliminate behavior it wants to get rid of by calling it "offensive."

See the entry on Sensitivity Training and the commentary "Sensitivity" Above All Else in Part III below.

# Open-Minded

PC agitators praise being open-minded. Their use of this term makes it sound like the reference means being tolerant. But that's not the case. The PC exhortation to be "open-minded" is an invitation to begin the process of conversion to PC Marxism. To be tolerant, however, means to respect the right of other persons to think and speak differently from the way you do; to be open-minded is to set aside one's ordinary standards of thought and judgment and put yourself in a frame of mind to consider the possibility that values other than those one grew up with might be worth accepting. PC Marxists promote that sort of "openness."

Following the Korean War (1950–1953), U.S. Army psychologists debriefed U.S. soldiers who had been held as prisoners of war in North Korea, and discovered that most of these POWs had been told they were going to be treated as "students" rather than prisoners. They were asked to be "open-minded" and listen to the North Korean reasons for invading South Korea. After all, hearing both sides of the story was only "fair." The Army psychologists discovered that American prisoners who were either commissioned or noncommissioned officers, older than twenty-five, or had been in the U.S. Army more than a few years were separated from the great majority of the prisoners who were young, had little institutional loyalty to the Army, and no leadership experience. The more mature, experienced Americans were put in heavily guarded prisons, and no attempt was made to make them doubt the rightness of their country's cause in fighting the Korean War or otherwise to control their perceptions and behavior.

There were libraries for the POWs in the North Korean "student" prison camps stocked with English-language novels, histories, and journals critical of life in the United States. The "student" prisoners were exhorted to use these libraries, and the tedium of prison life made them willing to do that. The "teaching" sessions for the comparatively immature American POWs consisted of indoctrination in Marxism, often conducted by instructors who had studied in U.S. colleges and universities before the war and spoke idiomatic American English. The "student" prisoners, bereft of their natural leaders, were encouraged to inform on each other; and those who did were rewarded with special meals and other privileges, which had the effect of breaking down group morale and unity. Also, their mail was screened, and only letters containing problems at home — notices of unpaid bills, announcements of divorce proceedings, suspicions of adultery or girl-friend infidelity, or other depressing news — got delivered.

By these simple means, the majority of American POWs in the Korean War were rendered dispirited and passive; and they made far fewer attempts to escape than in any previous war for which the U.S. Army had records. The Army psychologists designated the simple control techniques they encountered in debriefing Korean War POWs "brainwashing." The benefit of "brainwashing" to the North Korean military command was that fewer troops had to be assigned to guard these docile prisoners.

It is no coincidence that the Counter Culture indoctrination sessions about the Vietnam War on American college campuses in the 1960s were called "teach-ins," an echo of telling American POWs in North Korea that they were going to be treated as "students." Both the American POWs and the American college students were told it was only "fair" to listen to the communist side of the story.

## Oppression/Oppressor

These terms are in constant use by PC agitators and propagandists promulgating their line that America is a land of oppression, not opportunity.

## Oreo (slang)

A derogatory PC term deriving from a popular cookie which is black on the outside and white inside. The slang is applied to Negro

Americans who refuse to categorically hate their fellow, white Americans.

See commentary on Biological Class Consciousness in Part III below.

## Overreach

The constitutionally prescribed oath an elected U.S. president must take before assuming the office is: "I do solemnly swear (or affirm) that I will faithfully execute the Office of President of the United States, and will to the best of my Ability, preserve, protect, and defend the Constitution of the United States" (Article II, Section 1, U.S. Constitution). Section 3, Article II of the Constitution requires the president to "take Care that the Laws be faithfully executed." "Overreach" is the bland term (whose normal meaning is to be overly ambitious) PC Marxists use to pooh-pooh the violation of Sections 1 and 3 of Article II of the Constitution of the United States. By referring to President Obama's repeated violations of the Constitution as "overreach," his fellow PC Marxists made his behavior seem to be that of an ambitious but honest man in a hurry to achieve his goals. Such deceitful use of an ordinary word in reference to egregiously wrong behavior illustrates the insidious nature of agitprop.

## Overseas Contingency Operations

Using this term for U.S. military actions in foreign lands avoids calling war, war.

## Paranoia

A psychiatric term applied by Marxists to their opponents who, according to them, suffer from the delusion that Marxists want to take over the U.S. (The mental state clinically termed paranoia has been humorously defined as the person in the football stadium who believes the team huddling on the field is conspiring against him.) Despite what Marxists allege, such a state of mind is typical of Marxists, not their opponents.

Marxists typically blame their failures on "provocateurs," "deviationists," "saboteurs," or spies — anything except the nature of Marxism, the true cause of all their failures. Thus, the communist dictator of Cuba, Fidel Castro, attributed the dismal performance of his country's economy to the U.S. trade embargo, even though Cuba enjoyed such trading partners as China, the Soviet Union, and all the communist countries of Europe and had ranked high among Latin American economies before Marxists took over its management. It was Marxist dogmas, not U.S. refusal to trade with Castro, that destroyed the Cuban sugar industry, the mainstay of the country's economy, just as Stalin's collectivization of Ukrainian agriculture destroyed the Ukraine as Europe's most productive wheat-growing region.

Similarly, Hillary Clinton blamed her defeat in the 2016 presidential election on her opponent's "collusion with the Russians." Mrs. Clinton and her supporters did not use the word "conspiracy" in making this accusation because that would made them "conspiracy nuts," something they say only their opponents are.

See entries on McCarthyism and Witch Hunt.

## Partisan (adj.)

Putting the interests of one's political party above the interests of one's country is being partisan. PC Marxists are always and adamantly partisan.

See entries on Nationalism and Patriotism.

## Patriotism

One of the quotations once in vogue among PC Marxists in America was the saying of the eighteenth-century English author Samuel Johnson: "Patriotism is the last refuge of a scoundrel." PC Marxists often quoted this maxim in criticizing any American who refused to put the interests of "the international community" or "humanity" above their own nation's interests. In their fondness for this quotation, PC Marxists have shown their ignorance of the fact that Samuel Johnson was an eminent English patriot. They likewise reveal an inability to read English except through the red lens of their ideology, because Johnson was clearly not criticizing patriotism but the use scoundrels make of patriotism to cover up the fact that they are scoundrels.

See entries on Internationalism and Nationalism.

## People of Color

American Indians, Asian Americans, some "Hispanics," and Negro Americans are lumped together in this catchall phrase for persons of dark complexion, to create a broader spectrum of people allegedly being "victimized" by straight white American males.

## Person of Size

Someone who is extremely obese is "a person of size" in PC talk. The euphemism was invented as part of agitprop's insistence on the need for sensitive, inoffensive diction.

See entry for Sizeism and the commentary "Sensitivity" Above All Else in Part III below.

## Personal Responsibility

Personal responsibility is a paramount feature of American culture, a trait PC Marxists have targeted for vigorous attack because they believe environmental conditions rather than free will, individual decisions, and personal aspirations determine human behavior.

See entries on Crime and Environmentalism.

## Pluralism

Marxist agitprop in America employs the term pluralism as part of its misleading diction. The term is used to entice Americans into considering the dogmas of Marxism as being as valid as the beliefs of America's culture, which PC Marxism is trying to replace. The idea of pluralism requires that Marxism be regarded as just another political outlook and to overlook its pretensions as "science" and its constant use of threats and intimidation to impose its dogmas.

See entry on Open-Minded.

## Pop Culture

Popular (or "pop") culture is a set of self-conscious, ephemeral tastes in entertainment, manners, dress, and adornment. Culture, on the other hand, is not a matter of fashion and is notably stable. A pop culture creates bonds within age groups and classes, not a whole society. Culture is a set of beliefs guiding the general behavior of successive generations of an entire society and giving that society the moral unity and stability which it must have to make social life possible.

Agitprop lauds the ephemeral, fashion-driven concerns of Pop Culture to shift the attention of Americans away from the need for their culture's historical beliefs which have made America a great nation. Agitprop wants Americans focused on trivialities.

See entries on Culture and Multiculturalism.

## Pornography

Whatever destroys healthy male-female intimacy — for example, widespread use among males of hardcore pornography — is promoted and encouraged by PC Marxists as a way to weaken America's Christian culture by undermining Christian marriage, the foundation of America's most vital social institution, the family.

## Post-Truth

PC Marxists have recently coined this astonishing term and introduced it into American speech apparently to suggest that truth is something so problematic that no one should be concerned with searching for it. They claim Americans today are living in a "post-truth" era.

## Power

For people who are politically correct, truth is entirely a matter of *power* or the ability to make decisions and have them obeyed. Marxists are obsessed with getting and exercising power because having power is the main prerequisite for establishing Cultural Marxism in America. Whatever has to be done or said to gain power is legitimate; nothing else is. Concern for Judeo-Christian morality, the family, the Constitution of the United States, faith in God, respect for law and truth, all impede the pursuit of power which is the all-important Marxist endeavor. Therefore, these concerns must be discredited and their cultural importance derided. To a Marxist, everything is a weapon for gaining power, including matters no normal human being would regard in that way. Words are weapons. Addiction is a weapon. Law is a weapon. Sex is a weapon. Even food is a weapon — for example, the sixty years of food rationing in Cuba, the famine Stalin deliberately induced in the Ukraine to break the resistance of Ukrainian peasants to Marxist collectivization of their land, and the starvation now being induced by Marxists in Venezuela, including Russian state security police and Cuban soldiers, to establish communist rule in that once prosperous, democratic nation.

See entries on the Family, Religion, Truth.

## Preemptive Accusation

PC Marxists use preemptive accusation to undercut the credibility of their opponents. This technique consists of PC Marxists accusing their opponents of doing what they themselves are doing before the opponents can accuse them of that behavior. By accusing opponents of doing what they are doing, PC Marxists deprive their adversaries of any opportunity to speak the truth convincingly. After a PC Marxist preemptively accuses an opponent of doing what he (the PC Marxist) is doing, the opponent is prevented from credibly making that accusation against him, because if the opponent then accuses the PC Marxist of the same thing, his accusation will have an air of childish complaint, "Well, he did it first!"

The audacious hypocrisy of preemptive accusation leaves opponents of PC Marxism nonplused and speechless. Preemptive Accusation is one of agitprop's most effective tactics in the culture war being waged in America.

See the commentary A Standard of Double Standards in Part III below.

## Prejudice

PC Marxists like to think of themselves as free of prejudices. That only their enemies are prejudiced. But that self-image is false. Prejudices are the essence of Marxism, and have been ever since Lenin established the USSR in 1922 which required, as he said in his 1917 book *State and Revolution*, the ruthless application of Marxist dogmas for the good of "the masses." Revolutions like Lenin's in Russia in 1917 and Mao's in China in 1949 are nothing but murderously enforcing prejudices.

## Privacy

Privacy is the right PC Marxists invoke when they want to conceal something damaging to their cause. For instance, what country's passport did Barack Obama use in traveling from the United States to Pakistan when he was in college? Was it a U.S. passport or a passport from some other country? We were not allowed to know. Access to that information would violate Mr. Obama's "privacy," though in running for the presidency of the United States he was asking American voters to accept his assertion that he was a native-born U.S. citizen. In the same way, we are not allowed to know as a matter of fact whether he ever received, while in college or law school, financial aid as a foreign student. That too is a "private" matter.

## Progressivism

A reform movement in the United States in the late 1800s and early 1900s to root out graft in big-city, Democrat-party politics and corruption in electing U.S. Senators by State legislatures, progressivism came to an abrupt halt in April 1917 with U.S. entry into World War I. The ratification of the Seventeenth Amendment in 1913 providing for the direct election of U.S. Senators by the people of the States instead of State legislatures was the movement's most significant achievement, along with the federal Pure Food and Drug Act and the Meat Inspection Act, both enacted in 1903. Theodore Roosevelt and Wisconsin governor Robert M. La Follette were prominent progressives. Today's PC Marxists who call themselves "progressives" are too anti-religious (Judeo-Christian morality provided the impetus for the progressive movement) and too committed to imposing Cultural Marxism on America to merit being called "progressives."

## Race Norming

An invention of PC Marxists for achieving "diversity," race norming works like this. Suppose thirty promotions are available in a big-city fire department and to receive one requires a competitive written exam and a rigorous physical test; and suppose only white males make qualifying scores on both tests. To not give any of the promotions to "African Americans," "Mexican Americans," "Native Americans" or women would be politically incorrect. To prevent such "social" injustice, a politically correct point system is devised to take gender, ethnicity, and race into account and adjust test scores upward for "underrepresented" classes so they can receive promotions. That's race norming.

See entries on Diversity and Racial Profiling, and the commentary Biological Class Consciousness in Part III below.

## Racial Profiling

Any focus on a group that statistics indicate is prone to some kind of conduct PC Marxists want to shield is denounced as "racial profiling." Thus, the nineteen jihadist terrorists who commandeered four fully fueled, transcontinental airliners on the morning of September 11, 2001 and used them as mega-bombs to kill as many Americans as the Japanese Imperial Navy killed in it's attack on the U.S. naval base at Pearl Harbor, December 7, 1941, were allowed to board the airliners, even though they manifested every sign of being potential hijackers. All nineteen bought one-way tickets; all nineteen paid cash for their tickets; none had check-through luggage. These three kinds of behaviors were well-known markers of potential hijackers. But the only thing that mattered to the airlines was that they not be accused of racially profiling young Muslim men; so the nineteen hijackers were allowed to board the four planes, and thousands of Americans were killed that September morning.

See entries on Islamophobia, 9/11.

## Racism

The charge of racism — judging persons according to stereotypes associated with their race instead of by their individual character and personal qualifications and attainments — is the accusation PC Marxists most often make against Americans. According to them, all white Americans are racists. But isn't that accusation itself, "racist"?

See entry on Name-Calling, and the commentary Biological Class Consciousness in Part III below.

## Reactionary

A Marxist designates anyone who opposes Marxism "a reactionary." The American Marxist organizer Saul Alinsky describes in his handbook for Marxist revolution in the United States, *Rules for Radicals*, how to provoke reactions from political opponents and make their reactions the issue. For a Marxist, the term indicates that there can be no legitimate, rational objections to Marxism based on experience.

## Relationship

The expression "having a relationship" means in PC parlance having sex with the same partner ("a significant other," as such a person is called) for a significant length of time without getting married. To a PC Marxist, "having a relationship" is preferable to having a marriage because it forestalls family formation.

## Religion

PC Marxists find religion objectionable because the existence of God, God-given laws, God-given rights, the soul, and all other supernatural truths are highly abhorrent to them. They are abhorrent because they represent a kind of thought and feeling contrary to the materialistic determinism and scientism that characterize Marxism.

See Appendix B, Dogmas of Cultural Marxism.

## Revisionism

Revisionism, or the rewriting of American history to conform to the Marxist view of it, requires that American history be seen as a story of bigotry, "environmental rape," genocide, greed, hate, imperialism, racism, slavery, and "victimization" of the lowly by the high and mighty. The purpose of revisionism is to make young Americans ashamed of their nation's history and susceptible to conversion to Marxist thought and behavior.

See entries on Indoctrination and Open-Minded.

## Revolution

The word "revolution" since 1789, the year the French Revolution began, has meant the obliteration of an existing culture (an *ancien régime) and its replacement with a planned, or completely rationalized, culture.* A revolution is an attempt to totally alter a society's way of life. The destruction of the old regime or culture of France and the attempt to rebuild it as a regime of atheism, rationalism, and science was the first revolution in the modern world. The second was the Bolshevik Revolution in czarist Russia in 1917, and the third was the communist takeover of China of 1949.

America's War for Independence (1775–1783) was not a "revolution," as is plainly evident in the fact that there was no deadly struggle for power following it, no bloody "counterrevolution," as there was, for instance, in France, Russia, China, and Cuba in their revolutions. Americans in 1775 already had a new culture. Their war was a defense of that new culture's belief-behaviors. Most of the practitioners of England's culture in America left America for English territory during the war or soon afterwards.

See entries on Change, Culture, Transformation.

## Right-Wing Extremism

"Right-wing extremism" is one of the labels PC Marxists use to criticize their opponents, whom they regard as "extreme" because they put the interests of their nation above the revolutionary dogmas of global Marxism.

See entry on Extremism.

## Safe Space

A recent addition to the PC lexicon, a "safe space" is a designated place on a college campus where politically correct students can gather without anxiety about having their dogmas challenged by criticism. In other words, safe spaces are places at so-called "institutions of higher learning" from which free speech has been banned. But how, one may well ask, can knowledge ever advance to a higher level without free speech?

The creation of "safe spaces" on today's college campuses represents a sharp departure from the outlook PC Marxists promoted a couple of decades ago when they went around saying that the purpose of going to college was to have one's ideas challenged. But that was before Political Correctness gained its present ascendancy on American campuses. Now, "safe spaces" are needed and have been established by pusillanimous, politically correct college administrators. The formation of "safe spaces" indicates a fear of free speech and a desire to avoid it. "Safe spaces" represent the onset of a bunker mentality among PC Marxists who fear defeat if they engaged in debate. The creation of "safe spaces" suggests that the political tide is turning against PC Marxism. PC Marxists are becoming reactionary which is a sign of weakness in them.

See entries on Academic Freedom and Free Speech.

## Same-Sex Marriage

The Judeo-Christian teaching that marriage is the union for life — in every sense of those words — of a man and a woman for procreating and rearing children to healthy adulthood is being debased by the contention that two men or two women have a constitutional right to "marry." Like so many things PC Marxists claim as a constitutional right, this one is not in the Constitution of the United States. Rather, the Tenth Amendment in the Bill of Rights puts the definition of marriage under the jurisdiction of the States and excludes the federal government from having any say in what marriage is or is not.

Apologists for "same-sex marriage" rightly point out that not all marriages between a man and a woman result in offspring. But the couplings of two persons of the same sex are invariably sterile and can't ever result in the birth of a child, whereas the couplings of persons of the opposite sex usually do, which is the defining intention of marriage as Western civilization's primary social institution. "Same-sex marriage" contradicts the idea of the responsible creation of human life

## Sanctuary Cities

U.S. cities which pass local ordinances forbidding enforcement of federal immigration law and the arrest of illegal aliens are known as "sanctuary cities." Such cities apply federal law selectively and have abandoned the American ideal that the rule of law must be the same for everyone. They ignore the fact that offering "sanctuary" to illegal aliens attracts criminals, encourages lawbreaking, and endangers the lives of ordinary American citizens. According to Wikipedia, there are over 550 "sanctuary cities" in the United States. These enclaves of selective-lawlessness are in effect part of the plan to divide and destroy, or "deconstruct," American culture. PC Marxists have appealed to the compassion of Americans to establish "sanctuary cities.

## Scenario

The term for a movie storyline, "scenario" is used by PC Marxists in America in the same way the term "Party line" was used in the Soviet Union when it existed. Barack Obama as U.S. president sometimes used the term "narrative" for what the Soviets referred to as the "Party line."

## Science

Science is the ultimate authority Marxists use to validate their politics, as for instance in claiming "science" has proven human activities are causing "climate change," and therefore manufacturing and transportation must be controlled worldwide. A few decades ago, however, these same fear mongers were warning that science showed the planet was getting colder; then that it was getting warmer. The claim that human activities are causing "climate change" is not a scientific finding.

It's a political assertion. Just to say something is scientifically true does not make it so. The intent of this assertion appears to be to frighten human beings into consenting to global regulatory government, a goal Marxists have pursued since the founding of the USSR in 1922.

## Scientism

Invented by opponents of Marxism, this term characterizes the Marxist belief that science can solve every human problem because all human problems are material in nature, which is not so. The belief that science can solve every human problem is "scientism." It's a dehumanizing conviction because it denies the existence of the human soul and the fact that many problems experienced by human beings are spiritual problems, problems of the human soul.

## Secular/Secularism

PC newspeak uses these words as if they were synonyms for *atheistic* and *atheism*, terms too threatening to most Americans to be suitable for propaganda purposes in the United States where belief in God is still culturally vital. Hence agitprop in the United States uses the euphemistic terms secular and secularism in place of atheistic and atheism. By using the words secular and secularism, it becomes possible to espouse and advocate atheism without arousing middle-class American opposition to such propaganda.

## Self-Esteem

PC Marxists have put inculcating "self-esteem" at the top of their agenda for the public schools of the United States. Before the advent of agitprop in America, Judeo-Christian self-esteem was taught in U.S. public schools K through 12. American school kids respected themselves because their teachers and parents told them the Creator of the Universe had created them "in his image." Then in the 1960s, PC Marxists began agitating and propagandizing for the dogma

"Separation of Church and State" and jockeyed the U.S. Supreme Court into proclaiming it "unconstitutional" to invoke God in a U.S. public school. No brief exercises of prayer or Bible reading at the start of the school day. No displays of the Ten Commandments. Such things were offensive to persons who did not believe in God; therefore, the old basis for human self-esteem — the Judeo-Christian belief that human beings are made in the image of God — was eliminated, and a godless mantra for self-esteem was proclaimed. Public school students are now told, "You're special." This self-esteem ("You're special") has prompted self-centeredness, whereas being told that you and every human being has been made in the imagine of the Creator of the Universe fostered self-respect and respect for one's fellow students, one's teachers, one's parents, and human life in general.

Do you think there might be a connection between these observations and the fact there were no "school shootings" in America before the U.S. Supreme Court prohibited mentioning the Creator in the public schools?

## Sensitivity

By obtaining the suppression of behavior that allegedly offends the feelings of others, PC Marxists dictate the language Americans can use and thus the perceptions they will have. Any perception which would tend to affect the PC agenda negatively and impede the "transformation" of America is offensive speech to PC Marxists; language which promotes that agenda is "sensitive" speech. Agitprop dictates what is "sensitive" and what is "offensive."

See entries on Hate Speech, Sensitivity Training, and Speech Codes, and the commentary "Sensitivity" Above All Else in Part III below.

## Sensitivity Training

In countries with communist regimes, the need for remedial in-doctrination of persons who deviate from the "Party line" is called "re-education." In the United States, it is called "sensitivity training." Sensitivity training is now standard practice in American public schools, colleges and universities, and corporations. Sensitivity train-ing teaches conformity to politically correct dogmas.

See entries on Hate Speech, Sensitivity, Speech Codes, and the commentary "Social" Justice in Part III below.

## Sexism

The PC term "sexism" was invented to condemn the traditional family roles of men (fathers, bread winners) and women (mothers, home-makers). PC Marxism wants no distinctions made between male and female conduct. Thus, the one-man-one-woman family will be truly and completely destroyed, and government will become everyone's parent on whom everyone will be dependent.

## Sexual Orientation

This is the PC euphemism for homosexuality. The euphemism was coined to avoid the use of the words "homosexual" and "homosexual-ity." The phrase "sexual orientation" allows persons who are politically correct to praise and promote homosexual behavior without having to use the terms "homosexual" or "homosexuality," which are loaded with a historical burden of moral disapproval. The term "sexual orien-tation," however, has a scientific ring to it implying that homosexual-ity is merely one of various "orientations" toward sexual activity, so that no one should object to it. Homosexual practices ought to be considered as normal as any other erotic activity. That is the argument agitprop in America is making in its revolutionary assault on Judeo-Christian morality and its construction of Cultural Marxism.

## Sex Worker

The PC term for a prostitute, whether male and female. Re-classifying prostitution as "work" removes it from the context of moral judgment, and places it in the context of a career choice. And since one of the strongest beliefs of American culture is that everyone must work, this reclassification of prostitution as work makes it culturally respectable. *Sex worker* is one of the terms agitprop uses to make Judeo-Christian morality irrelevant. "Lifestyle" is the most effective and far-reaching of the terms agitprop has invented to render the Judeo-Christian moral tradition irrelevant.

See entries on Lifestyle, Sexual Orientation, and Value Free

## Single Parenting

The rhetoric of Political Correctness is full of praise for "single parenting" because it undermines the two-parent, mother-father family PC Marxists are eager to supplant with an open-ended definition of marriage which makes the family into whatever anyone wants it to be; thus obliterating Christian marriage. *The Communist Manifesto* by Karl Marx and Friedrich Engels, Part III, Section 3, identified "abolition of the family" as one of the aims of communism. Promoting "single parenting" is part of that effort.

See entries on Lifestyle, Same Sex Marriage.

## Situational Ethics

"Situational ethics" — the concept that the situation should dictate a person's conduct, not norms of moral goodness and sin — is encouraged by agitprop. When the situation determines conduct, the Judeo-Christian concept of inherent right or wrong no longer pertains.

See entry on Moral Autonomy and the commentary A Standard of Double Standards in Part III below.

## Sizeism

"Sizeism" is a PC term critical of treating a person of inordinate size in a different way from other people because of that size. For example, making someone weighing 400 pounds buy two seats on an airplane instead of one. In the lexicon of Political Correctness, sizeism is a type of prejudice or "discrimination" which must be eliminated.

See entry on Lookism.

## Snowflake (slang)

Someone who can't stand the heat of either criticism or personal responsibility.

See entry on Neoteny.

## Social Engineering

"Social engineering" is the construction of a Marxist society according to a Marxist ideological blueprint. The term is a bland reference to the revolution that's going on in the United States. Other terms for this are community organizing and transformation. The phrase social engineering reflects the importance which the ideology of materialistic determinism has in Marxist thinking and behavior.

## Socialism

The nub of socialism is dependence on the state. Although all communists are socialists (e.g. the Union of Soviet *Socialist* Republics), all socialists are not communists. Both communism and fascism are forms of socialism in which a single political party exerts total control of a society.

## Social Justice

Agitprop calls the goal it is striving to attain in America "social justice," a euphemism for Marxian socialism or justice for classes of people, not individuals. Historically, the ideal of justice in American culture has been what the American Pledge of Allegiance refers to as "justice for all." Amendments I through VIII of the Bill of Rights define the fundamentals of "justice for all."

See commentaries on Biological Class Consciousness and "Social" Justice in Part III below.

## Sophistication

The word sophistication is used by PC Marxists to entice intellectuals to become part of Political Correctness by getting them to think Marxism is a highly complicated, not easily understood theory of economics, politics, and humanism that only people of superior intelligence can appreciate and apply for the betterment of humanity. Anyone who accepts the idea that Marxism is too sophisticated to be understood by persons of ordinary intelligence is on the verge of being seduced by it. Elitism is a fundamental characteristic of the revolution being conducted by PC Marxists in the United States.

## Special Interests

A term of denunciation, "special interests" describes people who are extraordinarily self-centered. Those members of Congress, for instance, who have the overweening desire to remain in office for life represent a clearly defined special interest, even though they decry "special interests." PC Marxists dedicated to the cultural transformation of the United States are the most dangerous "special interest" in America today.

## Speciesism

One of agitprop's many invented words, "speciesism" is a term that criticizes the thinking of humans who value their own species, *Homo sapiens*, more than other species of animals.

See entries on Animal Rights and the Zoological Thesis.

## Speech Code

A speech code is a list of politically prohibited words and required substitutes. The faculties of some American universities and colleges today issue such lists to incoming freshmen. Speech codes have become a major tool for enforcing PC language and thus controlling the perceptions and behavior of college students.

See entry on Hate Speech.

## Status Quo

This phrase is the agitprop pejorative for the existing, allegedly oppressive conditions which "privileged," heterosexual, white American males have allegedly created to benefit themselves as a class.

See entries on Change, Revolution, Transformation.

## Supernatural, the

The supernatural is everything which transcends material reality and cannot be wholly explained in terms of it. The laws governing the natural world and the moral laws God has created to guide human freedom are paramount examples of the supernatural. Because God wanted to bestow on human beings a semblance of his own freedom to create what is good, he could not compel human beings to behave in a robotic or reactionary way as he did his other creatures in the animal kingdom. To persuade man to act as God wants him to act, God gave man a power of discernment far beyond any other creature.

## Superstition

The dismissive, derogatory term PC Marxists use as a synonym for religion.

## Supreme Court, the U.S.

The highest court in the United States and therefore the special target of PC agitprop. By controlling the Court (only five votes on it are needed to change or void a law), PC Marxists can control the Constitution. Dogmas of Political Correctness have attained legal status through decisions of the U.S. Supreme Court which has for many years been usurping from the people of the States their exclusive authority to amend the Constitution of the United States. The Court under color of interpretation is now routinely amending the Constitution.

## Taboo

By applying this word to the imperatives of Judeo-Christian morality, PC Marxists have reduced them to primitive superstitions. Thus, both Jewish interpretations of the Torah and Christian theology such as that of Thomas Aquinas, with their innumerable rational discriminations, are by the application of the word "taboo" reduced to the level of the ancient Hawaiian taboo against commoners casting their shadow on the sacred person of the king and the Comanche taboo against a human shadow falling on cooking food. The purpose of this diction is to make Judeo-Christian morality appear to be primitive, repulsive, and arbitrary.

## Tax Correction

One of the propaganda formulas of PC Marxism in the United States is, "The rich are not paying their fair share of taxes." (One can only wonder what "a fair share" of the federal government's gargantuan wastefulness and debt would be.) Because PC Marxists favor constant increases in federal taxes and consider the only correct tax to be a higher one, they have invented the term tax correction for an increase in the tax rate. "Tax correction" sounds so much more reasonable than "tax increase."

See entry on Budget Cut.

## Ten Commandments, the

Jews and Christians believe God transmitted to the tribes of Israel through the prophet Moses a set of ten eternal ordinances for human conduct suitable to all times and places. These Ten Commandments are the fundamental principles for human happiness and prosperity which God has laid down for the guidance of human freedom and understanding. And they might actually have that effect if PC Marxists had not used the federal courts to remove displays of the Ten Commandments from the public schools and court houses of America as if they were illicit, invalid guides for good behavior.

## Theory

Perhaps all that needs to be said about Marxism in its many manifestations was pointed out by the American home-plate philosopher Lawrence "Yogi" Berra in his observation: "In theory there is no difference between theory and practice; in practice there is." That pronouncement is, I think, the most pithy, most comprehensive observation ever made of the nature and history of Marxism, though the late Mr. Berra when he made it probably had the sense of common experience in mind rather than a critique of Marxist theory.

## Transformation

"Transformation" is a harmless-sounding euphemism for Marxist revolution.

See entry on Change.

## Transparency

Why should we speak of "transparency" instead of honesty; "transparency" instead of truthfulness; "transparency" instead of frankness? Making "transparency" seem to be a virtue produces moral confusion because it refers only to a means of perception, not what is perceived. PC Marxists use the concept of transparency to create an illusion of virtue. Barack Obama said his presidency was going to be "the most transparent" in the history of the United States. In hindsight, we know how little his promise to be transparent had to do with frankness, truthfulness, or honesty, and how much it had to do with telling people the shameless lies that they could keep the doctor and the health insurance plan they liked, and save thousands of dollars into the bargain, if they accepted "Obamacare."

## Trans Person

A shortening of "transgendered person." Janet Mock, in her piece in *The New Yorker* for August 1, 2016 on the beginning of the homosexual movement as a political force during a 1968 police raid on a gay bar in Greenwich Village, used this term in writing about the "L. G. B. T. [lesbian, gay, bisexual, transgender] movement." She also refers in her article to "trans people" and "trans women," as well as "trans-sexual, non-binary, genderqueer, femme, butch, cross-dresser, drag king or queen, and other gender identities and sexual orientations that challenge social norms."

## Tribalism

A term of quite recent origin, tribalism like so many other terms in the lexicon of Political Correctness is used to conceal something of fundamental importance to the movement, namely the fact that the inevitable reactions of normal persons to the aggressive and unyielding dogmas of Political Correctness is the reason civility, compromise, and the spirit of bipartisan decision-making are disappearing from the American political scene. The dogmatism inherent in Political Correctness is the cause of today's polarization in politics, which in turn is beginning to disgust the American public. "Tribalism," which suggests some sort of primitive mindset, has nothing to do with it.

## Triumphalism

This PC term was created by agitprop for special use when the Soviet Union collapsed in 1991. Its purpose was to dampen the impulse among Americans to celebrate their victory in America's forty-four-year Cold War with the Soviet Union. Had that impulse been allowed to run its natural course, there might have been the kind of miles-long cavalcades of honking automobiles full of jubilant, flag-waving Americans that spontaneously formed twice in rural and small-town America in May and again in August 1945 as the news arrived in America that first Germany and then Japan had unconditionally surrendered, ending the killing and destruction of World War II. But when the USSR disappeared from the political map of the world, everything was quiet in America. There was hardly a murmur of celebration or indication of triumph. PC Marxists thwarted what might have been by telling Americans not to say or do anything that smacked of "triumphalism" as they watched the Soviet empire fall apart.

U.S. leaders, particularly President George H. W. Bush (though he was not the only one), told their fellow Americans not to celebrate because that would only complicate matters for the leaders of the former Soviet Union and would do no good. The admonition to refrain from "triumphalism" was heeded. No widespread celebrations occurred in the United States as the Soviet flag was lowered for the last time from the Kremlin's ramparts. The lack of celebration in the U.S. of that wonderful victory (one of the greatest in American history) illustrates how much sway PC Marxism now exerts over Americans.

See entry on Gloating.

## Truth

Any claim or assertion that furthers the cause of Political Correctness is truth to a PC Marxist. Where Marxists are in control, even science must serve the cause of exercising political power. When truth becomes a matter of politics, a biological male can declare that he feels he is a female and everyone who is politically correct must solemnly accept the assertion as a brave and noble affirmation of "truth."

The Marxist's understanding of reality is like the way a child being read a story may ask, "Daddy, is that true?" and accepts whatever answer Daddy makes because children have no experience by which to form their own judgments. Party leaders to a Marxist are such authorities. The Apostle Paul, who besides being a rabbi was also a poet, wrote in First Corinthians 13:11: "When I was a child, I spoke as a child, but when I became a man, I put away childish things." Marxism, while it thinks its politics are advanced, is puerile.

## Underprivileged

This PC coinage, underprivileged, has a European context. American culture from its beginnings believed in equal privileges. (Slaves were chattel, and as such ineligible for equality with their owners.) To hear these days that an American, whether white or Negro or some racial mix, is "underprivileged" is startlingly un-American. PC Marxists in America are applying the now outdated cultural history of class privileges in pre-World War I Europe to America. They are using the idea of having or not having privileges to make Americans feel guilty for allegedly denying privileges to "victimized classes," as though chattel slavery still existed in the United States.

See entry on Entitled/Entitlement.

## Unfair

A favorite epithet of condemnation in the lexicon of Political Correctness.

See entry on Fairness.

## Unilateralism

"Unilateralism" is a PC term of disapproval for overseas actions by the United States undertaken without the approbation or participation of other nations. From this point of view, the options of the United States in foreign affairs are limited to actions that other countries signal their approval of, regardless of whether the U.S. has the means for acting alone to do something in its best interests.

## Urban Renewal

An environmental practice popular in the 1960s and 70s, the idea of urban renewal held that tearing down dilapidated neighborhoods, constructing new buildings, and moving the slum's former residents into the new housing would produce markedly better conduct. Experience showed, however, that urban renewal projects often produced high-rise slums, because unless slum dwellers undergo an inner, personal renewal which bolsters their respect for themselves as children of God and affirms for them their right and responsibility to determine their own lives, a radical change of environment is unlikely to change their behavior. The idea of environmental change without spiritual renewal comes from the Marxian mistake of regarding material conditions as all-important, which may be true for species which are dependent on the quality of their habitats for their well-being, but is not true for human beings. Historically, the well-being of Americans has not been determined by their environment. Rather, the confidence of Americans that they are "made in the image of God" and possess from God the right to self-determination has been the decisive factor in their long history of improving their environment.

## Useful Idiot

Anyone occupying a position of social, economic, or political influence is a potential useful idiot. Influential persons who sympathize with or promote the aims of PC Marxism in the United States are actual useful idiots. Lenin apparently coined this term during the Bolshevik Revolution to identify Russian leaders and opinion makers who would cooperate with him in bringing about their downfall.

## Victimless Crime

A crime which theoretically harms no one, according to PC Marxism, ought not to be prosecuted since it is "victimless." But an act which is said to be a crime probably does affect another human being. To speak of "victimless crime" serves only to condone conduct PC Marxists do not want to see punished and discouraged.

See entry on Consenting Adults.

## War on Poverty

The metaphor used in this phrase is significant: *war* on poverty. When President Lyndon Johnson launched his so-called "War on Poverty" in 1965, he said in the speech announcing the program that the only outcome he would accept would be "total surrender" (see similar language by a self-proclaimed Marxist on p. 38 above). For a president of the United States to use such phrases as "war on" and "total surrender" in connection with something whose causes are as complicated and individual as poverty is troubling.

Johnson's "war" had devastating consequences for the Negro American family. In 1950, 78% of Negro American families consisted of traditional married couples; and the advantages for the children of such marriages were palpable. But after Johnson's Aid to Families with Dependent Children — a major component of his "War on Poverty" — went into effect, it became profitable for black men and women *not* to marry and for Negro women to have children out of wedlock. *Within just one generation,* 68% of black mothers were unmarried, and the resulting lack of a father in these households contributed to a rise in delinquency and poverty among young Negro American males. (White American families having no male head suffered the same result.)

And let us remember that in the half-century between 1890 and 1940, "black marriage rates in the U.S. [were] higher than the white marriage rates"; that in the twenty years prior to the 1960s, the employment rate among Negro Americans exceeded that of white Americans; and that from 1940 to 1970, despite the segregationist (Jim Crow) laws then in effect, "the black poverty rate fell by 40 percentage points" and "the number of blacks in middle-class professions quadrupled." But in the 1960s, with the advent of agitprop about racism as the explanation for Negro American poverty, federal Affirmative Action laws granting Negro Americans special privileges, and Lyndon Johnson's "War on Poverty," all of that self-directed progress on the part of Negro Americans began to falter and then slide backwards as the Negro American family suffered the devastating effects of receiving government aid which destroyed their responsibility for themselves. The above information is from Jason L. Riley's column "Modern Liberalism's False Obsession with Civil War Monuments" in the *Wall Street Journal*, August 30, 2017, p. A15. Mr. Riley, a Negro American journalist, is the author of *Please Stop Helping Us: How Liberals Make It Harder for Blacks to Succeed.*

## Weaponize, to

This strange verb reveals the totalitarian character of agitprop. The notion that words are "weapons" indicates the nature of Political Correctness as all-out culture war against non-Marxist doctrines, ideas, sentiments, and persons. Only Marxists who regard politics as a kind of warfare would speak, as PC Marxists do, of "weaponizing" words. Such terminology is worse than appalling. It's dehumanizing.

## Wedge Issue

PC Marxists allege that "right-wing extremists" introduce "wedge issues" to drive an ideological wedge between people. The allegation is more descriptive of PC Marxist behavior, however, than the behavior of their opponents.

## Welfare

The general term for the distribution of "entitlements" by the U.S. government, "welfare," or the making of payments from the U.S. Treasury to classes of people, is not provided for in the Constitution of the United States. The reference to promoting "the general welfare" in the Preamble to the Constitution which is repeated in Article I, Section 8 (both times in conjunction with the common defense) has to do only with the *States of the United States*. Indeed, the States of the United States are the *only* reference in the Constitution's Preamble, which says the Constitution has been created "to form a more perfect Union" of the States; to "establish Justice" among the States; to "insure domestic Tranquility" within the States; to "provide for the common defence" [sic] of the States; and to "promote the general Welfare" of the States in order to "secure [i.e. protect] the Blessings of Liberty" for the people of the States and their posterity.

Delegates chosen by the people of twelve States wrote the U.S. Constitution to create a general government of, by, and for the people of the States. Each State had one vote (regardless of the State's size) in deciding what to put in or leave out of the Constitution, just as in amending the Constitution today each State has one vote. The one vote per State, regardless of a State's population, reflects the equal sovereignty of the people of the States. The Constitution is not of, by, and for a collective abstraction known as the American people but rather of, by, and for the equally sovereign, particular people of each particular State.

## White

Negro American youths influenced by decades of incessant racial agitprop now regard anything associated with white Americans as hostile to them as "African Americans." Because of the incessant agitprop on race which Negro Americans have been hearing for fifty years, "white" now has a highly pejorative meaning to these young Americans. They also have in many cases a sense of alienation from their American culture, as if they were not themselves Americans.

See entries on African American, Alienate/Alienation, Assimilation, Negro American.

## White Privilege

This is one of the racial accusations of Marxist agitprop, according to which all white Americans now enjoy and have always enjoyed special privileges. That will certainly be news to the poorer white residents of Appalachia.

## White Supremacy

This term is heard more and more often these days in PC propaganda aimed at destroying Donald Trump's presidency. Trump is being slandered by his politically correct enemies as a "white supremacist." Heretofore the term white supremacy was used only in reference to members of the Ku Klux Klan and Americans who approved of Adolf Hitler's theory of "Aryan" racial superiority, neither of which is generally admired in the United States. Racism, however, has long been the main anti-American accusation of Political Correctness in its campaign to obliterate America's culture. The great thing about this accusation for purposes of agitprop is that it doesn't have to be proven. It's presumptively true of all white Americans rather than particularly true of anyone. White Americans *in toto* can be accused of racism without having to demonstrate the truth of the claim. The accusation of racism must ignore or deny all of the recent evidence of growing good will between Negro and white Americans in the last twenty to thirty years and emphasize the past when racism was certainly commonplace in America, as any American in their eighties can tell you.

To say white Americans today are racists is the most destructive, recurring slander agitprop uses in its campaign to destroy America. That is why the accusation is so frequently made, and why it is being leveled against Donald Trump who is an arch enemy of Political Correctness. In fact, the appeal of the Rev. Martin Luther King to white Christians in the 1950s and 60s as a Christian minister and fellow American was effective. Jim Crow laws in the States were repealed by white State legislatures; and the U.S. Congress and U.S. courts finally started enforcing the Fourteenth and Fifteenth Amendments as they should have been doing since they were ratified in 1868 and 1870 respectively.

## Witch Hunt

Whenever anyone has alleged, as Joseph R. McCarthy, a U.S. Senator from Wisconsin, did in the late 1950s, and as I am doing in this book, that American Marxists are subverting U.S. institutions with the aim of destroying America's culture, PC Marxists say such persons are conducting a "witch hunt" against Marxists. The term "witch hunt" implies there's as much chance today that Marxists are out to destroy the United States as there is that witches are present in America and seeking to harm it. More importantly, the term witch hunt implies that anyone who thinks Marxists harbor a malicious intent toward the United States and its culture are the sort of people who think witches still roam the land. PC Marxists would have Americans think that believing in a Marxist threat to America is as stupid as believing in a threat from witches.

See entries on Culture War, McCarthyism, Myth.

## Xenophobia

An excessive suspicion or fear of foreigners, xenophobia is an accusation PC Marxists make against American patriots who want to put America's interests first.

## Zoological Thesis, the

The PC Marxist term for the Judeo-Christian claim that man is a unique creature. Marxists deny all such claims of human uniqueness. Man, to them, is only another species of animal, no different in essence from other creatures. According to Marxism, any other view of human beings is unscientific and dangerous.

PART III

# TRANSFORMATIONS

# Preface

THE FOLLOWING COMMENTARIES, comprising Part III of the book, identify and discuss seven related revolutionary concepts that PC agitprop is imposed on America. Each of them has been designed to make a significant contribution to the destruction of American culture and its reconstruction as Cultural Marxism. The ultimate goal of Political Correctness is to eliminate American culture as the chief impediment to global Marxism. The Appendices at the end of the book indicate the fundamental antagonisms between America's culture and Marxism which led to the conflict between the United States of America and the Union of Soviet Socialist Republics known as the Cold War which ended when the Soviet Union disintegrated in 1991. The conflict between the Beliefs of American Culture (Appendix A) and the Dogmas of Cultural Marxism (Appendix B) has continued beyond the end of the Cold War.

# Biological Class Consciousness

ECONSTRUCTING existing beliefs and behaviors of American
culture while constructing substitute Marxist dogmas
and behaviors sums up the general agenda of agitprop in
America. For example, replacing belief in self-determination with
dependence on government "entitlements." Agitprop has created two
antagonistic camps in the United States: an American camp and an
anti-American camp. As the goals of agitprop have become clearer,
most Americans, it seems, have become at least somewhat alarmed by
and opposed to what's happening in America, without becoming necessarily more *effective* in opposing Political Correctness, even though
the polarity of the two camps is growing more pronounced.

There was little conscious pushback to Political Correctness, the
anti-American camp, on the part of Americans until the loosely organized "Tea Party" movement of a few years ago. It was that pushback which, despite heavy media criticism and ridicule, led in 2015
and 2016 to the formation of the grassroots political organizations all
across America — many of them distrustful of the Republican Party
establishment — that coalesced behind the candidacy of Donald
Trump and elected him president of the United States.

But *how* has PC Marxism been destroying and rebuilding
American culture? That is the question for us here. What has been the
principal method agitprop has used for tearing down America's culture and rebuilding it as Cultural Marxism? In understanding how PC

Marxism has been accomplishing its twin goals, five things have to be stated from the Marxist perspective. (1) When one speaks of "Marxist revolution," one is speaking of the attempt to eliminate an existing culture and replace it with the dogmas of Cultural Marxism. Every revolution in the modern era, starting with the first one in France in the closing decade of the eighteenth century, has aimed to transform an existing culture. (2) The means for revolutionary change that Karl Marx identified and described in the middle of the nineteenth century, and that Vladimir Lenin applied in the early twentieth century in Russia, was class struggle which requires an absolute sense of class consciousness and historic class grievances. Marx expressed in his *Communist Manifesto* how indispensable class struggle is to Marxist thought and action by saying: "The history of all hitherto existing society is the history of class struggle." Without the dogma of revolutionary class struggle, there would be no Marxist regimes anywhere in the world. (3) The Soviet agents sent to the United States in the 1920s and 1930s by Lenin and his successor Stalin to foment class struggle did not appreciate the non-European nature of America's culture and class consciousness and were not trained in how to replace that consciousness with a class consciousness that would be conducive to Marxist class struggle. (4) The class consciousness that resulted from America's exceptional cultural history had to be replaced in order for Marxian class struggle to occur in America. (5) Starting in the 1960s and 70s, Marxist agitprop began the creation of a new, across-the-board *biological* class consciousness in America, which has proven successful in producing the Marxist class consciousness needed for class struggle in the United States.

To understand the new, Marxian class consciousness which has been growing stronger in America year by year since the 1960s, the class consciousness which existed in America prior to the 1970s and the causes of it must be grasped. Generally speaking, America had an exceptional demographical and political history and geography which influenced the behavior of generation after generation of Americans and led them to develop a quite different culture from the culture of Europe in the seventeenth and eighteenth centuries and the cultures in the other three main areas of European settlement in the Western Hemisphere: Brazil, Canada, and Spanish America.

Marx based his supposedly scientific theory of history on what he saw in Europe's history; and what he saw was a tiny class of "haves" which owned nearly all the continent's productive land and whose members claimed to have "noble" or "royal" blood which entitled them to govern the immense class of landless, "have-not" peasants of so-called "common" blood whom the ruling class regarded as fit only to serve them. (The recent Marxist nonsense that "99% of Americans" are being oppressed by the other 1% is an explicit reflection of Marx's view of history.) During the course of America's history, the largest middle class in human history formed in the United States, the class which collectively owns most of America's wealth, in the form of small family farms before the Civil War and afterward down to the present in land, homes, other property, and investments of various kinds. Indeed, the American middle class has amassed the largest amount of private property ever seen in one nation. Not surprisingly, a cultural belief that everyone must work arose in this immense American middle class because work leads to property ownership, and property is the basis for personal freedom and independence (beliefs already evident in the *Autobiography* Benjamin Franklin composed in 1771; 1784–88).

Work has great cultural value for Americans. Reverence for work goes back to the earliest colonial times when civilizing the continental expanse of Stone Age wilderness across the middle latitudes of North America from the Atlantic to the Pacific went on for fourteen successive generations and was the main occupation of Americans during the first three centuries of their history. It was from that Herculean labor that Americans developed their cultural belief in the value of work, which is one of the principal bases of America's exceptional wealth.

People of "noble" blood did not leave Europe to settle in the wilderness that was to become the United States of America. The culturally elite, hereditary ruling classes of Europe which owned nearly all the productive land in the nations of that continent stayed in Europe. They did not migrate and did not bring their antipathy for manual work with them to America. Thus, belief in privileged ruling classes founded on birth who considered manual and commercial work beneath their cultural dignity never got established in America. Only persons who wanted to determine their social rank through their own efforts and who did not regard the necessity of manual labor as demeaning came to the future United States of America.

In the formative generations of America's culture (1610–1770), the first eight generations of European settlement in the colonies that were to declare themselves the United States of America in 1776, persons who worked with their hands to create property and who recognized the imperative for hard labor in civilizing a Stone Age wilderness made up the bulk of American society, and expected to benefit from their labor. This is to say that even people of property in colonial America worked at the task of civilizing the wilderness. It almost goes without saying that the slaves who augmented that primary labor force did not derive any personal benefit from their labor which, among other considerations, is what made their status so terrible in a culture that valued freedom and a sense of equality.

To be sure, classes of rich and poor existed in colonial America. There are rich and poor in every society, even communist regimes like Cuba, North Korea, China, and Vietnam today. There were rich and poor in the USSR when it existed, as there are in its successor state, the Russian Federation. But in America's 400-year history, no ruling class based on supposedly superior blood or on an allegiance to a supposedly "scientific" political theory was ever established. Nor has property and political power in America ever been concentrated in a small, governing elite as it was in Europe before World War I. Rather, property and political authority have been historically widely

distributed in America. American society in the formative generations of its cultural development was bent on creating in the shortest
time possible as much property as possible from the superabundance
of wilderness that existed in the temperate, arable middle latitudes of
North America.

The new, non-European culture which formed in the English-
speaking colonies on the mainland of North America between 1610
and 1770 — that is to say, the new set of historical belief-behaviors that
formed there — developed from generations of lower and middle class
Europeans seeking opportunities for self-improvement in America.
These self-selected immigrants and their American-born descendants
living in America's opportunity-rich geography, where one's birth did
not automatically confer social, political, and economic privileges, had
left behind Europe's aristocratic cultures and their social and political
restrictions. Life in America was markedly freer than life in Europe
with its social classes defined by birth, forming a society shaped like
a pyramid, with a tiny, leisured class at the top ruling much larger
classes of workers at the bottom who in turn accepted the cultural
belief that they were inferior by birth to their so-called "betters." That
was the cultural structure of European society before the cataclysm
of World War I destroyed it. The experience of Europe's pre-World
War I social pyramid formed Marx's "scientific" idea of history as class
struggle.

The structure of American society has historically been, and remains, quite different. It is a diamond-shaped quadrilateral with an
extremely wide middle. Persons who thought of society as a gathering
of individuals who could determine their social rank through their
own efforts created this structure by the way they lived and related to
the majority of their peers. The self-selected immigrants and their descendants who made up the preponderance of America's population
also believed in the necessity of worshipping God in a way agreeable
to their own consciences rather than according to the dictates of a rul-
ing-class's church. The immigrants to the English-speaking colonies

of North America were seeking freedom to improve their class status and also freedom to worship God as it pleased their conscience. And the new culture they formed in the eight generations before 1770 embodies both of those desires for freedom.

America's class consciousness arose from two primary conditions not found in the countries of Europe. (1) A society almost entirely made up of descendants of ambitious immigrants who had chosen to become a member of it without having to meet particular criteria of European nationality or religion, as the immigrants to French Canada, Portuguese Brazil, and Spanish America all had to meet. (2) A wilderness of continental dimensions with a temperate climate and a high proportion of arable land and other desirable, accessible, seemingly inexhaustible resources: a combination of human and natural resources that no other part of the Western Hemisphere had to a similar extent. America's combination of unique demographic and geographic conditions produced an exceptional set of cultural beliefs on the Atlantic Coastal Plain of North America between 1610 and 1770.

America's declaration of its independence from Europe in 1776 stated the cultural difference between European and American culture in proclaiming "all men are created equal" in having from God the same birthright to "Life, Liberty, and the Pursuit of Happiness" and government by consent of the governed. America in the eight generations prior to 1770 offered a sense of equality, freedom, and opportunity not found in the other three major areas of European colonization in the Western Hemisphere: Canada, Brazil, and Spanish America. Consequently, a set of cultural beliefs developed there that was unlike Europe's culture and the cultures of other major areas of European continental colonization in the New World. The Declaration of Independence that Americans published to the world in July 1776 was an announcement of more than a political separation from Europe. It was also an announcement of cultural separation. One must again recognize that the slaves in American society from the 1660s to the 1860s — no matter how much we might regret their presence — were primarily regarded as live property or chattel, which could be bought and sold like a horse or a cow, rather than as human beings deserving and having the same rights as the free men and women in this society, who in the course of their colonial history developed the most self-determining, individualistic, and least personally restrictive culture in the New World.

The existence in the middle latitudes of North America of extraordinary freedom and opportunities for self-determination, and the cultural equality to take full advantage of these features of American society, resulted in an extraordinarily productive society with a relish for self-government. Because of the prevalent opportunities for gainful employment and upward mobility which existed in the future United States, few families in American society remained in a poverty-stricken situation generation after generation. To remain poor, an immigrant to America and his descendants almost had to be devoid of imagination and gumption. But lack of imagination was unlikely, since everyone in this society, aside from the slaves in it before 1865, had had ancestors with enough imagination and courage (what Americans once called "gumption") to find a way to leave their native places in Europe and go to an uncouth, far away continent in pursuit of opportunities they imagined awaited them there, opportunities which needed only to be discovered and used. And even some of the slaves developed marketable skills which allowed them to earn money, save some of it, and buy their freedom. America could be said to be the land of the free because it has historically been the home of many brave, hopeful, imaginative, and hardworking men and women.

During America's colonial period (1607–1775) when the formation of American culture took place, it was quite possible for immigrants from the lower classes of Europe to have families in America, rise to the vast middle class of American property owners, and for their descendants to remain in that class generation after generation. If a person in America was a diligent worker and had no wasteful habits, chances were he could become a property owner and belong to some level of America's broad middle class and live comfortably. If he worked extra hard and had enough talent, imagination, and ambition (plus some luck), he could hope to perhaps rise into that smaller but still sizeable upper class of affluent Americans. There was also of course the possibility of going broke and having to commence one's efforts to rise in American society all over again. But that, too, was possible with gumption and imagination.

Throughout its four centuries of history, America has been a country in which the great majority of Americans has been free to pursue their aspirations, whether modest or grand, and to strive to belong to whatever class of society they wanted to belong to. It would probably be safe to say that the United States of America has been the first large society in the history of mankind to have a consciousness of being "classless" in the sense that the classes in it for the most part *were not fixed by birth*. America in the 1700s was thought of in Europe as "the best poor man's country" because even poor persons in America having some ambition were generally better off than the well-to-do in some poor communities of "the Old World." The commonplace desire of America's poor before Marxist agitprop became entrenched in the United States in the 1960s was to improve their lives through their own efforts. Now, the poor in America, as well as an increasing segment of the middle class, look to Big Government to improve their lives. This has the appearance of a major change in American expectations, and could destroy the American belief in self-determination which lies at the heart of American culture. The election of Donald Trump to the presidency of the United States, however, has the appearance of an uprising of the American middle class against the alien dictates of PC Marxism or Political Correctness.

Karl Marx's dogma that *class struggle* (not individual struggle) is the universal character of human history derived from his consciousness that Europe's social classes were *fixed by birth*. The spire at the apex of Europe's social pyramid was limited to persons of the highest "noble" and "royal" blood, with classes of lesser persons below those, and immense classes of workers still lower down in the pyramid to serve the titled lords and ladies and royalty (their "betters"). The persons of exalted blood had a monopoly on arable land, in the form of huge landed estates maintained by passing them down intact to the firstborn males of the highborn families (the custom of primogeniture). Primogeniture never became a common practice in the thirteen English-speaking colonies on the mainland of North America during the period of their colonial history because too much wild, unowned arable land was available in those colonies at low prices, or just by "squatting" on it. An attempt was made in 1669 to introduce the English practice of primogeniture to America, and its system of hereditary government based on the idea of superior birth that England had. The plan, called *The Fundamental Constitutions of the Carolinas*, was written by the English political philosopher John Locke in the employ of the eight "Lord Proprietors of the Carolinas." It was a complete flop. In colonial Brazil, colonial Canada, and colonial Spanish America, however, classes of titled noblemen owning huge estates passed down father to son by the custom of primogeniture, whose proprietors constituted an hereditary ruling class, did develop and gave those colonial societies cultures similar to those of pre-World War I Europe.

In the 1920s and 30s, when first Lenin and then Stalin sent Soviet agents to the United States to foment Marxist revolution in America, they did not appreciate the class consciousness of American culture by which each person determined their class status through their own efforts. Because of this pervasive cultural consciousness that each person in American society determined their class status for themselves, the Soviet agents sent to America in the 1920s and 30s to arouse American workers to *class struggle* failed in their mission, even after the Great Depression of 1929. By the time that World War II broke out in Europe in 1939, it was clear that America's deeply ingrained, un-European class consciousness of self-determination and individual responsibility would have to be changed before Marxian class struggle would be possible in the United States.

Perhaps shortly before World War II, sometime in the 1930s, some advisor to the Central Committee of the Communist Party of the Soviet Union proposed a strategy by which America's peculiar class consciousness could be converted to a class consciousness suitable for Marxist class struggle. But the attempt to impose that transformation on America through agitprop could not be undertaken during the life-and-death struggle between Stalin's Soviet Union and Hitler's Nazi Germany. That titanic conflict in World War II between the two totalitarian socialist regimes of Europe was a fight to the death and took precedence over everything else. The Soviet dictator Stalin had to make a military alliance with Britain and the United States to repel the invasion of Soviet territory in June 1941 by his former ally Adolf Hitler, with whom he had collaborated in conquering and partitioning Poland in 1939.

Stalin called his alliance with Britain and the United States in the early 1940s "the United Front." (There never was a negotiated U.S.-Soviet treaty ratified by the U.S. Senate.) The pre-war Soviet agents in the United States stayed on in America during and after the war, gathering information on U.S. war plans for their Kremlin masters and influencing American policies in favor of the Soviet Union (see *America's Betrayal*, by Diana West, St. Martin's Griffin, 2013). After Hitler's invasion of the USSR in 1941, the Soviets of course suspended attempts at revolution inside America until they, in alliance with Britain and the United States, defeated Nazi Germany unconditionally.

In 1949, four years after Nazi Germany's defeat, the United States became the leader of a military alliance among Western nations called the North Atlantic Treaty Organization (NATO) to contain Soviet expansion from Central Europe (i.e. from the Soviet colonies of Poland, Hungary, Czechoslovakia, and East Germany) into Western Europe. That resistance to further Soviet expansion became known as "the Cold War."

The recovery of the Soviet Union from the devastation of World War II and the death of the longtime Soviet dictator Josef Stalin in 1953 (a major crisis for the Communist Party of the Soviet Union) postponed resumption of Soviet subversive activities inside the United States. But in the 1960s, a massive anti-American, pro-Marxist agitprop campaign was launched inside the United States, the long-range intent of which was to demolish America's culture and replace it with Cultural Marxism. This was the movement which significantly called itself "the Counter Culture" which was renamed by its American opponents "Political Correctness" because they saw in the Counter Culture a strong resemblance to the Chinese "Cultural Revolution" whose communist leader, Mao Zedong, referred to the politics of his movement as Political Correctness. Mao's "Cultural Revolution" like the Counter Culture in America was powered by the young who were most susceptible to agitprop.

The immediate purpose of the Counter Culture/Political Correctness Movement in America was to get American military forces out of Vietnam. Its more consequential, long-term purpose, as its name suggested, was to destroy America's will to contain the spread of communism by destroying its culture and rebuilding it as Cultural Marxism. After that was accomplished, nothing would then impede the conversion of every nation in the world to Marxism.

When the USSR collapsed in 1991, the Counter Culture/Political Correctness Movement was so firmly established in America and its momentum was by then so great that the Soviet collapse did not stop it. Unlike Soviet agitprop in America in the 1920s and 30s, the Counter Culture/Political Correctness Movement was not designed to overthrow the U.S. government by force. Rather, it aimed to co-opt America's most important institutions with a slow, steady persistence and convert them to a Marxist mindset. The professions, the unions, the public schools, the media, the political parties, the churches, every institution which influenced American opinion and behavior. The means to this subversion was the pretense to be fighting for American values like democracy, equality, freedom, and compassion. Though it has taken a long time, this deceptive, incremental approach to revolution has been effective. The pretense of representing the "liberal" and "progressive" elements in America's twentieth-century political history has worked. Tens of millions of Americans now approve of Political Correctness because they have been duped into believing that PC dogmas are a truer embodiment of America's historical cultural values and beliefs.

Biology has been the basis of Marxist class consciousness and class struggle in America. The idea of making class a matter of biology was the essential feature of the 1960s "Counter Culture" after an initial few years of basing class struggle on age and identifying young people as the "class" in rebellion. But of course for sustained revolution, youth alone was not enough; it lacked the requisite long-term stability needed for class struggle which the biological characteristics of gender, race, ethnicity, or homosexuality have, along with historical grievances that could be associated with those "classes." Youth, though a readily identifiable and strongly felt trait, is, after all, a characteristic of limited duration. The young rapidly become fully mature. They are not an enduring revolutionary cadre.

In the past five decades, PC Marxists in America have used agitprop to create a new class consciousness in America and to mount an unflagging class struggle through an intense class consciousness based on race, gender, ethnicity, and homosexuality. (According to PC Marxists "sexual orientation" is determined by birth.) Ethnicity and race have always of course played a role in U.S. politics. Every two years as congressional elections rolled around, especially when presidential elections coincided with congressional elections, there have always been appeals to the "German vote," the "Irish vote," the "Negro vote," the "Italian vote," etc., through a host of biological or birth groupings, including after the ratification of the Nineteenth Amendment to the Constitution in 1920 the "woman's vote." (Before the 1970s, homosexuals were not a politically important group.)

Nowadays ethnicity, race, gender, and "sexual orientation" define class consciousness in America. Prior to the advent of agitprop in America, with its strategy of biological class consciousness, Americans had not been divided into all-embracing, intensely felt, biologically defined class identities accompanied by intensely felt class grievances. The new, biological class consciousness is the most far-reaching result of the use of agitprop in America.

Now, after five decades of relentless Marxist agitation and propaganda promoting biological class consciousness in America, courses on U.S. history and Western civilization have dwindled and all but disappeared at American colleges and universities while courses on biological class consciousness have proliferated. Everywhere today in U.S. institutions of higher education, one find courses and degree programs in Women's Studies, African-American Studies, Mexican-American Studies, Asian-American Studies, and LGBT (Lesbian, Gay, Bi-Sexual, Transgender) Studies. And as college and university faculties have become more uniform in their Political Correctness, the courses on U.S. history and Western civilization which remain in the curriculum are almost invariably taught from the point of view of Marxian class struggle, which is to say from the standpoint that straight "Euro-American" males (SEAMs) comprise a ruling class which has "victimized" women, Negro Americans, Hispanics, Asian-Americans, homosexuals, and other biologically defined classes. College students today are being taught to hate SEAMs as a class for the "victimization" they have allegedly inflicted on all other biological classes in America.

The shift from a class consciousness of self-determination based on personal struggle and achievement to a class consciousness and set of historic class grievances based on birth (i.e. biology) has subverted the American sense of living in what used to be known in my father's generation as a "classless society," which is to say a society of volatile class identities, and has transformed it into an idea of class identities based on birth suitable for Marxian class struggle. Agitprop is conditioning Americans to think in terms of biological class struggle. Through agitprop, a class consciousness based on birth (biology) like that which prevailed in Europe prior to World War I (1914–1918) has been imposed on America.

The immigrants who left Europe for America before the twentieth century were choosing to live in a society they had reason to believe offered them opportunities for social and economic advancement. These immigrants and their descendants wanted to determine their class status through individual striving instead of having it determined for them by birth. They were conscious of having left the past behind them in "the old country." They were making a new start, a new life, on a new continent for themselves and their posterity. They were choosing to be reborn as Americans. Their hopefulness generation after generation formed a new, non-European class consciousness and set of cultural beliefs. They were future-oriented rather history-oriented.

But since Marxist agitprop came to America in the 1960s, America's exceptional culture has come under persistent assault and is in the process of being transformed into Cultural Marxism. Agitprop is establishing a radically different, backward-looking culture. Americans are being indoctrinated and trained to accept the idea of biological class consciousness and class struggle.

In the first three and a half centuries of American history (i.e. before the 1960s), property was the primary definer of social class in America, not biology. Persons moved up or down the social scale depending on how much property they individually acquired or lost. With biology now being established as the primary marker of class identity in America, that is no longer the case. Class identity in America today is fixed at birth. If a person is born female, that is her permanent class identity regardless of how much wealth she may come to control during her life or what her personal achievements may be. The same is true for "African Americans," Mexican Americans, Asian Americans, homosexual Americans, and other biologically defined "classes." No matter how much wealth they accrue and regardless of

their personal achievements, according to the new class consciousness they forever remain in the class of "victims" into which they
were born, and will continue to be "victimized" until the advent of
Cultural Marxism and the structure of "social" justice which that
advent will occasion. The same is true of straight "Euro-American"
males (SEAMs). They, too, forever have only the class identity of being
"victimizers," regardless of the individual characters they have. The
formula is absolute. The biological class consciousness agitprop has
created in America to prosecute the destruction of America's culture
and the construction of Cultural Marxism makes biological identity
all-important. Individual identity and character are quite secondary.

Perhaps the most un-American feature of the new class consciousness that agitprop is imposing on America is how *backward-looking*
it is. The class consciousness agitprop is creating is oriented to the
past as defined exclusively in terms of Marxism's theory of history as
class struggle. This class consciousness which emphasizes class grievances rooted in history leaves no room for an individual to overcome
their biological class history as that history is construed by agitprop.
According to agitprop, being "victimized" in the United States today
is essentially the same as it was in 1660, 1760, 1860, and 1960. Nothing
has fundamentally changed for victimized biological classes. The
American claim that American history is the history of individuals overcoming the limitations of their births to the extent that they
aspire to do that is according to PC Marxists a meaningless, unscientific assertion with no factual basis. The claim is just a collection of
meaningless anecdotes, a "myth," something of no consequence. And
what is the validity of that dismissal of American exceptionalism as
myth? It is the various and vehement assertions by PC Marxists of the
continued prevalence of "victimization" in America today. "African
Americans," women, ethnic minorities, homosexuals are still victims
defined by their biology and American society still awaits the liberating coming of Cultural Marxism. Slavery never really went away, according to PC Marxists; nor have women every been "liberated." The

Negro American Civil Rights Movement was an illusion. The need for comprehensive class struggle remains as urgent as it ever was.

Prior to the 1960s, Americans struggled as individuals to improve their lives. They thought in terms of their personal dreams and individual ambitions and their family's future. They wanted to be "self-made" men and women, and they believed they could achieve a better life for themselves and their families through their own efforts. Agitprop in America is whipping up a frenzy for class struggle and retribution for things which happened generations ago to other persons. Agitprop is deconstructing the allegiance of Americans to their families, their personal ambitions, and the beliefs of American culture and is calling for total allegiance to Marxian class struggle and "social" justice.

If agitprop fully accomplishes this transformation of allegiances, Americans will no longer regard their lives as a striving to "get ahead" as individuals but as a dependence on "society" to provide them with everything they need for their welfare and the welfare of everyone they love. People in a politically correct environment advance together as a class, in the Marxian "class struggle," or not at all. The agitprop about class struggle is making America's culture of self-determination obsolete. Signs of this transformation are all around us. Barack Obama announced what was happening when he said, just before he assumed the office of president of the United States, "We are five days away from fundamentally transforming the United States of America."

But this is not the whole story. Agitprop in America is presently making demands so extreme, so bizarre, and requiring such impossibly extravagant expenditures of borrowed money to accomplish them, that the Counter Culture/Political Correctness Movement in America is currently headed toward a precipitous collapse as monumental as that which the Marxists overlords of the Union of Soviet Socialist Republics experienced in 1991. For anyone who has given the matter much thought, it should be self-evident that a backward-looking movement like Political Correctness which requires Americans to renounce their individual aspirations in favor of "social" justice faces an ultimately insurmountable obstacle. Although agitprop has racked up some amazing ideological achievements in America in the last fifty years, its revolutionary goal of "social" justice remains way out of sync with America's true history of many tens of millions of individuals, who believe in the God that Moses and Jesus prayed to, struggling to achieve their middle-class dreams of success.

Certainly, anyone who lived in the American South in the 1950s or 60s when Jim Crow laws mandated racial separation knows that whatever racism remains in Atlanta, Birmingham, Charlotte, Memphis, New Orleans, Richmond, St. Louis, Washington, D.C. — or any other American city in the South, North, East, or West — is *not* the "institutionalized" racism Martin Luther King, Jr. overcame in the 1950s and 60s. PC Marxists, however, insist that nothing has basically changed in America with regard to racism since King's day. Racism, they say, is still at full throttle. PC Marxists invented their word victimization, which they employ with great fervor and frequency, to express their "talking point" that racial oppression is still rampant in America. One is born a victim, and will remain a victim, until the great liberating day of the class struggle's triumph arrives in America. That's the politically correct myth gripping the imaginations of millions of Americans today and alienating them from Americans who reject the agitprop of Political Correctness.

As Americans come to understand Political Correctness better and to see how retrograde it is and how much it is bent on taking revenge for what happened to one's ancestors, even those Americans it has persuaded to adopt the identity of "victimhood" may awaken to the plain truth that every straight white male alive in the United States today does not think like a slave owner on a nineteenth-century plantation, or a sex trafficker, or a would-be assassin of homosexuals. The backward-looking PC "scenario" or "Party line" of Political Correctness nonetheless makes every straight, white American male guilty for the chattel slavery which ended a century and a half ago, even though to do so is an affront to the most rudimentary concept of decency and justice, namely that only the perpetrator of a wrong be held accountable for it.

We do not hold every person in a family accountable for the crime one of its members commits. Why should an entire biological class be held responsible for what some of their ancestors may have done? To think in terms of "class enemies" is to think the way Marx and Lenin and Stalin (not to mention Hitler) thought. We are not holding accountable and punishing the entire German people for what the National Socialist Party (the Nazis) did before they were born. We do not think of holding the Japanese tourists who throng U.S. cities today accountable for what some of their forebears did in Nanking, China in 1938. (How many Americans even know what "the Rape of Nanking" was?) Nor should we hold straight, white American males alive today responsible for the evil of chattel slavery and the racism that existed in America before the Civil Rights Movement led by Martin Luther King, Jr. A recent op-ed in my hometown newspaper by a Negro American syndicated columnist (Leonard Pitts Jr.) was headlined: "Many Americans Can't Handle the Truth about Slavery" (*Arizona Daily Star*, Nov. 6, 2017). What PC Marxists can't handle is the truth that chattel slavery ended eight generations ago and that "institutional racism" died with the repeal of the Jim Crow laws on racial separation achieved by the Negro American Civil Rights Movement in the 1950s and 60s.

One sees in Marx's theory that class struggle is the universal feature of history the chief problem with Marxism: its rigid, mechanistic dogmatism and focus on the past. If Marxists were to admit that America's history is a departure from Marx's theory of history as class struggle, Marxists could no longer claim that their ideological progenitor, Karl Marx, was a "scientist" and would have to cease believing in his infallibility. In the 1920s and 30s when Marxists invented the term exceptionalism to ridicule the American claim that they lived in a "classless society," Marxists of course did not want to concede that

American history was different from the history of Europe because to do that would have been to destroy their confidence in Marxian "science." America's history as a land of opportunity for individuals makes a mockery of Marxism's class thinking; therefore, agitprop insists, America isn't a land of opportunity for individuals with "get up and go" but a land of class oppression, of "victimization," requiring class struggle to attain "social" justice.

The revised, dumbed-down version of American history as the story of "victimization," which agitprop is imposing in the nation's public school classrooms, is a rewriting of America's cultural history. If this Marxian indoctrination in the public schools continues for another two generations, the slow-motion Marxist revolution that has been going on in America since the 1960s might well triumph. To enforce that Marxian indoctrination, America's youths are being told over and over again that the opportunities which have attracted count-less millions of immigrants to America over the centuries are "myths." Agitprop wants young Americans to believe that the American middle class from which most U.S. public schools students come somehow never existed. PC Marxists are making the ludicrous claim that America is a country where "99%" of the people are "victimized."

The agitprop version of American history in U.S. public schools and on college campuses attributes all virtue to "victimized" bio-logical classes and all wrongdoing to SEAMs (Straight Euro-American Males), whether living or dead. These straight white males, according to PC Marxists, are an omnipresent ruling class of despicable oppres-sors. It's as if all the straight white males who ever lived in America were bound up in a monolithic class of "victimizers" all of whom were trashing day after day the human rights of other Americans.

The idea that wrongdoing is class-specific is the mentality of every revolution: get rid of the "exploiting" class and all will be well. That idea was clearly present in the French Revolution in the 1790s and has been evident in every communist revolution of the twentieth century. In a culture like America's, however, in which the Christian view of human nature as "fallen" plays a major role, wrongdoing is not class-specific. Rather it is attributed to sinful human nature. In that Christian view of wrongdoing, man is continually misusing his God-given freedom and stands in need of a redemption which can only come from God. It is an axiom of American culture that all human beings, whatever their biology may be, are prone to sinful behavior, which is why Americans have believed so stoutly in constitutionally limiting the powers of government, since neither the persons who are governed nor the persons who are governing are sinless. When governmental powers are unlimited and go unchecked, tyranny is the inevitable result, the American Founding Fathers believed. In Marxist theory, however, Marxist leaders can do no ultimate wrong because the doctrines of Marxism represent "scientific" truth. The Marxist "vanguard" are merely applying the principles of science to the needs of society. Therefore Marxist "changes" to the structure of society will lead mankind to utopia, no matter how harsh the benevolent leaders have to be in effecting that "change." That is how Marxists rationalize the need for their violence, intimidation, and contemptuous disdain for whoever disagrees with them. Agitprop regards Western civilization as the work of an historically corrupt ruling class which must be replaced by a "scientific" Marxist elite.

In the Marxist revolution being perpetrated in the United States today, one must never have an opinion which deviates from the idea that America is and has always been a land of oppression. American history must never be regarded as the story of extraordinary individual successes, of ambitious persons choosing to abandon their birthplaces to take advantage of the extraordinary opportunities America offers to those with enough imagination to see these potentials. Such hard-working visionaries have created America's great and widely distributed wealth. Whoever deviates from the Marxist line about America as a land of oppression is dismissed and scorned as a "bigot," a "fascist," a "homophobe," a "racist," a "sexist," or a "xenophobe." Imagine every character in Nathaniel Hawthorne's novel of seventeenth-century

Puritan Boston, *The Scarlet Letter*, in which an adulteress is sentenced in a court of law to wear the stigma of a red letter A, having to wear a red B identifying them as a Bigot, or a red F for Fascist, or a red H for Homophobe, or a red R for Racist, or a red S for Sexist, or a red X for Xenophobe, *without even a trial based on evidence.* Such stereotyped labeling is the America agitprop is creating. That is the America that politically correct Americans want everyone to believe is a "scientific" truth. That is the procrustean nightmare which is being taught in our schools, colleges, and universities.

According to PC agitprop, the polarization of politics in America in recent decades is the fault of America's culture, and not until that culture is replaced by Marxism will "social" justice be possible. And not until "social" justice is attained will life in America be redeemed from its "deplorable" condition. Young middle-class Americans are being indoctrinated in these views. Because of unrelenting agitprop, fewer and fewer Americans appreciate America as the most attractive land of opportunity in history judged by its unequalled volume of immigration.

# "Social" Justice

THE BIBLE REFERS many times to justice and being just, both with regard to God and human beings. The Bible indicates that human beings yearn for and seek justice. The yearning for justice is part of our nature as God has created us. Only man among the creatures God has created wants justice, which doubtless has a lot to do with that passage in the first book of the Bible which says God gave man "dominion" over all the other creatures of the earth (Genesis 1:26, 28).

But what exactly do we mean in saying human beings want justice? And what is meant these days by "social" justice? In what ways may "social" justice differ from ordinary justice?

"Social" justice is Marxist language. It refers to the transformation of the United States into a socialist country. It expresses the hope for that transformation, without specifying its Marxist nature. It is the victory that believers in Political Correctness have been working for and continue to work for, the "change" they want to impose on America. "Social" justice is justice for classes of people as opposed to justice for individuals. It is "class action" justice. "Social" justice is wholesale justice obtained through class struggle. It is justice for the "victimized" classes PC Marxists claim are "underprivileged" and "marginalized." According to PC dogma, it is the justice that heterosexual white males in America deny other biological classes.

"Social" justice is a system of government-run programs for re-distributing wealth. It is the justice whose administrators feel, "Ten million dollars isn't much money," or fifty million, or a billion, or even a trillion dollars because the credit of the United States is supposedly inexhaustible. (The United States according to this way of thinking can run up a national debt without limit.) "Social" justice is the justice which creates class privileges, benefits, and immunities to compensate for historical injustices. To use Karl Marx's diction, "social" justice will give "the have-nots" the benefits which in the past have belonged only to "the haves." It is the idea of justice the Counter Culture/Political Correctness Movement introduced to America in the 1960s: a system for distributing wealth that will satisfy historic inequities.

Justice for all — the ideal of justice which American culture es-pouses — means judging everyone's conduct by the same rules of judi-cial procedure. Justice for all is egalitarian. It is the belief that no one is above the law, not even the highest government official or wealthiest citizen; and the belief that everyone's conduct ought to be examined by the same standard of accountability which ultimately derives from God's moral laws for the guidance of man's unique freedom. Thus a sculpture showing Moses receiving God's Ten Commandments has been placed in the chamber where the U.S. Supreme Court hears cases.

Justice for all is the belief that the political views and personal in-terests of a judge should not enter into how he or she applies the laws. It is the justice predicated on the assumption that an accused person is innocent until a jury of his peers unanimously decides on evidence presented at a public trial according to rules of due process and after due deliberation, that he is guilty. Justice for all provides protection against self-incrimination, being tried repeatedly for the same offense, prompt trial, legal counsel for the person accused of a crime, and aid in collecting evidence and witnesses in his defense.

"Social" justice, on the other hand, is based on the idea of pref-erential treatment for members of allegedly oppressed classes. It is justice dispensed according to class history. It is the justice that comes from rifle barrels when revolutionaries take over a nation's institutions of law. Victorious revolutionaries see people in terms of either having opposed or having supported their revolution. "Social" justice is political justice. It expresses political favoritism that will advance the revolution. It is justice which starts in the sort of violence one sees in the histories of Russia and China when communists took over those countries, in Spain when *los rojos* (the Reds) took power there, and in Cuba when Marxists became the ruling class there. "Social" justice is an instrument for revolutionary cultural change.

In the United States, two of the slogans of the Counter Culture/ Political Correctness Movement in the 1960s and 1970s were "Question Authority" and "Don't Trust Anyone Over Thirty." These admonitions interrupted, for those young Americans who took them to heart, the transmission of cultural beliefs by preventing them from imitating their elders' behavior which transmits the culture's beliefs from older to younger generations which happens only if the young respect their elders.

The justice that agitprop is preaching and promoting in America today is a milder form of the justice Lenin and Stalin dished out in the years from the Soviet takeover of Russia in 1917 to the death of Stalin in 1953, milder in the sense that it lacks the peremptory bullet to the back of the head for opponents of the revolution (this was ghoulishly called "liquidation" by the Soviets in mockery of a common financial practice of capitalism). If not summary execution, the justice Lenin and Stalin dispensed was incarceration in forced-labor camps or internment in psychiatric hospitals. As the Soviet revolution entered its third generation, after Stalin's death in 1953, Soviet justice seemed to become milder. The reverse may be true, should the incremental revolution that's been going on slowly in the United States ever gain total control of life in the United States. One thing, however, about "social" justice in the United States has been constant from the outset of the PC revolution in America. As in the Soviet Union, in the United

States membership in an oppressed or "victimized" class has defined a person's eligibility for privileges under the law. The American cultural ideal of justice for all has nothing fundamental to do with the class membership of a person, except that persons who have more wealth can hire more knowledgeable, more experienced lawyers to defend them.

In the days when the Soviet Union existed, Soviet citizens jokingly referred to "telephone justice," which meant a communist party official would telephone the judge in a case being tried in his court and inform him how the Party wanted the case decided. A recent example of this kind of justice in America, by which a person's politics decided the justice they received, was the following. The Attorney General of the United States conferred in 2016 on the tarmac of Sky Harbor Airport in Phoenix, Arizona, with the husband of the Democrat candidate for president who was under investigation by the U.S. Department of Justice, which the U.S. Attorney General heads, for numerous flagrant violations of national security laws. All three of these persons — the former Democrat U.S. president Bill Clinton, his wife Hillary Clinton the Democrat presidential nominee for 2016, and the Democrat Attorney General Loretta Lynch — are politically correct Marxists with degrees from elite U.S. law schools that teach courses in Marxist Critical Theory (see entries for the Frankfort School and Critical Theory in Part II above). Lynch, following her meeting on the tarmac in Phoenix with former president Bill Clinton, said she'd follow whatever recommendation the head of the FBI, James Comey, made regarding Mrs. Clinton's use of an unsecured computer server to conduct secret government business. Comey then said in a formal public statement that although Mrs. Clinton had repeatedly violated national security laws during her tenure as U.S. Secretary of State, she should not be prosecuted because she had "intended" no harm. (Mrs. Clinton destroyed thousands of records of her crimes under subpoena by Congress, but she denied having done anything wrong. She admitted only to having made "a mistake.") The most significant thing here is that FBI directors do not have statutory authority to make recommendations regarding prosecution whereas the Attorney General is under a statutory obligation to study the FBI's findings and make that decision.

The kind of justice displayed in the investigation of Hillary Clinton's criminal conduct is revolutionary, or political justice. It exonerated a person who supports the PC Marxist revolution that has been going on in America since the 1960s. This is the justice all Marxist revolutions dispense. It is the political justice Mao Zedong dispensed in the "Great Proletarian Cultural Revolution" that he launched in China in 1965 and continued until his death in 1976. Mao called the politics of his Cultural Revolution "Political Correctness."

Estimates vary, but the dictators of the one-party Soviet state "liquidated" probably thirty million human beings in dispensing their political justices in the Union of Soviet Socialist Republics during their attempt to create "social" justice in the former empire of the Russian czars. The death toll in Red China after the inception of Marxist government there in 1949 has been much more than that. The Chinese communist state is now the same age the Soviet state was at the time of its collapse, and the question must be asked whether it will survive beyond four generations (eighty years) and thus establish a communist culture in the world's most populous nation. If it does, the culture it establishes will not be orthodox Marxism, because China has not practiced orthodox Marxist economics for almost two generations now (forty years), the sort of Marxist economy the Soviet Union had at the time of its collapse. It has had during the last two generations a state-controlled capitalism. Recently, the Communist Party of China amended the Chinese constitution to allow the chairman of the Party to be president for life (a regression to the era of Mao's rule), which suggests a possible fear among Party leaders that rank-and-file Marxists in China want to move in the direction of an American-style multi-party government which would be the end of the attempt to "build communism" in China as the Chinese people have known it since 1949. Will the current Marxist government in China ever permit candidates nominated for election to government office by independent non-Marxist political parties to stand for office?

In the 1970s and 80s, Political Correctness got into high gear in America. College students influenced by the agitprop of the 1960s took jobs in law, economics, television, banking, journalism, public school teaching, churches, consulting firms, libraries, social services, think tanks, entertainment, universities, foundations, local, State, and federal government, unions, writing, publishing, politics, finance, advertising, and various other vocations influencing public opinion. In the 1970s and 80s, the counter-culture agitators of the 1960s worked on the next generation of Americans to join the revolutionary class struggle for Marxian "social" justice. As one repentant PC agitator of the 1960s said at a reunion of former radicals in 1989: "The difference between the '60s and the '80s is that the radicals in the '60s were on the outside beating on the doors, demonstrating, trying to get in. In the '80s they're on the inside running institutions" (Hilton Kramer in *Second Thoughts: Former Radicals Look Back at the Sixties*, Madison Books, 1989, p. 176).

The emphasis which Political Correctness puts on "social" justice is contrary to the U.S. Constitution, which neither recognizes the need for "social" justice nor makes any provision for it.

The part of the U.S. Constitution which deals most directly with justice is the Bill of Rights. This set of ten amendments to the U.S. Constitution was written and ratified to specify personal liberties and put them under the jurisdiction of the States by declaring unequivocally a separation of State and federal powers. The State governments were to have exclusive jurisdiction over the exercise of personal liberties. The purpose of the Bill of Rights was and is to prevent the general government from encroaching on the personal liberties of the people of the States and on the constitutional powers of the State governments.

The Bill of Rights is the eighth article of the U.S. Constitution. While delegates of the people of the States were meeting in State conventions to decide whether to ratify the seven Articles of the Constitution of the United States that had been presented to them, those State conventions made known their desire to have "a Bill of Rights," or eighth article, added to the Constitution. This eighth article would identify the personal liberties of the people of the States and put their exercise under the authority of State government. It also declared in unequivocal terms the principle that the powers of the proposed new general government were limited while the powers of the people of the States were not. The proponents of the new Constitution — the first constitution, the Articles of Confederation, having proven intolerably defective — promised the State constitutional conventions that if they ratified the seven articles of the proposed constitution, the desired Bill of Rights would be added to the Constitution as an eighth article as soon as the new government began operating. That promise was kept. Within twenty-seven months after the new federal government began functioning, the Bill of Rights had been written by Congress, sent to the States for ratification, and ratified by the required three-fourths of the States: a rapidity which shows how earnestly the people of the states wanted the new U.S. Constitution to protect their personal liberties from encroachments by the federal or general government. The First Session of the First Congress submitted the Bill of Rights to the States on September 25, 1789; it became part of the Constitution, on December 15, 1791.

Amendments I through VIII of the Bill of Rights enumerate twenty-five freedoms, immunities, privileges, and rights of the people of the States. Amendment IX declares that the U.S. government has no authority to define the liberties of the people of the States; that only the people of the States can do that. "The enumeration in the Constitution, of certain rights, shall not be construed to deny or disparage others retained by the people." Amendment X of the Bill declares with great precision and clarity: "The powers not delegated to the United States by the Constitution, nor prohibited by it to the States, are reserved to the States respectively, or to the people." By giving the State Courts exclusive jurisdiction over disputes arising from the exercise of the personal liberties enumerated in the Bill of Rights, the Tenth Amendment of the Constitution prevented any possibility of federal encroachment on those liberties.

The people of the States in ratifying the Bill of Rights were reconfirming their consent to have the Constitution of the United States replace the Articles of Confederation which had no Bill of Rights. One of the most fundamental differences between these two constitutions was that the Articles of Confederation (the first constitution) had been ratified by the legislatures of the States, while the Constitution of the United States (the second constitution) was ratified directly by representatives of the people of the States in special State ratification conventions elected for that explicit purpose. Thus, the constitution Americans have lived under for 230 years derives its authority directly from the people of the fifty States, since the thirty-seven States that subsequently joined the Union, after the initial thirteen ratified the Constitution of the United States, have each consented to living under its authority by joining the Union.

The most important governmental features of the Bill of Rights are: (1) its exclusion of the federal courts from deciding disputes arising from the exercise of freedom of religion, freedom of speech, bearing arms, trial proceedings, and the other personal liberties the people of the States declared for themselves in Amendments I through VIII of the Bill of Rights, and (2) the distinction which the Bill makes between the "retained" or reserved powers of the people of the States (Amendment IX) and the general government's "enumerated" powers (Amendment X). That distinction may be said to be the most important separation of power in the entire Constitution because it shows, in no uncertain terms, that the people of the States are the sovereign, government-making power in the United States while the powers of the general or national government are limited to those the people of the States specify it can have.

The people of the States have made the Constitution, including the Bill of Rights, the supreme law of the nation by their unanimous ratification. *They are the Constitution's lawful proprietors.* The persons the people of the States put in Congress, the White House, and the federal courts under *their* Constitution to serve their *permanent interest in limited government* are their servants, not their masters. These servants are *in office,* not in power.

In recent decades, federal officeholders have acted as if they were the Constitution's proprietors; as if they, not the people of the States, had given the Constitution its authority and were "in power." More often than not these days, after fifty years of agitprop, federal officeholders openly refer to themselves as being "in power." Federal officeholders these days seem to think they can do whatever they want to do, regardless of the restraining principles, procedures, prohibitions, and provisions of the Constitution. This attitude has led to the unwarranted habit among federal officeholders of amending the Constitution through acts of Congress, executive orders, and federal court rulings in defiance of the Fifth Article V of the Constitution, which specifies that only the people of the States, acting through elected assemblies in their respective States, have the sovereign power to amend the Constitution of the United States, just as they alone by ratifying it in their respective States gave it supreme authority in the first place.

Moreover, in recent decades the government's three branches have created an extra-constitutional monstrosity which concentrates in itself legislative, executive, and judicial powers, which the Constitution takes pains to keep separate. The three branches of the general government acting in concert with one another (apart from the will of the people of the States) have created this "Administrative State" which serves their interests but not necessarily the interests of the people of the States. Federal officeholders in Washington bloviate about an abstraction they call "the American people." They have given up thinking of the people of the States as the framers of the Constitution did (see the numerous references to "the people of the States" in James Madison, *Notes of Debates in the Federal Convention of 1787*, Bicentennial Edition, W. W. Norton, 1987). In the past fifty years, the States of the United States have become, it seems, in the thinking of federal officeholders, under the influence of agitprop, mere administrative units of the federal government.

Judged by their actions, federal officeholders no longer regard themselves as servants of the people of the States controlled by the requirements of the Constitution of the United States which the people of the States have ratified, under whose authority the people of the States delegate some of their sovereign authority to the representatives they elect to serve them in the general government, to do things, following the principles, procedures, prohibitions, and procedures of the Constitution that no State, or several States, can do for themselves. To give a salient illustration of this development: Congress has delegated a large part of its federal legislative authority, which Article I, Section 1 vests *solely* in Congress, to the executive branch of the general government. This illicit amendment to the Constitution of the United States is a gross violation of Article V (the amendment article) of the Constitution. Instead of adhering to their oath of office to uphold the requirements of the Constitution, congressmen now seem to think primarily in terms of getting re-elected, and presidents give a great deal of thought to the histories which will be written of their administrations (their "legacy"). Even federal judges seem too often to be mainly concerned with manipulating the Constitution to allow them to do what they wish to do. Nowadays, it often seems that America no longer has a constitutional, republican form of government, but rather a government not unlike what the Soviet Union had when it collapsed: a politically correct regime of men, rather than a government of laws.

The president of the United States is sworn to "preserve, protect, and defend" the Constitution of the United States. Congressmen, federal judges, and the officers of the State governments are likewise sworn to uphold the U.S. Constitution. But are they obeying their oaths of office? In too many cases, it seems they are not. They are amending the Constitution of the United States by legislative acts, executive orders, and judicial decisions. The so-called Administrative State is becoming a law unto itself, having little or no connection to the American ideal of justice for all or the Constitution. Federal officeholders are becoming servants of the alien PC idea of "social" justice.

The federal government now routinely disregards the requirements of the U.S. Constitution the way the eleven States which seceded from the Union in 1860–1861 did. And some Americans, it seems, have begun to think, like the secessionists of 1860–1861, that the right of a State to secede unilaterally from the Union is one of the unspecified, reserved powers of the States. But such a unilaterally State power does not exist under the Constitution of the United States, for when a State unilaterally secedes, it impairs the sovereignty of the other States. It was the States *in Union with each other* that won for each of them their independence from foreign rule, the essential characteristic of sovereignty; and each State's sovereignty under the Constitution of the United States exists only in Union with the other States. This Union was formed by three-fourths of the thirteen States that existed in 1787 when the Constitution of the United States was written in Philadelphia by delegates from twelve of those States and proposed to all of them for ratification. Without the consent of three-fourths of the States that existed in 1787, there would have been no Union of States called the United States of America today.

When it is believed that each State has a unilateral right to secede, no Union constituted by the consent of three-fourths of the States exists, because each State has a nullifying veto over the Union. It is not that each State acting alone created the Union, and therefore can withdraw from it on its own. Rather, three-fourths of the States acting together withdrew from the original Union under the Articles of Confederation (see Article VII of the Constitution of the United States) and formed a new Union organized on a new principle of Union under a new constitution. This new Union can only be dissolved if three-fourths of its members acting together should decide to dissolve it. No single State or group of States less than three-fourths of the whole can canceled the Union formed under the Constitution of the United States.

In ratifying and amending the Constitution of the United States, each State has had one vote, but no State has ever had a veto over the amendment and ratification process set forth in Articles V and VII. In other words, while each State has an equal and coexistent sovereignty, no State has unilateral, that is to say autonomous, sovereignty apart from every other State, the kind of autonomous State sovereignty that existed under the Articles of Confederation. Each State's sovereignty under the Constitution of the United States exists in union with the other constituent States of the Union. This coexistent, equal State sovereignty is what principally distinguishes the Constitution of the United States from the nation's initial form of government, the Articles of Confederation, which the U.S. Constitution replaced in 1788 by consent of three-fourths of the original thirteen States after the Articles had been in effect only seven years.

To amend the Articles of Confederation required the consent of every State (see Article XIII in the Articles of Confederation) which meant that each State had a nullifying veto over the will of all the other States, as if each of them was a wholly independent, autonomous nation whose actions were not contingent in any way on the other States in the Union. Since under the Articles each State's sovereignty was *autonomous*, an individual State's secession from that Union was conceivable. The Union organized and ratified in 1787–1788 under the Constitution of the United States, however, was not like that. The Constitution of the United States could be amended by three-fourths of the States, and thus the compliance of a State which dissented from an amendment was required as part of the new terms of union which went into effect in June 1788 when New Hampshire's ratification of the Constitution of the United States of America completed the required three-quarters of the States to put it into effect for those States (see Article VII, U.S. Constitution). State sovereignty under the U.S. Constitution is not *autonomous* but contingent on the will of three-fourths of the States, which is why the Articles of Confederation lasted only seven years while the Constitution of the United States has lasted more than 230 years and has made possible the growth of a great nation. It is significant that the States which seceded from the Union in 1860–1861 designated the government they set up a "confederacy," as if the principle of union in the Articles of Confederation was still in effect and had not been canceled by the Constitution of the United States.

The serial secessions of one-third of the States from the Union in 1860–1861 were not constitutional acts because they violated the principle of union in the Constitution of the United States which was contingent on the will of three-fourths of the States. The secessions carried out by less than three-fourths of the States in the following sequence: South Carolina, Mississippi, Florida, Alabama, Georgia, Louisiana, Texas, Virginia, Arkansas, Tennessee, and North Carolina over the issue of Abraham Lincoln's lawful election to the presidency of the United States under the terms of the Constitution of the United States temporarily and unlawfully disrupted the Union established by the Constitution. As George Washington pointed out in 1796 in his "Farewell Address," the remedies for any serious grievance a State may have under the Constitution of the United States are an amendment to the Constitution or the impeachment of the offending federal officeholder, *not* secession (unless the aggrieved State is part of a super majority of three-fourths of the States).

After the principle of unitary sovereignty was established by the Constitution of the United States and the government organized under it began operating in 1789, the Congress of the United States vetted the constitutions proposed by each territory seeking admission to that Union. Had any of these would-be States petitioning Congress for admission to the Union submitted a proposed State constitution with a clause allowing it to unilaterally secede from the Union, its petition to join the Union would have been denied, because such a clause would have violated the principle of unitary State Sovereignty under which the Constitution of the United States was framed. It was to defend that principle that the two-thirds of the States which did not secede in 1860–1861 fought the Civil War to restore the Union by force of arms and nullify the unconstitutional secessions of the one-third of the States that withdrew from the Union, which had unconstitutionally injured the sovereignty of every State by their illicit actions.

Another vital principle of the Constitution of the United States is that the personal liberties of the people of the States which the Bill of Rights was written to protect against federal encroachment are exclusively under State jurisdiction. How else except by denying the federal government any jurisdiction over them can the personal liberties of the people of the States be protected from federal encroachment? As Chief Justice of the U.S. Supreme Court John Marshall said in articulating the Court's reasoning in *Barron v. Baltimore*, 32 U.S. 243 (1833), the people of the States demanded the addition of the Bill of Rights to the Constitution to defend themselves "against the apprehended encroachments of the general government" on their personal liberties. The exclusion of the federal judiciary from having any say in adjudicating disputes arising from the exercise of the personal liberties of the people of the States is a mandatory requirement for safeguarding those liberties from the federal government.

The twenty-five personal liberties the Bill of Rights protects, which are vital to the American ideal of justice for all, are stated as follows in its first eight articles:

**First Amendment:** Congress shall make no law respecting an establishment of religion or prohibiting the free exercise thereof; or abridging the freedom of speech, or of the press, or the right of the people peaceably to assemble, and to petition the Government for a redress of grievances.

**Second Amendment:** A well regulated Militia, being necessary to the security of a free State, the right of the people to keep and bear Arms, shall not be infringed.

**Third Amendment:** No Soldier shall, in time of peace, be quartered in any house, without the consent of the Owner, nor in time of war, but in a manner prescribed by law.

**Fourth Amendment:** The right of the people to be secure in their persons, houses, papers, and effects, against unreasonable searches and seizure, shall not be violated, and no Warrants shall issue, but upon probable cause, supported by Oath or affirmation, and particularly describing the place to be searched, and the persons or things to be seized.

**Fifth Amendment:** No person shall be held to answer for a capital, or otherwise infamous crime, unless on a presentment or indictment of a Grand Jury, except in cases arising in the land or naval forces, or in the Militia, when in actual service in time of War or public danger; nor shall any person be subject for the same offence to be twice put in jeopardy of life or limb, nor be compelled in any criminal case to be a witness against himself, nor be deprived of life, liberty, or property, without due process of law; nor shall private property be taken for public use without just compensation.

**Sixth Amendment:** In all criminal prosecutions, the accused shall enjoy the right of a speedy and public trial, by an impartial jury of the State and district wherein the crime shall have been committed, which district shall have been previously ascertained by law, and to be informed of the nature and cause of the accusation; to be confronted with the witnesses against him; to have compulsory process for obtaining witnesses in his favor, and to have the Assistance of Counsel for his defence.

**Seventh Amendment**: In suits at common law, where the value in controversy shall exceed twenty dollars, the right of trial by jury shall be preserved, and no fact tried by a jury shall be otherwise re-examined in any Court of the United States, than according to the rules of the common law.

**Eighth Amendment**: Excessive bail shall not be required, nor excessive fines imposed, nor cruel and unusual punishments inflicted.

Since the people of the States gave their State courts jurisdiction over disputes arising from the exercise of these personal liberties, how is it that for decades now the federal judiciary has exercised plenary jurisdiction over them? The reason is that the U.S. Supreme Court in a series of decisions amounting to a series of illicit amendments to the Constitution of the United States put all twenty-five of the personal liberties enumerated in the Bill of Rights under federal jurisdiction. This series of illicit verdicts, starting in the 1940s and lasting until the 1960s, were orchestrated by an associate justice of the Court distinguished for his intense political partisanship, unyielding tenacity, and charming Southern manners, all of which he brought to bear on his fellow "New Deal" justices on the Supreme Court to obtain their acquiescence to his argument that the Fourteenth Amendment to the Constitution had transferred jurisdiction over all of the personal liberties enumerated in the Bill of Rights (Amendments I through VIII) from the States to the federal government in 1868.

Hugo Lafayette Black was put on the U.S. Supreme Court by Franklin Roosevelt in 1937 and served until his death in 1971. As a member of the Court in the 1940s, 1950s, and 1960s, he tirelessly insisted on his idea that Sections 1 and 5 of the Fourteenth Amendment had transferred jurisdiction over the Bill of Rights from the States to the federal government. The Fourteenth Amendment to the

Constitution was the second of the three Civil War Amendments. The Thirteenth Amendment, abolishing chattel slavery in the United States and its territories, was ratified in 1865. The Fourteenth, ratified in 1868, bestowed citizenship on the many thousands of freeborn and naturalized Negro Americans then living in the United States and the millions of just-emancipated Negro slaves. (Many Americans today, I daresay, are unaware that before the Fourteenth Amendment was ratified, States had withheld citizenship from *freeborn and naturalized* Negro Americans.) In 1870, the Fifteenth Amendment conferred the right to vote on Negro Americans.

Hugo Black, because of his fervent "New Deal" politics, found it impossible to believe that the federal courts could be excluded from so important a constitutional matter as jurisdiction over the personal liberties in the Bill of Rights. He therefore contended that the Fourteenth Amendment had conferred such power on the federal government, and made it his personal mission to get the Supreme Court to accept his reading of the Fourteenth Amendment. He called his reading of the Fourteenth the Incorporation Doctrine because his reading of it "incorporated" under federal jurisdiction all of the personal liberties enumerated and protected in the Bill of Rights.

Getting the U.S. Supreme Court to accept his "Incorporation Doctrine" was the most consequential of Hugo Black's actions in support of the politics of the "New Deal," as President Franklin Roosevelt called his administration. Roosevelt used the designation New Deal because, as he said in his First Inaugural Address on March 4, 1933, he did not intend to allow the Constitution's requirements to interfere with acting on whatever he considered necessary to do to relieve the economic crises of the Great Depression. "We must act and act quickly," he said in his first address to the nation as president. The "unprecedented demand and need for undelayed action" might, he announced, require "temporary departure" from "normal" constitutional requirements. He promised to exercise "broad Executive power" like that which would be given to him if the United States were "invaded by a foreign foe," and likened the American people to "a loyal army" which had elected him its commander in a "time of armed strife" to provide "discipline and direction under leadership." In short, Roosevelt's First Inaugural Address all but stated flat out that one of his "New Deal" policies would be to exercise executive powers not granted presidents in the Constitution of the United States.

The U.S. Supreme Court did not, of course, go along with this concept of the Constitution and found, not surprisingly, some of Roosevelt's "New Deal" actions as president unconstitutional. In 1937, at the beginning of his second presidential term, Roosevelt conceived a plan to solve this problem with the Court, and put Hugo Black, then senior Senator from Alabama and an extremely loyal New Dealer, in charge of getting his Supreme Court bill through the U.S. Senate. Roosevelt thought that there was urgent need for such a bill, and Black agreed with him, because the Court was blocking major legislative components of the "New Deal" as unconstitutional. The most strenuous efforts of Hugo Black in the Senate, however, failed to win passage of Roosevelt's "Court-packing bill," as it was called, which likewise failed to win passage in the House of Representatives, despite the administration's enormous majority of seats in both houses of Congress: 76 Democrats to 16 Republicans in the Senate; 334 Democrats to 88 Republicans in the House. The reason Roosevelt's "Court-packing bill" failed to pass was obvious. Democrats in Congress as well as Republicans recognized it for what it was: an out-and-out attempt to politicize the Supreme Court of the United States, the branch of government supposed to be above politics in its reverence for preserving the integrity of the Constitution of the United States. Those Democrats in the House and Senate who voted against Roosevelt's Supreme Court bill felt greater loyalty to the Constitution than they did to the Democrat Party.

Had Roosevelt's "Court-packing bill" been enacted, it would have given him as president authority to appoint an additional, younger justice to the Supreme Court for each justice on it older than seventy, up to a total of six new justices. (The Constitution does not specify how many justices there shall be on the Court.) When Roosevelt's unconstitutional machination to "pack" the Supreme Court failed, the president made Hugo Black his first appointee to the Court. By putting Black, one of his most trusted and combative "New Deal" lieutenants, on the Court and by getting himself elected to a third term as president of the United States, Franklin Delano Roosevelt achieved the politicization of the Supreme Court which he had wanted but failed to obtain through his "Court-packing bill."

In his first term on the U.S. Supreme Court, Hugo Black set a record for filing dissenting opinions and created such a politically charged atmosphere in the Court's chambers that vacancies on the high Court began occurring at the unprecedented, unnatural rate of one a year because of Black's intense New Deal politicking. Since Franklin Roosevelt remained president for another eight years after he appointed Black, he got to do what no other president except the first has done: appoint an entire Supreme Court. (President Washington had to appoint an entire Supreme Court because none existed when he took office.) Roosevelt nominated and appointed a total of eight Associate Justices and one Chief Justice. Roosevelt's appointments to the Supreme Court were of course all staunch New Dealers. And, as other loyal New Dealers joined Hugo Black on the U.S. Supreme Court, he conceived his bone-jarring plan to assert federal jurisdiction over the exercise of the personal liberties enumerated in Articles I–VIII of the Bill of Rights.

Black based his Incorporation Doctrine on the meaning he assigned to Sections 1 and 5 of the Fourteenth Amendment. With capitalized emphases added, here is the text of Section 1 of the Fourteenth Amendment:

ALL PERSONS BORN OR NATURALIZED IN THE UNITED STATES, and subject to the jurisdiction thereof, are citizens of the United States and of the States wherein they reside. No State shall make or enforce any law which shall abridge the privileges or immunities of citizens of the United

States; nor shall any State deprive ANY PERSON of life, liberty, or property, without due process of law; nor deny to ANY PERSON within its
jurisdiction THE EQUAL PROTECTION OF THE LAWS.

Hugo Lafayette Black alleged that this language, in conjunction with
Section 5 of the Fourteenth Amendment's ("The Congress shall have
power to enforce, by appropriate legislation, the provisions of this article") proved that the Fourteenth Amendment intended to place the
personal liberties of every American under federal jurisdiction.

But the first statement in Section 1 of the Fourteenth Amendment:
"All persons born or naturalized in the United States, and subject to
the jurisdiction thereof, are citizens of the United States and of the
State wherein they reside," could not have been a reference to white
Americans born or naturalized in the United States for the obvious
reason that they were *already* citizens of the United States and of
the States wherein they resided and did not need State and national
citizenship conferred upon them by the Fourteenth Amendment.
The first sentence in the Fourteenth Amendment is a reference to the
Negro slaves emancipated in Amendment XIII and to the freeborn
and naturalized Negro Americans whose citizenship had never been
recognized by the States in which they resided. Hugo Black wanted
white Americans to believe that their "equal protection under the
laws" derives from the Fourteenth Amendment. But it does not. Only
Negro Americans derive equal protection under the law from the
Fourteenth Amendment which extended to freeborn, naturalized,
and emancipated *Negro Americans* the equal protection of the laws,
including the Bill of Rights, which white American *citizens* already
enjoyed. The Fourteenth Amendment extended the rights of U.S.
citizenship to the just-emancipated Negro slaves and to all freeborn
and naturalized Negro Americans whose citizenship rights had never
been recognized by the States where they resided. Sections 1 and 5 of
the Fourteenth Amendment had nothing to do with white Americans.

The second statement in Section 1 of the Fourteenth Amendment:
"No State shall make or enforce any law which shall abridge the

privileges or immunities of citizens of the United States; nor shall any State deprive any person of life, liberty, or property, without due process of law; nor deny to any person within its jurisdiction the equal protection of the laws," notified the States of the United States that the personal liberties enumerated in the Bill of Rights now applied to every Negro American the same as they applied to other Americans. Section 1 of the Fourteenth Amendment in conjunction with Section 5 of the Amendment further notified the States that the federal government was being empowered to enforce the personal liberties of Negro Americans. But only the personal liberties of Negro Americans were being place under federal protection. The Fourteenth did not otherwise enlarge the powers of the federal government. It did not, as Hugo Black alleged, grant the government plenary jurisdiction over the personal liberties of every American. Sections 1 and 5 of the Amendment are *race specific*. They apply only to Negro Americans.

The phrases "All persons" and "any person" were used in writing Section 1 of the Fourteenth Amendment because of the infamous phrase "other Persons" in paragraph three of Section 2, Article I of the Constitution in reference to Negroes which stated that only three-fifths of them, whether freeborn, naturalized, or enslaved, were to be counted in calculating the seats each State would have in the House of Representatives. The emphasis in Section 1 of the Fourteenth Amendment on "all persons" and "any person" (repeated twice) established beyond any doubt and emphasized the full (as opposed to "three-fifths") personhood of Negro Americans.

Hugo Black's interpretation of "All persons" and "any person" was quite different. He contended the words any and all made the federal government the overseer of the civil rights of *every* American, whether white or black. He paid no attention to the fact (already noted) that Section 1 of the Fourteenth Amendment could not have been a reference to white American since at the time the Fourteenth Amendment was framed and ratified they were already citizens of the United States and the State where they resided. Black's interpretation of "all" and "any" was intended not to make sense but only to give federal courts jurisdiction over every American's personal liberties. His Incorporation Doctrine made no sense unless his claims about the meaning of "all" and "any" were accepted.

To demonstrate that politics had a higher priority in Hugo Black's thinking than either judicial sense or constitutional history, one need look no further than the opinion he wrote for the U.S. Supreme Court in *Everson v. Board of Education*, 330 U.S. 1 (1947), the first case regarding religious freedom the Supreme Court illicitly took on appeal, applying Black's Incorporation Doctrine.

The question at issue in *Everson* was whether the State of New Jersey had made a religious establishment by enacting a law authorizing use of State funds to transport school-age children to religious schools. Although the Supreme Court illicitly applied Black's Incorporation Doctrine to justify taking this case on appeal, the Court properly ruled that New Jersey's transportation law was *not* an establishment of religion because religious establishment laws always single out one religion which the law names for preferential government treatment. The New Jersey transportation law did not do that. It treated the children of all religious faiths the same, without showing any preference for one religion over others. (Unless the religion being established is named, it is impossible for an establishment law to show the preference for that religion which it is the purpose of every religious establishment law to do.)

In writing up the decision in *Everson v. Board of Education* for the Court, Black crafted four resounding definitions of a religious establishment and declared:

> The "establishment of religion" clause in the First Amendment means at least this: Neither a state nor the Federal Government can set up a church. Neither can pass laws which aid one religion, aid all religions, or prefer one religion over another.

The first, second, and fourth of these assertions — that neither a State nor the general government can establish a church, pass laws which aid one religion or "prefer one religion over another" — were false because when the Bill of Rights became part of the Constitution of the United States in 1791, half the States then in the Union (Connecticut, Delaware, Maryland, Massachusetts, New Hampshire, New Jersey, and South Carolina) had religious establishment laws enacted by their State legislatures. The establishment clause in the First Amendment could never have been ratified by the required three-fourths of the States if the States then having religious establishment laws, which comprised half the States in the Union, had thought its ratification would cancel the establishment laws then in effect in their States.

The Massachusetts establishment law, for example, required the State government to pay the salaries of the ministers of the Congregational Church (the religion established by law in Massachusetts) from the State treasury and made membership in the Congregational Church a prerequisite for voting and holding public office in Massachusetts. The religious establishment thus created by State law in Massachusetts continued in effect for forty-two years after ratification of the First Amendment to the U.S. Constitution and neither it nor any of the other religious establishments in the States of the United States was rescinded until the State legislature which had enacted them did so. Eventually, all seven State religious establishments in effect when the First Amendment was ratified as part of the Bill of Rights were rescinded by the State legislatures which created them.

Given these historical facts, despite what Hugo Black said in the opinion he wrote for *Everson*, the First Amendment most certainly *did allow a State to establish a religion* — and for that matter still does since the Constitution has never been amended to deny a State that constitutional authority. Hugo Black's contention that no State can pass a law establishing a religion contradicts the history of the Constitution. "Respecting" is the key word in the First Amendment's establishment clause: "Congress shall make no law respecting an establishment of religion." The word meant two things at the same time. It meant the federal government could not pass a law regarding any of the religious establishments in the seven States that had them when the First Amendment was presented for ratified, and it meant that the federal government could not itself establish a religion. Either Hugo Lafayette Black did not know this constitutional history, which in my opinion is unlikely, or he knew the history and deliberately ignored it because he was intent on transferring jurisdiction over religious liberty — along with the other personal liberties guaranteed in the Bill of Rights to the people of the States — from the States to the federal government.

The third of Black's four definitions of religious establishment in his write up of *Everson* — that neither the federal government nor a State can make a law aiding "all religions" — is more than nonsensical. It is astounding (one might even say breathtaking) in the priority it gives his political determination to give the federal government jurisdiction over the Bill of Rights. Remember: the Supreme Court decision in *Everson v. Board of Education*, the case Black was writing up, was that the State of New Jersey had not, in enacting its transportation law, made a religious establishment, precisely because the law aided all religions. Thus, when Hugo Black, who had voted with the majority in that decision, wrote: "Neither a state nor the Federal Government … can pass laws which … aid all religions," he was contradicting his vote and the judgment of the Court he was writing up! All of Black's four resounding definitions of religious establishment in *Everson* were nonsense. But they did not have to make sense to be cited as legal precedents. They became legal precedents simply by being published as part of an official write up of a Supreme Court decision.

Let it here be stated forthrightly: the Fourteenth Amendment does *not* grant the U.S. Supreme Court appellate jurisdiction over religious liberty, nor any of the other personal liberties enumerated in the Bill of Rights, except for appeals in which the plaintiff is a Negro American who claims the State where he lives is violating his rights under the

Bill of Rights. In that case, the Supreme Court would not only have appellate jurisdiction but would be obliged to exercise it, under the terms of Sections 1 and 5 of the Fourteenth Amendment.

It is comforting to know that the U.S. Constitution puts the appellate power of the Supreme Court (its authority to hear appeals) under "such Regulations as the Congress shall make" (Article III, Section 2, Paragraph 2). Congress, therefore, has constitutional authority to annul Hugo Black's nonsensical Incorporation Doctrine, which must be annulled because it represents an illicit amendment to the Constitution. State jurisdiction over the personal liberties enumerated in the Bill of Rights must be restored to the States, bearing always in mind the Supreme Court's obligation under the Fourteenth Amendment to hear appeals from Negro Americans on possible State infringements on their personal liberties granted in the Fourteenth Amendment and the Bill of Rights.

Of all the constitutional separations of power between federal and State government, none is more essential to the cause of liberty than the exclusion of the federal government from exercising plenary jurisdiction over the Bill of Rights. By accepting Hugo Black's Incorporation Doctrine and allowing the federal courts jurisdiction in the exercise of the personal liberties enumerated in the Bill of Rights, we have allowed the federal government to usurp a constitutional power it cannot justly exercise since it is impossible for the federal government to protect the people of the States *from itself.* The only authority in matters of personal liberty that the Fourteenth Amendment granted the federal government was to protect the personal liberties of Negro Americans from infringement by a State, which of course was a quite rational, necessary protection, given the history of the States in denying freeborn and naturalized Negro Americans their rights as freeborn and naturalized Americans.

Ever since Franklin Roosevelt's "New Deal," the separation of State and federal powers required under the Tenth Amendment has been frequently ignored. The federal government today appears to be attempting to make itself ubiquitous and omnipotent in all matters of government. The three branches of government seem to have developed a mutual deference to one another whereby none of them is keeping an eye on the actions of the other two to make sure every branch of the federal government obeys the requirements of the Constitution. Disobedience of the Constitution by any federal officeholder, including associate justices of the Supreme Court like Hugo Black, is an intolerable infringement on the rule of law and the American ideal of justice for all. The problem must be addressed and remedied. As long as it goes unaddressed, the American ideal of equal justice for all is in jeopardy. The remedy lies in passing an amendment to the Constitution giving the States power to impeach and try federal officeholders.

The amendment might read:

**Section 1.** The power to impeach federal officers who may have committed the high crime of violating a requirement of this Constitution is hereby expanded to include the chief justices of the several States, who shall assemble as a body at a place of their choosing to exercise that power; and the State chief justice of greatest age and longest service in that office shall preside over their meeting. The concurrence of two-thirds of the chief justices present shall be required to bring an impeachment.

**Section 2.** The power to try an impeachment brought in this way is hereby granted the governors of the States who shall assemble as a body at a place of their choosing to exercise it; and the governor of greatest age and longest service in the office shall preside over their meeting. The concurrence of two-thirds of the State governors present shall be required for a conviction.

**Section 3.** Judgment in such cases shall not extend further than removal from office and disqualification to hold any office of honor, trust, or profit under the United States; but the party convicted shall nevertheless be liable and subject to indictment, trial, judgment, and punishment according to law.

Granting the people of the States, acting through assemblies of their highest State judicial and executive officers, the power to impeach and try federal officeholders for violating a requirement of the Constitution of the United States would not have to be exercised often to induce among federal officeholders a more faithful obedience to the Constitution than they presently exhibit. Such a constitutional amendment, in conjunction with an amendment limiting the terms of members of Congress to six years, would go a long way to restoring constitutional, representative government in the United State to what it was supposed to be: constitutional and representative.

# Mandatory "Diversity"

THE AMERICAN POPULATION has always been diverse. From the start of European settlement in what is now the United States of America, there were immigrants from many nations and religions. Thomas Paine in his pamphlet "Common Sense," published the year America declared its independence, rightly said, "Europe, and not England, is the parent country of America." Four of the original thirteen American colonies were founded as asylums for Europeans fleeing persecution for their religious beliefs. The first Negro Americans to land in America were a group of twenty *freeborn* blacks from the Caribbean who arrived at Jamestown, Virginia, in 1619 of their own free will as indentured servants seeking opportunities, just twelve years after the first European settlers (John Hope Franklin, *From Slavery to Freedom: A History of Negro Americans*, Fifth Edition, Alfred A. Knopf, 1980, pp. 54–55). The practice of importing slaves from Africa and laws instituting Negro chattel slavery because free laborers did not provide enough laborers for hire did not begin until the 1660s. Perhaps as many as half the white immigrants to America during the colonial era and the early years of the republic were, like the first Negroes to settle in Virginia, too poor to pay their own passage to America and came in the condition of indentured servants, a kind of short-term, contractual slavery whereby a fixed number of years of unpaid labor was agreed to (three to seven years was the usual duration of the contact or "indenture") in exchange for having their passage to America provided.

The cause of the extraordinary diversity of America's colonial population was the English crown's unique immigration policy. The kings of Spain, Portugal, and France allowed only subjects from their European kingdoms who were communicants of their state religion to immigrate to their colonies in the New World. The kings of England, however, allowed persons from any nation and any religion to take up residence in their colonies on the North American mainland, provided they took an oath of fealty to the English crown. The reason for England's unique immigration policy was simple. The English monarchs wanted to attract as many settlers as quickly as possible to their colonies in North American to create transatlantic commerce which the crown could profitably tax. The colonists would export agricultural products, lumber, ship spars, and marine stores to England and import English finished goods, thus making these colonies a source of growing revenue for the English crown.

The colonies of Spain in the New World — the conquered Indian civilizations of Mexico, Central America, Colombia, and Peru — already had a long-civilized population larger than that of the Spanish homeland to work the mines and plantations which made Spain's American possessions highly profitable. Portugal, with its small population, sent from its trading stations on the Atlantic coast of Africa millions of slaves to convert the wilderness of Brazil into lucrative agricultural plantations. French-ruled Canada during its first century and a half as a European colony depended on indigenous Indian trappers to supply the valuable fur trade at Montreal with luxurious winter pelts.

France, the most populous of Europe's four main overseas imperial powers, sent the fewest settlers to the New World because Canada's main value to France was as a military base to block England, her chief European rival, from expanding into the North American interior. The French crown maintained Canada's forts and rotated royal troops from France into them. No large resident French population was needed in Canada, and the French monarchs did not encourage immigration to that immense part of the Americas. The French kings wanted France's manpower to stay in Europe to fight its wars there.

Thus, the English-speaking colonies on the North American continent facing the Atlantic were the only colonies in the New World having a diverse European population of various nationalities and Christian denominations which doubled in size every twenty years after the first viable settlements were established in the early 1600s. There is no reason to mandate diversity in America because diversity has been an inherent part of America's demographic history from the earliest colonial times; and the diversity only became more pronounced as increasing numbers of immigrants began arriving during the post-colonial period of the nineteenth and twentieth centuries from southern and eastern Europe, Mexico, Central and South America, the Caribbean, Asia, and Africa.

The "diversity" that Political Correctness is mandating is part of its agenda to replace America's culture with Cultural Marxism by giving "diversity" an economic value and making "diversity" mandatory in the American workplace. Mandatory "diversity" has become a major basis for Marxian class consciousness and Marxian class struggle in America. Which is why PC Marxists oppose so adamantly any step to reduce illegal immigration into the United States by building a barrier-wall across the southern border of the United States and the enactment of State laws requiring proof of U.S. citizenship to register to vote in U.S. elections. They want hordes of aliens entering the United States illegally and voting in U.S. elections, thus putting and keeping PC Marxists "in power."

Mandatory "diversity" in the workplace and higher education has become since the 1990s a major factor in making an ever-larger portion of the American population dependent on PC Marxists for political protection and privileges. Mandatory "diversity" in the workplace increases the power of PC Marxists and undermines belief in self-determination. The more mandatory "diversity," the more biological class consciousness there'll be, and thus the more demand for "social" justice and Marxist class struggle. Mandatory "diversity" creates loyalty to the political party which engineers it.

Agitprop in agitating and propagandizing for mandatory "diversity" is transforming the American work place. Demands for "diversity" give priority to membership in a "victimized" biological class in filling a job, instead of the applicant's knowledge, experience, character, and skills. Insistence on "diversity" is adding a political consideration to the workplace.

The same thing has happened in higher education. America's oldest private universities and biggest public universities alike have instituted administrative offices with such titles as "Diversity and Inclusion," and "Gender and Campus Culture," and "Pluralism and Leadership" which purport to show a connection between "wellness," academic success, and "diversity." Administrative officers boasting such pretentious titles as "Dean of Diversity" are common on today's college and university campuses. America's college admission officers now regard a student's membership in a "victimized" biological class as having a significance as great as, if not greater than, their academic and extracurricular records. Because of agitprop, "diversity" quotas have become an important feature in the landscape of American higher education. Federal "Affirmative Action" legislation led the way to mandatory "diversity," and agitprop has succeeded in getting mandatory "diversity" quotas enacted by State and federal levels of government. The hiring and the promotion of college and university faculty is subject to the demands of mandatory "diversity" today.

The concept that some sort of superior socio-political merit is inherent in such biological traits as race, gender, ethnicity, homosexuality was introduced into America in the 1960s and 70s as a way to create biological class consciousness and class struggle, intently developed in the 1980s, and took America by storm in the 1990s. Like the PC dogmas "multiculturalism" and "environmentalism," mandatory "diversity" had its origin on the campuses of America's colleges and universities, was elaborated in the publications of American academics and journalists, and is now as sacrosanct as those other two PC Marxist dogmas. On almost all the more than 3,000 college and university campuses across the United States, there are now degree programs in "Women's" Studies, "African American" Studies, "Mexican American" Studies, "Native American" Studies, "Queer" Studies, and so on. These courses teach biology-based class consciousness, the history of biology-based class grievances, and the need for biology-based mandatory "diversity" to compensate for past "victimization."

On the largest campuses in America, and many of the smaller and midsized ones, there are not only "diversity" offices but "diversity" programs and workshops and "diversity" standards for faculty recruitment, retention, and promotion and student admission — all of them based on the dogma that mandatory "diversity" is imperative to compensate for America's atrocious record of injustice to "minorities" in the past. The obsession with "diversity" in American higher education is replicated in American corporations, businesses, and industries as well as in city, county, and State governments. The largest corporations employ salaried "diversity" supervisors, specialists, and consultants. Upwards of 15,000 fulltime corporate "diversity" trainers are now working day in and day out in America explaining the benefits of mandatory "diversity" and how to establish and maintain "diversity" in the corporate world. The Ford Foundation, the MacArthur Foundation, the Rockefeller Foundation, the Mellon Foundation, and other well-funded private organizations have taken up the cause.

A reputation for being "diverse" is something institutions throughout America today are eager to acquire. Being "diverse" has become a political, economic, and academic requirement, a much-coveted accolade, a shibboleth attesting to one's Political Correctness. From the politically correct point of view, mandatory "diversity" is part of the class struggle for "social" justice.

The alleged benefits to society from mandatory "diversity" were enshrined in American law by the highest court in the United States in 1978. That year in *Regents of the University of California v. Bakke*, the U.S. Supreme Court, in an opinion written by Justice Lewis Powell, designated diversity "a compelling interest" of the federal government; thereby giving it inestimable economic value as well as the highest legal approbation. Thinking in terms of "diversity" now permeates the U.S. government. No bill proposed in the House of Representatives or the Senate of the United States which opposed or weakened a requirement for mandatory "diversity" would stand a chance of getting out of committee for a vote on the floor of the House or the Senate. It is doubtful any congressman would even think of writing such a bill.

Part of the concept of mandatory "diversity" according to such PC Marxist authorities as Senator Elizabeth Warren (D-MA) and former president Barack Obama is that wealth is not created by the ingenuity, initiative, and hard work of individuals. No. Wealth is created by "society." And classes which have been "victimized" deserve to have some of society's wealth distributed to them through "diversity quotas" because they have participated as members of society in the creation of the wealth without receiving a fair share of it.

PC Marxists say an assured job, a "livable" income, "affordable" housing, government-provided healthcare and subsidized pharmaceuticals, free college tuition, etc. etc. are "rights" — never mind that no "rights" of this sort are hinted at in the Constitution of the United States. The Constitution of the USSR when the Soviet Union existed guaranteed a whole panoply of such "rights," provided that Soviet citizens obeyed Article 59 in the Soviet Constitution, which required them to uphold "the honor of Soviet citizenship," an obligation so broad and abstract it might mean whatever Soviet authorities wanted it to mean so they could withhold benefits from unenthusiastic Marxists in the Soviet Union.

To an increasing segment of the American population, mandatory "diversity" has become more valuable than freedom, equality, or opportunity. In the agitprop Political Correctness spews forth in America every day to advance the cause of Cultural Marxism, mandatory "diversity" plays a key role. It is a new kind of morality, an almost mystic boon. Regulations mandating "diversity" and conferring "entitlements" are justified by saying they compensate for centuries of "sexism," "institutionalized racism," and "victimization." According to PC Marxists, "social" justice for the weak, the "vulnerable," the "victimized," the "underprivileged" can only be attained through mandatory "diversity" and class struggle.

Mandatory "diversity" takes Affirmative Action to a higher level. It makes proportional representation of "victimized" biological classes mandatory throughout America's economy. Proponents of mandatory "diversity" claim that it benefits every American, but its benefits cannot be realized until it prevails everywhere, a claim not unlike the Marxist promise that the state will "wither away" once Cultural Marxism has been implemented worldwide. Mandatory "diversity" requires people of different ethnic, sexual, and racial identities to work and study together to foster "intercultural" or "multicultural" understanding and "healing." The revolutionary idea here is that each "victimized" biological class has its own culture and needs to be in organized contact with the cultures of other "victimized" classes to create a revolutionary force moving toward Cultural Marxism.

PC Marxists would have Americans believe their nation has never had a culture which gave them a sense of having a common American identity, regardless of gender, race, ethnicity, or "sexual orientation." If we believe the politically correct "line" about America as a land of oppression, the United States has never had a culture which Americans of all conditions and backgrounds shared. PC Marxists contend that the motto *E Pluribus Unum* (Out of Many, One) which, according to the Pledge of Allegiance, has made the fifty States of America "one nation under God," is a fraud. The only thing Americans have in common, according to PC Marxists, is multiculturalism. There isn't any such thing as a unifying culture in America, never has been, and won't be until Cultural Marxism has been fully constructed. Mandatory "diversity" by celebrating and praising the "mosaic," the "rainbow," the "salad bowl" of multiculturalism is moving America in the direction of true, Marxian unity. Education in America today from kindergartens to professional schools is indoctrinating students in the underlying beauty and potential unity of multiculturalism.

In contrast to Political Correctness and its thinking, the Civil Rights Movement of the 1950s and 60s led by the Rev. Martin Luther King, Jr. aimed to integrate Negro Americans into America's culture, without of course obliterating the identity each race, gender, and ethnicity naturally has. (This was before PC agitprop invented the term African American and substituted it for the term Negro American.) The desire for integration is an aspiration of Negro Americans as old as the Fourteenth Amendment (1868) and Booker T. Washington's autobiography *Up From Slavery* (1901). King's most memorable expression of his convictions on the matter of integration was his speech "I Have a Dream," delivered at the Lincoln Memorial in Washington, D.C. in 1963 which declared his faith that all persons in America would one day be judged by the "content of their character" not the color of their skin. King's most poignant statement in that speech was perhaps this passage:

> But there is something that I must say to my people who stand on the warm threshold which leads into the palace of justice. In the process of gaining our rightful place we must not be guilty of wrongful deeds. Let us not seek to satisfy our thirst for freedom by drinking from the cup of bitterness and hatred.

To be sure, the organized, massive, peaceful solidarity which the Negro American Civil Rights Movement brought to bear on federal and State governments in the 1950s and 60s to enforce "the equal protection of the laws" promised Negro Americans in the Fourteenth Amendment in 1868 was, without a doubt, a class struggle. But it was an American class struggle that had as its ultimate goal individual freedom for Negro Americans as *self-determining Americans*. The prize Martin Luther King, Jr. sought for Negro Americans was not perpetual dependence on Big Government, either as individuals or as a class. Equal freedom, equal opportunity, and self-determination were what Martin Luther King sought, as an American, in the Civil Rights Movement he led. His published speeches and essays are full of eloquent expressions of that American aspiration of integration, the Out-of-Many-One idea. It was the same aspiration which motivated immigrants who came to America to want to be "Americans" instead of perpetuating the cultural identity of the country of their origin. That aspiration, not the desire to receive government handouts, has been at the center of American immigration history. Government-assured uniformity of outcomes and dependence on Big Government are, however, the acme of Marxist aspirations.

PC Marxists in America preach that equal opportunity is dead-end freedom. They promote government guarantees of economic equality as true liberty and equality. Likewise, the Constitution of the Union of Soviet Socialist Republics regarded total control by a single political party as "true democracy" because it promised "social" justice. However, the comrade leaders of the Communist Party of the Soviet Union apparently enjoyed what might be thought of as "more freedom" and "extra equality." Everybody was free and equal in Marxist theory, but in practice the comrade leaders, "the vanguard" of the revolution to attain communism, were indubitably more equal and free. They had to be, it seemed, because of their singular responsibility to assure the attainment of communism, whose coming would systematically wipe away, forever, all the accumulated sins of human history.

The difference between self-determination and the promises of Marxism is the difference between having one's life regulated by what a government considers "fair" for each person to have and the freedom to make one's own decisions about what one wants out of life and the right to struggle personally to attain it. The contrast is that between mediocrity with minimum security on the one hand and the risk of failure with the possibility of great personal accomplishments on the other. In launching his "War on Poverty" in 1965, President Lyndon Johnson chose the former. He proclaimed the Marxist ideal: "We seek not just equality as a right and a theory but equality as a fact and equality as a result." That's dependence on Big Government. That's Soviet-style socialism and PC Marxism.

Membership in a "victimized" biological class and participation in class struggle based on biological class consciousness now represents to many Americans the correct way forward. PC Marxists slander Booker T. Washington as "an Uncle Tom" because he devoted his talents and energies and dreams to the development of the Tuskegee Institute in Tuskegee, Alabama, to teach Negro Americans marketable skills that would make them self-supporting Americans. PC Marxists scorn his achievements because he did not spend his talent and energy hating his "class enemies" and organizing the Marxist class struggle in Alabama, as he ought to have done, according to Marxist theory. See Booker T. Washington's *Up From Slavery*, one of the most powerful and moving American autobiographies of self-determination ever written.

Mandatory "diversity" is racism packaged as liberation from racism. But it is neither diverse nor liberating because what PC Marxists call "diversity" is the promotion of conformity to PC dogmas and the perpetual subservience (enslavement) of individuals to class consciousness. As a Christian minister, the Rev. Martin Luther King, Jr. preached compassion and forgiveness. He also preached equality based on the Christian belief that every person has equal worth in God's eyes and the same birthright from God. As an American, King believed every American had the God-given birthright to liberty and the pursuit of happiness, and had the same responsibility to strive to improve their God-given lives. One has only to read such public addresses and essays of his as "I Have a Dream" and "Letter From a Birmingham Jail" to see how much his American outlook and

Christian convictions differ from the mentality of PC Marxists today with their "correct" dogmas. The achievement of self-determination for Negro Americans was his goal. He believed in people respecting themselves and other human beings as creations of God. Marxist hatred for "class enemies" played no part in Martin Luther King Jr.'s thoughts and feelings. He appealed to white Americans and Negro Americans alike as fellow Christians and fellow Americans.

The mandatory "diversity" which agitprop advocates is not diversity at all. It is the slow lockstep shuffle of the politically correct chain gang as it moves in unison toward socialism.

# A Standard of Double Standards

HYPOCRISY IS AN inherent characteristic of Political Correctness. PC Marxists have one standard for their own conduct and another for that of their enemies. The "enemy" is never right, even if he does what PC Marxists do, because he is not politically correct. How, therefore, can he ever be right in what he does or thinks? Having two standards is part of the revolution. The revolution's success will justify everything that must be done on the way to victory. The hypocrisy of a PC Marxist is never hypocritical to him because his goal is true and just, according to his "scientific" pretensions.

A Marxist revolution to get started must have some degree of tolerance from adherents of the existing culture. Then as the revolutionary movement gains adherents and momentum, the need for tolerance shifts to the practitioners of the formerly dominate culture which the revolution is displacing. The former dispensers of tolerance — the practitioners of the culture which once prevailed — must then ask for tolerance from the former recipients of their tolerance: the revolutionaries who have begun to gain dominance. But those who received tolerance when they were initiating their revolution cannot tolerate their "enemies." Tolerance to them is never a two-way street. A politically correct Marxist cannot tolerant his opponents because his allegiance is completely absorbed by his goal of destroying the existing culture and rebuilding it as Cultural Marxism.

For revolutionaries, the revolution is what gives their lives direction and meaning. They live for no other purpose than the revolution. To destroy and rebuild the existing culture according to their ideological specifications is their reason for being. Because of the totality of their revolutionary commitment to "transform" America's culture, they cannot reciprocate the tolerance of those who embody the existing culture's belief-behaviors, even though they tolerated the revolutionaries at the outset of the Marxist revolution. The hatred revolutionaries feel for the existing culture is absolute. Their identity is defined by that hatred. Whether they're correct to feel that way is beside the point. A revolution is not a matter of rational purpose. It is a matter of feeling, of passion. To tolerate anyone identified with the existing culture would be a betrayal of the revolution. A revolutionary cannot be tolerant of his enemies and still "transform" the existing culture. He must be an ardent, uncompromising dogmatist whose political cause is his purpose in living, just as Lenin was when he stepped off the train at the Finland Station in St. Petersburg in 1917. The revolution fills the void left in the lives of Marxists by their rejection of belief in God. A true believer in Marxism rejects everything his opponents believe, everything related to the culture he wants to replace. His opponents are, he thinks, blocking the way forward to the utopian future for mankind which he ardently imagines his revolution will inaugurate.

PC Marxists think of themselves as the party of the future, and their opponents as the party of the past. But in truth they are obsessed with the past, with rectifying the wrongs of the past. They are the party of the past, the party of envy and covetousness which wants to strip their enemies of everything they wrongfully possess through outright confiscation or destruction of their property, or through confiscatory taxation. An obsession with the past consumes the thoughts and energies of Marxists. All their talk of a perfect society sometime in the future is to justify the revenge they want to take in the present on their "enemies" for things which transpired in the past. Forgiveness for wrongdoing in the past in the interest of reconciliation never enters into a revolutionary's mind or feelings. However, it is not their enemies who are causing their failure but the inherent faults of their ideology, their obsession with *Marxist theory.*

Absolute and total trust in and obedience to the dogmas of their leaders have been characteristic of revolutionaries since the one that started in France in 1789, the year George Washington was sworn in as president of the United States under the authority of the U.S. Constitution. Revolutionaries regard their leaders as infallible and as serving only "the good of the people." They see opponents of the revolution as self-serving enemies of mankind. The revolutionary's sense of his mission's righteousness is absolute, and in his mind what advances the mission has to result in his becoming more powerful. Their identification with benefit to "the masses" makes Marxist revolutionaries exceptionally ruthless.

To a politically correct revolutionary — and every revolutionary is certain he's 100% correct — the revolution's righteousness is its attractiveness. He thinks his opponents are stupid because they reject the "scientific" dogmas of Marxism. To a Marxist, the distinctions between progressive and regressive ideas, between piecemeal and "structural" (i.e. environmental) solutions to human misery are obvious. Any slightest tolerance of the cultural behavior of his enemy (that is to say tolerance of opposition to Marxism) or compromise of any kind with those who oppose Marxism would, in the thinking of a Marxist, be a betrayal of the revolution. Political opponents must be seen as morally inferior ignoramuses, and condemned.

Marxist leaders consider themselves more knowledgeable than anyone else about everything connected with social, economic, and political progress and the needs of human beings, and they are revered by their followers as absolutely worthy of obedience. Marxism offers, Marxists think, the only serious solutions to the world's social, economic, and political problems because all of mankind's problems are material in nature because man is only another species of animal, PC Marxists believe.

Maximilien Robespierre (1758–1794), one of the bloodiest-minded leaders of the French Revolution, believed in giving revolutionary government unlimited power. He distinguished between the terror of the revolution and the terror of the ruling class he and his fellow revolutionaries wanted to supplant. The difference for Robespierre was the *intention* of revolutionaries to make a qualitative change in culture for "the good of the people" while the intention of the enemies of the revolution, was to maintain "the status quo" of continuing to oppress the people. In accordance with such distinctions, revolutionaries regard their enemies as subhuman and called them names. Stalin, for instance, called non-Marxists parasites. In Cuba, whoever rejected the revolution by wanting to leave revolutionary Cuba were called *gusanos* (worms), one of the lowest form of visible animal life. And when Marxist agitprop came to the United States in the 1960s, capitalists and everyone who tolerated or supported capitalism (for instance the police who protected private property) were called "pigs." Revolutionaries do not grant their enemies human status. Because they regard their opponents as subhuman impediments to the revolution, they deserve only ridicule, abuse, suppression, and eventual elimination. Character assassination is a standard tactic for eliminating a political enemy. Bankruptcy from having to hire lawyers to defend themselves from false accusations is another. The use of existing laws to eliminate political enemies is a sure sign of being in the presence of Marxist revolutionary activity.

The violence practiced by liberators, Robespierre argued, differs from the violence practiced by oppressors. Both inflict pain, to be sure. But the end served by the revolutionary's violence is justified while that of the enemies of humanity is not. This distinction is the usual one of revolutionaries, that their end justifies their means. Experience shows the flaw in the argument. Violence and coercion, once initiated to eliminate "enemies" and create the new culture, become a procrustean way of life. The revolution's demands become ever more extreme, demanding, and destructive. Cultural warfare, which is always initiated without consent of the majority, "the people" in whose name the revolution is made, in the end becomes a debacle of incompetence. Once the revolution has attained absolute power in the name of benefiting the downtrodden, it finds the second part of its formula Destroy and Rebuild troublesome because rebuilding requires practical solutions to problems, whereas Marxists have only theoretic solutions. The revolution gets over this difficult not by actually addressing and solving problems but by controlling communications and producing "images" of success and excuses for nonperformance, including the accusation of others for their failure.

Robespierre and the other leaders of the French Revolution wanted, they said, a humane, rationally organized, atheistic culture led by "enlightened" revolutionaries with knowledge grounded in science. They claimed to be liberating mankind from the "superstition" of Christianity and wanted to establish a cult of "reason" in France. Instead, they instituted a regime of terror and coercion. The French revolutionaries believed in their absolute right to destroy every vestige of the church, the monarchy, and the nobility of France, because they alone stood for liberty, fraternity, and equality. They were totally justified, they thought, in their desire to root out and replace the ancient regime of France; and since their motives were beyond reproach, whatever violence they deemed necessary to attain their goals was justified, regardless of the suffering it entailed.

Revolutionaries who theoretically serve "the people" never in fact consult those they supposedly serve. "Government by consent of the governed," one of the primary beliefs the Declaration of Independence proclaimed, never touched the hearts of the French revolutionaries. Nor has it played any role in the communist revolutions of the twentieth century. Revolutions are movements in which a small group of dictators decide what is good for everyone and then impose their supposedly beneficial ideas.

John Adams, Benjamin Franklin, Nathaniel Greene, Thomas Jefferson, Alexander Hamilton, Daniel Morgan, George Washington, and hundreds of thousands of other Americans who waged America's war for independence from Europe were not the same sort of men as those who directed the Terror of the French Revolution. For one thing, they did not aim to destroy a culture and replace it with a new culture based on a rationalized plan. They already had a new, non-European culture: the way of life their ancestors in America had created between 1610 and 1770. What they wanted was to break away from the restraints of their "Allegiance to the British Crown" and all interference from London. They were already living in accord with a set of cultural beliefs and behavior different from England's way of life, a set of belief-behaviors committed to the proposition that God has made all men equal in their natural rights. Jefferson said that the American idea of equality which he expressed in the Declaration of Independence came down to this: No man is born with a saddle on his back and another man born booted and spurred to ride him (*Thomas Jefferson Writings*, ed. Merrill D. Peterson, Library of America, 1984, p. 1517). In English culture, as elsewhere in Europe, some men *were* born booted and spurred to ride on the backs of other men who were born metaphorically saddled by their cultural belief in their inferior birth.

The Counter Culture Movement which American Marxists and their sympathizers launched in the United States in the 1960s pretended to represent true Americanism by portraying America's existing culture as conformist, elitist, and materialistic which is ironic because these are all traits of Marxist regimes. Using this "line," agit-prop has pounded into the minds of Americans since the 1960s the idea that they must reject their country's culture in favor of Political Correctness, which, they say, represents true Americanism. The 1960s marked the beginning of the culture war which is still being waged in America with as much anti-American fervor as it was in the 1960s, but on a broader front.

The Marxists on American college campuses in the 1960s and 1970s loudly proclaimed their right to freedom of speech and tolerance. As usual, they appealed to these American values — free speech and tolerance — to get their movement started. The tolerance the revolutionaries asked for and received in the 1960s and 70s made the war on American belief-behaviors possible. Tolerance of the enemy within — the PC Marxists in the public schools, universities, the media, the government, the political parties, the entertainment industry, the churches, and the other opinion-shaping institutions of America — has allowed the recruitment of Americans of goodwill to participate in the sustained attack on America's culture that is about to enter its sixth decade. The election of Donald Trump to the presidency of the United States in 2016, however, suggests that the tolerance of the American middle class for the dogmatism, coercion, and anti-Americanism of Political Correctness is coming to an end.

Politically correct American Marxists in the 1970s spoke like true-blue American patriots interested only in liberty and equality — not in the destruction and rebuilding of American culture. A generation after PC Marxists took over the Democrat Party and got a second-generation member of the Counter Culture Movement and trained deceiver (Barack Obama, born 1961) elected president of the United States, politically correct newspapermen in America switched the traditional color for Democrat States (red) to blue and the color for Republican States (blue) to red on the Electoral College map of the United States. In reporting Obama's election, States that voted for him were portrayed in the media as *blue;* those that voted for the Republican candidate were portrayed in *red.* This reversal of colors signified that with the election of Obama PC Marxists had become the cultural majority in America. That switch in the traditional electoral map colors was propaganda announcing a revolutionary change in America. The former "reds" were now the "blues," which is to say with Obama in the White House PC Marxists had gained control of the U.S. government. The party of Political Correctness was no longer the radicals or "reds" but the "true blue" Americans. Donald Trump's election has shown that that conclusion was wrong.

When he needed to, Obama talked like a true-blue American. But during his eight years in the White House, he acted like the PC revolutionary he truly was and has always been as a teenage disciple of Frank Davis, a member of the Communist Party USA; an instructor in Alinsky's school for "community organizing," a euphemism for training Marxist agitators in America; and a parishioner in Jeremiah Wright's Liberation Theology church in Chicago. Electing a PC Marxist to the most powerful office of government in the United States ushered in eight years of bigger and bigger government, more and more "entitlement" programs, and skyrocketing national debt. So enormous was the increase in the national debt as the government borrowed ever-larger amounts of money to finance "social" justice, that the credit rating of the United States of America on the international money market was downgraded from AAA+ to just AAA.

Month after month in the first two years of his administration, Obama said one thing while doing another. He asked Congress, both houses of which were controlled by his PC political party, for an appropriation of close to one trillion dollars to fund, he said, "shovel-ready jobs" to stimulate the economy and upgrade and repair America's aging infrastructure; and Congress gave him the $900 billion dollars he asked for. However, the promised improvements to highways, bridges, and airports and the jobs he said he would create never materialized. Nonetheless, the 900-billion-dollar appropriation disappeared. It went somewhere. Where did it go?

Also, when Obama bailed out the auto industry which he said had to be done for the good of the U.S. economy, he gave the autoworkers unions first crack at the bankruptcy settlement funds instead of the creditors *as federal law required*. This violation of federal law was likewise given a pass by Republicans as well as Democrats. There was no talk on Capitol Hill of Obama's impeachment for violating Article II, Section 3, Clause 5 of the Constitution which says, "[The President] shall take Care that the Laws be faithfully executed." Republicans were terrified of standing up to Obama's violation of his presidential oath of office and his use of the U.S. Treasury for political and personal purposes. America's "historic African-American president" violated his oath of office with impunity to benefit himself, his cronies, and his cause.

Obama moved health care in the U.S. in the direction of socialism by systematic deceit. He said of his proposed socialist healthcare plan, "If you like the medical plan you have, you can keep it." He said: "If you like your doctor, you can keep your doctor." He said his 2010 Patient Protection and Affordable Care Act ("Obamacare") would save American families thousands of dollars annually. These were all lies, as he well knew. "Obamacare" neither allowed patients to keep the health insurance they had and liked nor the doctors they had and liked; and it did not save American families money. Under Obama's direction, his plan for expanded healthcare coverage in the United States was passed in a great rush because, as he and his associates insisted, the need for it was so extremely urgent. But once passed by the Democrat Congress and signed by Obama, "Obamacare" became, all of a sudden, non-urgent. *The requirements of the Patient Protection and Affordable Care Act were not implemented for two years after it became a federal law.* Why rush a piece of complex legislation affecting one-sixth of the American economy through Congress in a matter of days, claiming its immediate enactment was desperately needed; then delay its implementation for two years? Obama needed to hide the results the legislation would have until after his re-election.

Obama's healthcare bill was a giant stride forward on the road to socialism. It gave Americans what Obama wanted them to have, a socialist healthcare system, and what he said the country needed, even though under the Patient Protection and Affordable Care Act, premiums and deductibles both went up, and Americans had less choice in their health care. The title of this legislation was 100% fraudulent. Yet it was the act of his administration that Barack Obama and his PC Marxist allies were most proud of. It was the most socialist single act of his presidency.

The falsely designated Patient Protection and Affordable Care Act was presented to the American public as a *reform* of the existing healthcare system. But it wasn't. It was a socialist healthcare system. It was an act only Democrat members in Congress voted for, a 2,700-page behemoth that none of the Democrats who voted for it — and only Democrats did vote for it — knew what they were voting for because neither they nor their staffs had time to read the bill they voted for. They voted for it because their leader told them to vote for it. Not even the Speaker of the House, the loyal PC Marxist Nancy Pelosi, seems to have known much about its contents. She knew only that Obama wanted the bill passed. With a bemused smile and tone of voice, Pelosi in telling the members of her party in Congress to vote for the Patient Protection and Affordable Care Act made the astounding observation that *after its passage* there would be time enough to study the bill's provisions and learn how wonderful they were. That's how corrupt the Congress of the United States has become.

There wasn't enough time in the few days the Democrat Party leaders allowed before the vote was taken in Congress on "Obamacare" to read a bill thousands of pages long. What sort of congressmen vote for something they haven't read? To do so makes a mockery of representative government. Yet that's what the Democrats in Congress did in enacting "Obamacare." Obedience to the Party "line" in such ways as this was standard procedure for the Communist Party of the Soviet Union before the collapse of the USSR.

The same kind of fear of punishment for disobeying the will of the Party typified the Marxist revolution in Cuba. Only at the outset of the Marxist takeover of Cuba, the punishment for disobeying the Party "line" was likely to be death. Thousands of Cubans who opposed implementation of Marxism in Cuba after January 1959 were executed. The execution and imprisonment of not just non-Marxists but communists who objected to terror as a mode of government continued through the 1960s and 70s in Cuba as the revolution there made its power absolute and impoverished an entire society in the process. Today everyone in Cuba is poor except the leaders of the

Communist Party of Cuba and those whose loyalty the Party needs to stay "in power." The leaders of the Party and their top supporters are wealthy because they own the whole island of Cuba in the name of "the Revolution," which theoretically was for the benefit of the Cuban people. Under communist dictatorship, poverty has engulfed Cuba. The Cuban revolution, which every useful idiot in the world praises as marvelous, has made a nation which before the Marxist revolution had the best economy in Latin America (the eighteen Spanish-speaking nations of the Western Hemisphere plus Brazil) into the poorest nation in the Western Hemisphere, poorer even than Haiti.

The only Cubans better off today than they were before the revolution are the leaders of the Communist Party of Cuba. They are so wealthy they have secret bank accounts in Switzerland. (A cousin of my wife whose father died in the revolution and was declared by Fidel Castro "A Hero of the Revolution" was given a secretarial job in a government office building for important Party officials, and was asked to take a deposit of money to Switzerland by Raul Castro, the dictator's brother.) Cubans today on average, even medical doctors, make a dollar a day, eighty cents less than the $1.80 a day economists estimate is the average income in the world's poorest nations. But that doesn't matter. What matters is that Cuba is now a communist regime which Marxist propaganda says has greatly improved the lives of Cubans.

Food has been strictly rationed in Cuba for the Cuban people since 1962. Leaders of the Communist Party of Cuba and their top supporters, however, have all the food they want and servants to prepare and serve it to them in the splendid, expropriated mansions of pre-Revolution wealthy Cubans which they now inhabit. Healthcare in Cuba for ordinary Cubans is execrable, despite what the propaganda films of the American PC Marxist Michael Moore say about the superiority of Cuba's socialist healthcare. Even common medicines like aspirin are in short supply; syringes are reused without sterilization; hospital patients must provide their own bed linen, towels, and food. The country's leaders, however, have up-to-date, well-equipped, well-staffed, well-supplied clinics for their exclusive use just like Party leaders in the Soviet Union had before the collapse of the USSR. The statistics on infant mortality in Cuba, which according to Michael Moore's propaganda films is better than the infant mortality rate in the United States, does not include data on infant mortality. The communist rulers of Cuba forbid the deaths of Cuban kids below the age of two to be recorded and reported in statistics on Cuba's infant mortality. The leaders of the Communist Party of Cuba and their chief supporters also have access to special stores where they can get all the good-quality consumer goods they want.

Cuba's pre-revolution economy has been destroyed through Marxist incompetence in substituting Marxist theory for practical behavior. The mainstay of Cuba's economy, its centuries-old sugar industry, which made Cuba the world's leading exporter of sugar, has been ruined by sending city dwellers into the countryside to harvest sugar cane to teach them political lessons. Sugar cane is a perennial plant which will grow back year after year if properly cut. Whole fields of this valuable plant were killed by inexperienced harvesters. Today, the nation which before the Marxist revolution in Cuba was the world's largest exporter of sugar does not under communist government always produce enough sugar to supply its own domestic needs. The Cuban cattle industry has likewise been devastated through the application of Marxist dogma about collective ownership of agricultural production.

Cuba is an island larger than England whose climate and extraordinarily rich soil are ideal for agricultural production. Why would food have to be rationed there for three generations? Marxism is the cause of the agricultural de-development of Cuba. Cuban Marxists seem to have found food rationing to be an effective means of controlling the Cuban population. Cubans who dare to complain about the lack of food, the scarcity of consumer goods, the slave wages of a dollar a day, the erratic supply of electricity and crumbling buildings, or who refuse to embrace the regime's explanation that "the U.S. embargo" is responsible for the unprecedented economic problems in Cuba, are subject to imprisonment, "re-education" in government camps, or worse. Three generations after Marxists took over Cuba, there are still thousands of political prisoners on the island. But the Marxist regime says there aren't any, not a single one, and technically there aren't. There are no political prisoners in Cuba because political malcontents are tried and found guilty of bogus charges of having committed theft, fraud, graft, rape, and so on before being sent to prison. There are no political prisoners in Cuba because political dissidents are imprisoned as common criminals for crimes they didn't commit. They are not imprisoned for being political dissidents.

Why are lies, fear, and hypocrisy common attributes of life under Marxist rule? Because Marxist government depends on deceit and terror to gain and to retain power.

For PC Marxists to have obtained the level of influence they currently enjoy in the United States, hypocrisy has been essential. For instance, Obama's red-white-and-blue, Star-Spangled-Banner keynote address praising American culture and the need for American unity at the 2004 Democratic National Convention. His behavior as president demonstrated that he actually harbored a good deal of hostility toward America's culture. This kind of PC hypocrisy is entirely different from American politicians making promises to get elected without intending to keep their promises. Marxism is different because it is an unmitigated, systematic sham, a pretense from start to finish.

The same pretense which characterized the speech Obama made in 2004 at the Democrat Convention and the promises he made in regard to his healthcare plan in 2010 likewise characterized Hillary Clinton's presidential campaign in 2016 as the PC Marxist-Democrat candidate to succeed Barack Obama. Throughout her political career, a defining pledge of hers has been to "fight" for "equal rights" and "equal pay" for women, not only in the United States but around the world. Indeed, her accusation that the Republican Party is waging a "War on Women" was her bread-and-butter issue not only as the 2016 candidate for president of her party but as First Lady of the United

States, U.S. Senator from New York, and U.S. Secretary of State. Women were the subject of her first public talk after losing her campaign for the presidency. Reported in the *New York Times* for April 7, 2017, Mrs. Clinton spoke to a New York City audience of women and denounced the Republican who had defeated her five months earlier by saying he was waging a "War on Women." Yet tens of millions of American women voted for Donald Trump. Why did they vote for him instead of her? Did they know that as Secretary of State Hillary Clinton did not see to it that the women employees in the Department of State received equal pay with men; that she was a hypocrite about equal pay for women?

Hypocritical behavior, however, is no problem for Mrs. Clinton because as a PC Marxist she must never be judged by the same standard as other people. She must be judged by the standard of Political Correctness which means she can never do wrong. However deceitful PC Marxists actually are, theoretically they always have the interests of the "have nots" at heart. Just trust them, and everything will turn out OK. Ignore Mrs. Clinton's use of her government position for personal gain (her sale of U.S. supplies of uranium to Vladimir Putin, for instance) and her decades-long history of crookedness, that ominous cloud of suspicions of wrongdoing that has been so evident a part of her life. Just embrace wholeheartedly her Political Correctness. If you do that, you'll feel as righteous as she does.

We have Mrs. Clinton's word for it that the women who voted for Donald Trump in November 2016 were being dictated to by the men in their lives. They weren't thinking for themselves. Had they been thinking for themselves, as women, members of an aggrieved allegedly "minority" class, every woman in America would have voted for Hillary Clinton, and she would have been elected president of the United States, not Donald J. Trump. That's what she said five months after being judged unfit by the people of the States to occupy the White House.

# "Sensitivity" Above All

A S I'VE SAID, middle-class American mothers are prone to teach their children to be polite and considerate of other people's feelings. PC Marxists having noticed this tendency have used it. By claiming to be experts on what is "sensitive" speech and what is "offensive" speech, PC Marxists have manipulated Americans into adopting, or at least tolerating, politically correct language, and thereby controlling their perceptions. By changing the language Americans use, PC Marxists have changed their perceptions and behavior, and thus American culture itself, which, like every culture, is transmitted from generation to generation through behaviors which express the culture's beliefs. Unless each generation of a society as it comes of age imitates the behaviors of their elders which express the beliefs of that society's culture, the culture of that society will decline and, should the refusal to imitate persist and worsen, eventually perish.

The present insistence, for instance, of using "African American" in place of the allegedly insensitive term "Negro American," and the change in perception which the new usage conveys, has been accomplished entirely by appealing to the American middle-class desire to be considerate of other people's feelings. First, Negro Americans were convinced through agitprop that they should take pride in their African heritage by calling themselves "African Americans" instead of Negro Americans. Once that had been accomplished, PC propaganda then in short order convinced white Americans that the term "Negro American" was offensive to "African Americans," and they shouldn't use the traditional form of polite reference to Americans with dark skin. Consequently, use of the term "Negro American" has been largely discontinued in America. With that change in diction, the term "African American" and the perception it conveys has been established. And what is that perception? That Americans with some tinge of blackness to their skin are Africans forced to live in America because ancestors of theirs were brought here against their will as slaves. In other words, use of the term "African American," instead of "Negro American," is a constant reminder of the chattel slavery that was part of America's history from the 1660s to the 1860s. This elementary change in diction from "Negro American" to "African American" has created a sense of general alienation among Negro Americans, a class consciousness conducive to Marxist class struggle. The term Negro American merely identified Americans having some Negro ancestry. "Negro American" did not challenge their identity as Americans as "African American" does.

Another example of an appeal to "sensitivity" concerns the use of a large category of words in English containing the suffix "man" in reference to women. Agitprop has convinced Americans it's insulting to women to use such words in reference to the childbearing gender, though one of the oldest meanings of the word "man" in English makes it perfectly clear why referring to women using words containing the suffix "man" is appropriate. The word "woman," for instance, contains it. That meaning is "A human being, regardless of sex or age" (*American Heritage Dictionary*, second edition, 1985), and is found in written English going back more than a thousand years. Nonetheless PC Marxists claim that words containing the suffix "man" when used in reference to women, are affronts to women. And so they are, after half a century of agitprop making that claim. This censorship which agitprop has imposed includes such words as chair*man* (a human being in charge of a group), congress*man* (a human being elected to

Congress), and flag*man* (a human being using a flag or other signaling device to control traffic at a highway construction site). Similarly, to be "sensitive," one must never call a first-year female high school or college student a fresh*man*. One must call a first-year female high school or college student a "freshperson"; a female highway traffic controller, a "flagperson"; a female member of Congress and a female in charge of a group, "congresswoman" and "chairwoman" (even though both of the latter terms contain the allegedly offensive suffix "man").

"Man" does, of course, mean an adult male. But it also has that other, generic meaning which, as *Webster's Third New International Dictionary, Unabridged* (1970) points out, can be found in the earliest surviving texts of English as far back as the 7th century. *Webster's* defines that meaning as, "a member of the human race, a human being," as in "all men, both male and female" (David Hume, 1776). The Declaration of Independence could likewise be cited as an example of this generic meaning of the word because it says "all men are created equal," in having been given by God life and free will, or liberty. To think that statement in the Declaration of Independence applies only to men, and not women, one would have to assume the Founding Fathers were idiots who did not regard women as human beings. If the word "man" could only mean adult male, then PC "sensitivity" should ban the word "woman" in reference to women as insensitive and insulting since it contains the suffix "man," which is supposedly an affront to women.

Such agitprop language theory has just one purpose: to make American women feel they're being "victimized" by a male conspiracy to demean them. Agitprop uses the phrase "war on women" to refer to this alleged male conspiracy against women which agitprop urges women to combat. (The attitude which allegedly motivates men to make "war" on women is called in PC newspeak: "male chauvinism.") Such folderol if taken seriously creates divisions between men and women. But it also creates divisions *among women* because it pits women who buy into the PC sensitivity theory against women who know that one of the meanings of the word man is "a human being, regardless of sex or age." Women who feel that the meanings assigned to words should derive from the way an entire community uses them over time, and should not be arbitrarily given political meanings, are likely to feel some antagonism toward women who think deliberate changes to language for political purposes are OK.

And what about that word "female"? Shouldn't politically correct language theory insist that it be banned in reference to the childbearing gender on the grounds that its use is "insensitive"? How can the use of the word female in reference to the child-bearing gender of the human race be "sensitive" when its second syllable has only one, unequivocally masculine meaning? But I suppose that from the PC point of view, being that I am a male, I have no right to analyze such matters, even though I write books and the English language belongs to me as much as it does to the PC language police. The PC language police have, of course, acquired their authority simply by asserting it. I have as much right as they do to assert such authority.

In truth, of course, male speakers of English cannot legitimately be accused of starting over a thousand years ago to create meanings of English words to demean and insult women. PC Marxists in their pronouncements on sensitive language are "weaponizing" words for use in their war against American culture. Indeed, language is their principal weapon in that war.

To PC Marxists, the sensibilities of millions of Americans like me who see Marxism as a threat to humanity are irrelevant. Indeed, PC Marxists are obliged to be verbally abusive toward us because we are "the enemy": non-homosexual white males who are allegedly oppressing every other biological class of Americans. The "sensitivity" which PC Marxists profess to zealously uphold comes into play only with regard to "victimized" classes of human beings. Agitprop is obliged to heap ridicule, slander, and hatred on the heads of SEAMs (Straight Euro-American Males) as was abundantly evident in the media coverage in 2018 of the U.S. Senate confirmation hearings on the nomination of Judge Brett Kavanaugh to the Supreme Court. The atmosphere in that Senate hearing room was thick with hate, slander, and ridicule for him and his entire "victimizing" class. There's no limit to the *insensitive treatment* such "enemies" deserve.

The hypocrisy of PC agitators and propagandists who profess such exquisite concern for "sensitivity" is especially evident in the linguistic vulgarity they have introduced into American speech. The most convincing examples of this are the broadsides of accusation PC Marxists fire at anyone who refuses to submit to their tactics. Call an American with a black skin a "Negro American" instead of referring to him or her by the PC authorized term "African American," and see how instantly and vehemently you will be labeled a "racist" and accused of "racism." Defy the authority of the PC language police to censor speech in any regard, and you will be vilified as a member of the "alt-right," the agitprop term for fascism.

The real purpose of the sensitivity game is intimidation. Its goal is to change American perceptions by changing the words Americans use. PC Marxists want to create perceptions that will promote class struggle. Therefore, the language used in referring to American women, Negro Americans, American Indians, Americans of Mexican or Asian ancestry must convey the impression that these biological classes are being "victimized" by straight white males. Agitprop, which asserts that "99%" of the American people are being oppressed by the other "1%," has made the idea of "victimization" ubiquitous in America. Name-calling under the influence of agitprop is replacing normal political discourse. You're a dirty rotten "sexist" if you call a female member of Congress a congressman or a first-year female college student a freshman. You're a dirty rotten, mean-spirited Christian "bigot" if you point out that many verses in the Koran tell Moslems they have a duty to their God Allah to kill non-Moslems and apostate Moslems. You're a dirty rotten "racist" if you call an American Indian an American Indian instead of a "Native American," the term PC Marxists insist Americans use because it indicates the Western

Hemisphere was inhabited before Europeans arrived to deprive them of their land, freedom, and lives.

Several summers ago, in a coffee shop in Portland, Oregon, I experienced how the "sensitivity" game is played. A guy about my age whom I had never seen before came in, got his coffee, and took a chair that was available across from mine, and we got to talking. It turned out he and I had the same views on the Supreme Court decision in 1973 overturning State jurisdiction in matters of abortion. As we were sharing our thoughts and feelings on these matters, a mature woman seated by herself at a table within earshot of ours, got up and came over and said in a firm voice, looking down at us, that she found our speech "offensive" and didn't want to hear any more of it. We stopped our conversation. The alternative, I suppose, would have been to tell the lady she could go somewhere where she wouldn't hear what we were saying. But, of course, as American males of a certain age, we had been raised to respect the feelings of women. That's the way the "sensitivity" game works. The discourse of two old guys was silenced out of deference to a PC lady who said with considerable feeling and firmness that our conversation on abortion was offending her.

Here's another instance of PC language policing. This time the offensive word was "God" and the offended person was the Clerk of the U.S. House of Representatives. The occasion was the planting in 1992 of a grove of 500 California coastal redwood trees (*Sequoia sempervirens*) on the wet, foggy Atlantic coast of Galicia, the northwest region of Spain, to commemorate the 500th anniversary of Columbus's world-changing transatlantic voyage. To plant these redwoods and name them the Columbus Grove (in Spanish "el Bosque de Colón") in honor of Columbus was my idea, and I was organizing the plantation with the help of persons in Spain and the United States, including especially my wife, a native speaker of Spanish. My memory of Galicia from having visited that mountainous, remote region of Spain in 1968–1969 when I taught at the University of Salamanca and did background research for a history of Columbus I was editing, gave me the idea for such a plantation of these noble New World trees. The forested, precipitous, foggy coast of Galicia with its maritime climate much resembles the coast of Northern California where the redwood trees flourish.

Having lived and worked in Spain, I knew how fond Spaniards are of proclamations, and being an American, I wanted the 500 redwood trees that would be planted on the Galician coast to be an official gift from the people of the United States to the people of Spain. Therefore, a part of the Columbus Grove project would have to be a congressional proclamation making the 500 trees an official gift to the people of Spain from the people of the United States. Only a congressional resolution could do that; so I recruited a former graduate student of mine at the University of Arizona, an American of Italian descent, the late Joseph Crapa, and his wife Barbara, who both worked in the U.S. House of Representatives in 1992 as chiefs of staff, to gather the necessary signatures to create a Columbus Grove resolution of the Congress of the United States (House JR 529 of the 102nd Congress, Second Session) officially bestowing the 500 sequoias on the people of Spain as a gift from the people of the United States in honor of the 500th anniversary of Columbus's world-changing round-trip crossing of the Atlantic in 1492–1493.

This Joint Resolution of Congress declared the trees a commemoration of the voyage which "established permanent communications between the Eastern and the Western Hemispheres and launched the greatest migration of human beings in the history of the world"; which "stimulated the first circumnavigation of the globe and other explorations that gave mankind their first genuine understanding of the Earth's geography"; and which "inaugurated a new world that led to the formation of the United States." The Resolution concluded by saying that the 500th anniversary of Columbus's voyage was an especially appropriate moment to honor his achievements by planting a grove of unique, long-lived, noble trees from the Western Hemisphere on the northwest coast of Spain facing the formidable, unknown ocean he crossed, so that during the next five centuries, as the trees reach their full grandeur and growth in the soil of the Eastern Hemisphere, "they will give to each individual who visits [the Columbus Grove] an experience of the awesome potentials and wondrous beauty of God's Creation...."

The Clerk of the U.S. House of Representatives found the word "God" politically incorrect and insensitive. He refused to allow a resolution containing it to be printed at federal expense and circulated among the members of the two chambers of Congress for approval. The phrase "God's Creation" offended him because, you see, some people (Marxists, for instance) don't believe in God, and mustn't be offended by using the word God in any document originating in the government of the United States. This clerk had the authority to decide what would be shown to members of the House for their approval before being passed on to the Senate to become a Joint Resolution of Congress, and it was unthinkable to his politically correct sensibility to ask congressmen to put their names to something acknowledging God's existence. His PC sensibilities took precedence over the fact that a 1956 act of the U.S. Congress made the phrase "In God We Trust" the motto of the United States of America. And over the fact that the House of Representatives emblazoned that motto in outsized letters above the Speaker's Chair in the chamber where the House meets, so everyone who enters there will be sure to see it.

The refusal of the Clerk of the House to allow H.J. Res. 529 of the 102$^{nd}$ Congress, Second Session, to go forward as written, with my insensitive phrase "God's Creation," forced the removal of the word "God's" from the Resolution. After majorities in both houses of Congress had signed the censored Resolution, the President of the United States (George H.W. Bush), the President of the Senate pro tempore, and the Speaker of the House signed it; and I took the printed resolution to Spain and personally handed it to Juan Carlos de Borbón, the king of Spain, at his palace of Zarzuela outside Madrid; then distributed copies of it to the president of the Autonomous

Region of Galicia, the chief executive of the province of Pontevedra, and other Spanish dignitaries and officials. Lacking the reference to "God's Creation," the Resolution did not have, in my opinion as its author, the proper spirit for presenting a gift which God, not human hands or ingenuity, had created. But such is the pernicious influence that PC Marxism has acquired in the United States.

The people of the village of La Communidad de Montes San Juan de Poio took land of theirs used for commercial tree farming and donated it for planting the 500 sequoia seedlings. The Simpson Timber Company, a California business enterprise, donated the 500 hundred seedlings. U.S. Airways donated cargo space to fly the cartons containing the seedlings to Spain. The little trees were taken through Spanish customs under licenses for importing plants belonging to a Spanish friend of mine, Juan Manuel Cremades, an importer-exporter of agricultural products, and were stored in a warehouse of his in Madrid, awaiting their planting. American teenagers belonging to 4-H clubs in Columbus, Wisconsin, Columbus, Georgia, and Columbus, Texas and 4-H clubs in Northern California and in Maine were invited to go to Galicia to plant the seedlings with Spanish kids their age, and these "Columbus Kids" from America (as they came to be called) raised the money in their home communities to fly themselves to Spain to team up with Spanish teenagers to plant the Columbus Grove on December 4, 1992 under the supervision of Jonathan Rea, an American forester on loan to the Columbus Grove Project from the California Department of Forestry. Many persons in Spain and the United States were thus involved in making the ceremonial planting in Galicia of the 500 sequoias possible.

All but twenty of the ten-inch sequoia seedlings have survived and have already grown to heights between thirty and forty feet. I am also pleased to report that the people living in the highlands above Poio in the Galician province of Pontevedra overlooking the ocean Columbus crossed in 1492 have adopted the "bosque de Colón" as their own. And as news of the Grove has spread, people from other parts of Spain are beginning to visit it. One wedding has already taken place in the nascent Columbus Grove, though the trees are nowhere near the full majestic grandeur God created them to attain. I am quite certain, however, as the sequoias reach their full growth in the soil of Galicia, that they will give every person who visits them, as I said in writing the joint resolution for congressional approval, "an experience of the awesome potential and wondrous beauty of God's Creation."

The Clerk of the U.S. House of Representatives who removed the word God from my Columbus Grove Resolution in his righteous, politically correct zeal to be "sensitive" likewise censored another part of its text. He didn't like the way I said Columbus's Atlantic voyage led to further maritime explorations which gave "mankind their first genuine understanding of the Earth's geography." He could not stand the word *man*kind which apparently suggested "sexist" speech to him, and was therefore a "hateful" insult to the female half the human race. He therefore struck out the word mankind and substituted the word humankind, though his PC substitute diction also contains the supposedly offensive syllable "man." One wonders if this son of PC Marxism even noticed that his supposedly more "sensitive" term humankind contains the allegedly hateful syllable man in the sense of all human beings regardless of sex or age. (One can only pray that the days of PC Marxist speech in America are approaching their end.)

"Sensitivity training," as it's called by PC Marxists, is a common method these days of enforcing PC language use. This unprecedented means of thought control is now widespread in the United States. If a student or a teacher in a public school or a university in the United States, or an employee of an American corporation or other large enterprise, says or does something contrary to the "sensitivity" dogmas of Political Correctness, they are subjected to the bullying termed "sensitivity training." In communist regimes, this sort of bullying goes by the name of "re-education." Despite their different names, the procedures are identical in purpose, and that purpose is to ensure the use of PC Marxist speech.

"Sensitivity training" in America takes the form of an intense short course in correct Marxist thinking in regard to some "victimized" biological class and its history to squelch ideas that are deemed to deviate from that PC perception. That is why lists of prohibited words and politically correct substitutes for them are handed out these days to entering freshmen at American institutions of so-called higher learning, and "speech codes" approved by faculty and administrators are in use at American colleges and universities to ensure the uniform use of "sensitive" language. Such lists of forbidden terms and their PC replacements are also in common use these days in the editorial offices of U.S. newspapers, magazines, and book publishers.

Let two further examples of PC language policing illustrate this politically correct phenomena of "Sensitivity" Above All. In 1991 at Duke University, an assistant vice chancellor was screening applicants for a job and mentioned to his assistant that the candidate he had just interviewed (who was no longer in the room) had had "homosexual mannerisms." Half a year later, a confidential memo containing Larry Nelson's private remark was leaked to a local giveaway newspaper known for its dogmatic Political Correctness, which immediately published it and raised the issue of whether Nelson's "homophobia" (!) had influenced who had been hired for the position at Duke. The politically correct article was brought to the attention of the president of Duke University; he ordered an investigation into the matter which turned up no evidence of prejudicial behavior on Mr. Nelson's part and ample proof that the best-qualified candidate had been hired. Nevertheless, this assistance vice chancellor of a prominent, once-liberal, now politically correct American university was suspended from his job for a month without pay (a fine of thousands of dollars), ordered to perform community service at a local soup kitchen, and made to undergo "sensitivity training."

The publicity on this episode moved Donald L. Horowitz, a Duke University law professor, to write a letter to the *Durham Herald-Sun* in protest, saying the punishment meted out to Mr. Nelson "smacked of the Chinese cultural revolution, of reeducation ... in thought reform camps." Prof. Horowitz's observation is absolutely right.

The same fierce insistence on "sensitivity" is also evident in regard to a novel by Mark Twain (1835–1910) criticizing slavery and the theory of Negro inferiority which was used to justify slavery. Set in Missouri (Twain's home State) before the Civil War and narrated by a boy from the class in that society known as "poor white trash," *The Adventures of Huckleberry Finn* (1885) shows Huck overcoming his racial prejudices as he discovers that a runaway Negro slave he has joined up with in fleeing the abusiveness of his drunken father, "Pap" Finn, has the same human feelings he has. *Huckleberry Finn* dramatizes the effects of slavery on whites as well as blacks, and shows how one poor white boy overcame his racism.

Before PC "sensitivity" came along, this anti-slavery novel was a much-respected classic of American literature — Ernest Hemingway famously said American literature started with *Huckleberry Finn* — and the novel was a commonly assigned reading in high-school and college literature courses in America. But because Huck's vocabulary naturally, given the time and place of the setting of the novel, included the word "nigger," *The Adventures of Huckleberry Finn* has been removed from many American high school and college literature courses. There is special irony in this since Twain told in Huck's language the story of his growing awareness of his Negro companion's human sensibilities: the story of Huck's dawning *sensitivity* toward the feelings of his fellow runaway Jim, who is running away from his status as property just as Huck is running away from the drunken abuses of his father. But that didn't matter. Huck used a word that Political Correctness has classified as "hate speech," the word "nigger," which therefore made *The Adventures of Huckleberry Finn* a racist novel, despite its manifest denunciations of racism and slavery.

If Twain, writing long before agitprop's "sensitivity" dogma appeared in America, had only avoided the PC prohibited word "nigger" and used the correct PC term "African American," all would have been well. But how could Twain have done that in the 1880s when "African American" wouldn't be invented by PC Marxists until the 1970s? And how could he have created an authentic pre-bellum Missouri boy-narrator from the lowest white class of that society and avoided his narrator's use of that then ubiquitous term?

How *insensitive* of Twain to use the n-word! How deplorably *racist*! And how deplorably insensitive of me to use the word to make a point.

# "Correct" Free Speech

WITHIN THE MEMORY of living man, there was a time in the United States, believe it or not, when the f-word was never heard in movie dialogue or seen in novels or encountered in "polite company" (a gathering of middle-class American men and women). Such language was socially banned in those olden days fifty years ago by common consent. In those days, before the PC Marxist "sexual revolution" had been accomplished, with all its many glorious results, respect for women took a quite different form from today's PC ban on using words in references to women that contain the suffix man, in the sense of a human being of any sex or age. In those olden days before Political Correctness became fully entrenched in America, burning an American flag in public or any other hateful or disrespectful act toward it was not condoned as "protected free speech." Also in the days before the smelly camel of Political Correctness got his entire body inside the tent of American respectability and culture, the fake groans of a female porn actress was not regarded as a form of "free speech."

As we have seen, agitprop in America in the last five decades has worked fundamental changes in American speech, perceptions, and cultural norms. Agitprop has taught Americans that they must tolerate vulgarity and regard violence as constitutionally protected "speech." Such notions did not exist prior to the advent of agitprop in America. Extremely vulgar language may have come naturally to the lips of drunken American sailors who associated with low women in foreign ports of call, women who did not mind hearing the f-word and who used it themselves. But it was understood before the 1960s and 70s that American men of good will and upright intentions would not put up with foul language in the presence of their ladies, no matter how American males might talk when they were in the company of other men and hard liquor was being imbibed.

Evidence that these social behaviors were beginning to change surfaced in the late 60s when the Counter Culture made "mind-altering drugs," "free love," and "liberation from bourgeois morality" fashionable on America's college campuses and condemned middle-class distinctions between male and female conduct as "inequality." It was then, in the 1960s and 70s, that the notion was planted and took root in American society that women to be considered "equal" to men had to have the same "right" as men to be promiscuous, loud, vulgar, and "drunk out of their minds" in public places. This was the beginning of the "gender equality" that has had such a devastating effect on the formation of families in America. In the 1960s and 70s, all previous distinctions between the permissible behaviors of American men and women in company with each other went out the window along with the idea that "sex" was not a topic for explicit conversation in mixed company. In those two decades, American speech became "liberated."

However, as time passed, experience showed that if you wanted to criticize abortion in a Portland, Oregon, coffee shop or refer to "God's Creation" in writing a joint congressional resolution, well, PC Marxists deemed those forms of speech intolerable and made sure they were suppressed.

In the 1960s, Marxist disdain in America for "bourgeois" cultural values became quite evident and began its present rise to ascendancy in the thinking of many Americans. The idea of "genteel company" itself has become in the last fifty years quaint and outdated, a throwback to a time when distinctions were made between male behavior and female decorum. (Decorum — now *there's* an old-fashioned word!)

I vividly recall the occasion on which I became aware of the Marxist intention to "liberate" America from middle-class restraints regarding speech. It was during my years as an Assistant Professor at the University of Wisconsin-Madison in the late 1960s. I was then in my early 30s, having spent a couple of years at sea aboard a U.S. Navy destroyer escort after college, two years teaching at a prep school in Honolulu, and six years getting my PhD. Another untenured professor in my department at the University of Wisconsin, Frank Battaglia, a tall, lean, smiley, soft-spoken, pubescent-looking Italian-America who made no bones about his Marxist convictions (a poster of China's communist dictator Mao Zedong adorned his office door) who lived in the same neighborhood in Madison that I did, invited me to hear him give a talk in a church basement, and I accepted his invitation.

When I showed up, the place was already jammed. I don't recall the subject of Frank's talk. What I remember is that every third sentence of it contained the f-word. I had not heard the f-word used with such abandon since my stint in the Navy; and I never imagined I would ever hear such language used in a church, even if it was in the basement of the building, and especial not with such calm, matter-of-fact aplomb by an educated, respectable-looking middle-class American who had an innocent, clean-cut look. As soon as I could get a word in private with Frank after his talk, I asked him why he had spoken like that. He said he was trying to get his audience over their "hang-ups" about language (i.e. he was attacking America's middle-class sense of decorum). He wanted to make vulgar speech acceptable in public discourse, even churches. My evening listening to Frank Battaglia assault American language decorum was a big revelation to me, one of the several learning experiences I had at the University of Wisconsin-Madison.

Another lesson occurred my last year there, before my wife and I left Madison because of the violence on campus to accept an offer I had had from the University of Arizona. This lesson came during an all-faculty meeting in the spring semester of 1970. The purpose of the meeting was to have a full-faculty vote on the left-wing faculty motion to close the University of Wisconsin, as campus Marxists like Battaglia wanted to do. The Marxists and their sympathizers represented perhaps one-third of the tenured and tenure-track faculty. They wanted the University shut down to protest U.S. military involvement in Vietnam. Roughly another third of the faculty was too afraid to come on campus because of the daily late-afternoon clashes between Madison police and the "protestors" (i.e. rioters) which left enough tear gas still hanging in the air the next morning to make your eyes water as you walked up Bascom Hill. The other third of the faculty — the third I belonged to, the conservative third — was continuing to meet classes and keep the University open, though there were helmeted Wisconsin National Guard with fixed bayonets in every classroom building on the campus.

The faculty voted at that full-faculty meeting held in one of the mammoth agricultural exhibit halls on campus ("the Cow Palace"), which had been set up with folding chairs, that the University of Wisconsin should remain open and not shut down. Various people addressed the meeting, but the only speech that left a lasting impressing on me was by the vice-president of the student body who told the assembled professors and instructors that we shouldn't be upset by the campus violence, because, he said, "Violence is just another form of speech." As if a pair of drunks slugging it out in the parking lot of a bar ought to be regarded as having a vigorous debate and the firebomb which had been tossed down the return-book chute of the University of Wisconsin's main library had been just the expression of an idea. I did not believe in 1970, and still do not believe, that violence is a form of speech.

During those weeks of daily rioting on the Wisconsin campus in the spring semester of 1970, I was privileged to have yet another epiphany. I was late to class one day (or so I thought) and took the stairs to my upper-floor classroom two at a time, entered, and confronted an empty, silent space. During that awful moment when I thought, "Nobody came to class," I realized with a completeness I would never otherwise have obtained, that without students I wasn't a university professor. That was my epiphany. Then it dawned on me. I had come to the right classroom at the right hour, a little after the appointed time for the class, *but on the wrong day*! That's how confusing things were on the campus of the University of Wisconsin that tumultuous spring of 1970 when I thought I had failed to inspire a single student of mine in that course to continue attending the class. Besides teaching me how essential students are to the profession I had chosen to make my life's work, that epiphany also made me realize that a university is a bond of trust between teachers and students which brings them together in mutual respect, without fear or intimidation, in the pursuit of truth. A commitment to truth in an atmosphere of free inquiry defines what a university's purpose is. Everything that Political Correctness is — its dogmatism, its indoctrination, its fondness for bullying and intimidation, its acceptance of violence as "speech," its uniformity of thought and servile conformity to whatever the leader says to believe — is opposed to the idea of a university. PC Marxists believe only in the "party line." Truth to a PC Marxist is whatever puts politically correct persons "in power" and keeps them "in power."

The Marxist notion that violence is just another form of speech still exists in the United States. The Democrat Party hired thugs during the 2016 presidential campaign to create violence at the Republican candidate's rallies so the violence would be attributed to what he said. And when he won the election, supporters of the defeated Democrat candidate expressed their disappointment by rioting and destroying property in American cities, most notably in Berkeley, California where the Counter Culture/Political Correctness Movement began in the 1960s as a "Free Speech Movement" on the University of California campus.

The breakdown of the distinction between violence and speech in the 1960s is still with us today in America. Now, however, we have a fifty-year perspective on violence as speech which we lacked in the 60s. Now Americans are justifiably reluctant to tolerate the proposition that violence is just another form of speech protected by the First Amendment.

In 2000, the idea of non-verbal "speech" reached the U.S. Supreme Court in *United States v. Playboy Entertainment Group, Inc.* (529 U.S. 803, 2000). This lawsuit concerned a federal statute prohibiting sexually explicit television programming at times when children might be awake to see it. Was that statute a violation of the First Amendment's free speech clause? The U.S. Supreme Court said it was. The Court ruled that the law prohibiting scheduling hardcore porn on television at times when children might see it was an unconstitutional infringement on the free speech guarantee in the First Amendment.

The verdict the Court handed down was full of lofty sentiments. "It is through speech that our convictions and beliefs are influenced, expressed, and tested. It is through speech that we bring those beliefs to bear on government and society. It is through speech that our personalities are formed and expressed." The highest court in the United States also proclaimed: "Basic speech principles are at stake in this case." Thus, the U.S. Supreme Court identified free speech as an indispensable part of American culture, which it surely is. But what, exactly, was the "free speech" at issue in *United States v. Playboy Entertainment Group, Inc.*? It was the feigned groans of ecstasy of a professional porn actress pretending to masturbate. It wasn't even words. The Court did not explain how seeing and hearing a female porn actress groan and writhe in phony pleasure helped Americans form and support their "convictions," which was one of the Court's lofty pronouncements on the importance of free speech. The effect which such "speech" would have, however, on children who might see it was plain enough. It would make them more hedonistic and self-indulgent, less likely to develop self-control.

While the Supreme Court of the United States was not responsible for equating hardcore pornography with "speech" (that was something the CC/PC Movement did in the 1960s and 70s), the Court's ruling in *United States v. Playboy* gave hard porn the highest possible legal respectability. The ruling that hardcore porn fell within the meaning and purpose of the free speech clause in the Bill of Rights is an outright perversion of civil rights and puts pornography in the same category as showing disrespect for the American flag, which has also been designated as "speech" by the federal courts. This is one of several ways that human nature is being reduced in America to the level of an animal for which no symbol can be sacred.

And please remember what I have already pointed out in my commentary on "Social" Justice: the U.S. Supreme Court has no constitutional jurisdiction to hear appeals on any Bill of Rights issue (freedom of religion, free speech, the right to bear arms, etc.) unless the plaintiff is a Negro American who, under the authority of Sections 1 and 5 of the Fourteenth Amendment, can appeal to a federal court should the State where he resides attempt to deny or abridge the personal liberties the Fourteenth Amendment has conferred on Negro Americans. Only Supreme Court Justice Hugo Black's nonsensical reading of the Fourteenth Amendment (his so-called "Incorporation Doctrine") has given federal courts the cockamamie notion that they have jurisdiction over the personal liberties of every American enumerated in the Bill of Rights. Let it be stated once again here that the Bill of Rights was written and ratified to protect the personal liberties of the people of the States from encroachments by the federal government which means no federal jurisdiction over them.

In 1972, twenty-eight years before the *Playboy* case, the Supreme Court illicitly took under appeal, invoking Black's illicit amendment of the Constitution known as the Incorporation Doctrine, three free speech cases: *Rosenfeld v. New Jersey*, *Lewis v. New Orleans*, and *Brown v. Oklahoma*, cases in which each defendant had been found guilty in State courts of using language harmful to public peace and order. In all three of those cases, the high court overturned the State verdicts and found in favor of behavior which broadened the meaning of free speech. In the Rosenberg case, the word "motherf***ing" had been used repeatedly in addressing a school board meeting to characterize teachers, board members, and the United States of America. In the Lewis case, the same epithet was hurled with menacing vehemence at police officers making an arrest. In the Brown case, violent language was used to break up a meeting in a university chapel. The Supreme Court found that Rosenfeld, Lewis, and Brown had used language that had been condoned on college campuses in the 1960s, and that that standard had become established and protected "free speech." (Remember, we have the word of the campus Marxist Frank Battaglia on his purpose in bludgeoning a respectable American audience with the f-word in a Wisconsin church basement in the 1960s. He was attacking middle-class American culture. His efforts that evening were part of the incipient PC Marxist culture war in the United States.)

In her presidential campaign in 2016, the Democrat candidate Hillary Clinton promised that if elected she would spend half a billion dollars from the U.S. Treasury on "anti-bullying" programs in the public schools. "Bullying" is the current explanation the teachers' unions are using as their excuse for why the public schools of America are failing in their mission. The teachers' unions claim "bullying" is so widespread in the public schools that a proper learning environment no longer exists in them. Not many years back, they blamed "American culture" for the failure of American public schooling; then they said "the decline of the American family" was causing it. (They have never suggested that the politicization of America's public schools might have a lot to do with the decline of academic standards and performance in the schools.) According to the teachers' unions, students are failing to learn because bullying is so pervasive in the public schools. Union ads to that effect have been on the radio for quite awhile. Apparently, we are supposed to believe bullies are running the schools. The teachers' unions bear no responsibility. It is interesting to note, in regard to the promise the Democrat candidate in 2016 made to spend half a billion federal dollars to combat "bullying" in the public schools, that the teachers' unions are among the biggest contributors to the Democrat Party. (The biggest all-around bully in America today, of course, is Political Correctness.)

Politically correct restrictions on free speech have become more common and more explicit recently. The former governor of Arizona, Janet Napolitano, was Barack Obama's secretary of Homeland Security for most of his presidency and now heads California's university system, the largest consortium of public institutions of higher learning in the country. In June 2015, she issued an order to the state universities and colleges she oversees, informing their faculties that they must not express any of the following ideas in their classrooms and publications because these ideas constitute "microaggressions" detrimental to the well-being of college students:

"America is the land of opportunity."

"I believe the most qualified person should get the job."

"Everyone can succeed in this country, if they work hard enough."

"When I look at you, I don't see color."

"There is only one race, the human race."

(David Horowitz, *Big Agenda*, Humanix Books, 2017, pp. 73–74.) Each of the Napolitano-banned ideas plays a momentous part in the belief-behaviors of America's culture, and each is opposed to some aspect of the PC "Party line" that America as a land of oppression.

Suppressing these ideas strengthens the PC Marxist dogmas that America is a land of "victimization," that racism is rampant in America, and that America must be "transformed" for "social" justice to prevail.

The ideas Janet Napolitano wants to ban from California's public universities and colleges: that America is a land of *opportunity*, that the most *qualified* person should get the job, that *personal success* is possible in America if you work hard enough, that it's best *not* to see "color" when looking at a fellow American, and that there's only *one race* ("the human race") are inimical to the Marxist orchestration of class struggle in America, which Napolitano and her fellow PC Marxists around the country are promoting. She knows as a PC Marxist that one of the surest ways America's culture can be destroyed is through strengthening "correct" free speech on America's university and college campuses.

Violence as speech is a PC Marxist idea. America as a land of opportunity where success is possible if you work hard is part of America's history. Violence as "speech" is an agitprop concept; America as a land of opportunity is an historical truth.

# A Culture Without Belief in God

A CULTURE IS a set of beliefs having historical authority which is formed and transmitted through behavior. A culture's beliefs acquire historical authority by being acted on continuously for at least four generations. Of necessity, cultural beliefs are extremely simple. Otherwise they would lose coherence before they attained historical authority. When we say a culture is complex, we are referring to *the set of its beliefs*. A further characteristic of cultures is that their beliefs are acted on without consciousness of doing so. This is one of the main differences between so-called "pop cultures," whose behaviors are extremely self-conscious, and cultures. This is to say that pop cultures consist of ephemeral, self-conscious *fashions* in dress, manners, food, and entertainment which affect only some groups in a society, whereas a culture's belief-behaviors are acted on by virtually every mature person in a society and are a shared inheritance created by the society's deceased generations. These belief-behaviors are acted on unself-consciously and, once they are established by behavior, are long lasting. Cultures satisfy the human need to know how to behave in society with other human beings. Their purpose is to satisfy that need. Without a stable set of simple beliefs to provide a shared, automatic guide for behavior, living in society with other human beings would be impossible, especially in large societies.

The need for culture makes its appearance in the lives of individuals at the time a person enters puberty, the onset of sexual maturity, when two things happen. (1) Human beings become aware of their sexuality and the sexuality of others, and (2) they become aware of their mortality. Awareness of the certainty of personal death is the only human knowledge which may be said to be truly universal and absolute. The acquisition of this knowledge around the time of puberty marks the beginning of the transition from childhood to adulthood. How the universal knowledge of personal mortality arises is puzzling in that it occurs at a time when humans are entering upon their fullest physical vigor and sexual potency.

Naturally, from the moment human beings become aware of their mortality, they begin asking themselves what is the meaning of life. Why am I alive if I must die? From this question arises a need which though also more or less universal varies greatly in intensity, urgency, and duration from one person to another: the need to be connected with something eternal, to offset one's awareness of one's mortality. Thus, we find in every culture some indication of belief in a reality which transcends the natural world to which one's body belongs. Human burial rituals imply this need to connect with something transcendent. Anthropologist have found evidence of such rituals in the most remote periods of history and in a great variety of locations. The pyramid-tombs of Pharaonic Egypt are perhaps the most spectacular proof of this aspect of human nature.

The current era in human history, however, presents an anomaly to these observations. The development of modern science has produced among some human beings a strident philosophy of materialistic determinism which categorically and emphatically insists that no transcendent, eternal spiritual reality exists. In this aggressively materialistic outlook, man is just another animal having only physical needs. The theories and dogmas of Karl Marx in the nineteenth century were particularly emphatic in this regard. Marx and his followers as materialistic determinists have aggressively campaigned for a world culture devoid of religious beliefs, a completely godless way of life unconnected with anything believed to transcend the material world. To the atheist — and all Marxists are atheists — death is annihilation of consciousness because life is merely a fortuitous combination of material elements which has occurred by chance, without purpose. To an atheist, man has no spiritual needs which distinguish him from other animals.

The attempt to establish Marxism as a world culture represents a radical departure from previous human history. For the first time, it appears, an intellectual movement (modern science) has been adopted by a militant political movement whose members reject any belief in a transcendent reality. In the past century and a half, Marxists have made innumerable converts to their pretentious claims. But to their dismay, no society has accepted the dogmas of materialistic determinism and acted on them for the requisite four consecutive generations to create an atheistic culture anywhere in the world.

Marxism's rejection of the ancient, universal function of religion to provide human beings with a belief in something transcendent and eternal is its most astonishing feature. Marxism's insistence on believing man is only one more species of animal, having no consciousness which survives the death of the body, appears to be unprecedented. Marxists, insofar as they may be said to worship anything, could be said to worship science for its ability to manipulate the material world. They believe science capable of answering every question human beings can pose and of solving every human problem given enough time and resources to make its experimental inquiries. Critics of Marxism have designated this exalted reverence for science "scientism."

Christianity represents in the person of Jesus of Nazareth, the Christ, the "Son of God," a particularly powerful invitation to believe in the truth of an eternal, nonmaterial reality mightier than death. Many people witnessed the crucifixion of Jesus of Nazareth, who was a well-attested historical rabbi with numerous followers in Judea two thousand years ago, and saw the excruciating, slow destruction of his mortal flesh by a squad of Roman soldiers who specialized in conducting crucifixions. Then, three days later, some of those same witnesses saw this same crucified Jesus of Nazareth alive in body and soul. His resurrection from the dead had the effect of assuring them that there is life after the death of the body.

The death of Jesus must be understood in the context of the ancient Judaic theology of making propitiatory blood sacrifices for sins against God's moral laws. Jesus and his disciples were raised in that theology, which demanded that a sin against a law of God be atoned for through a blood sacrifice. Hence the followers of Jesus, once they knew he had risen from the dead, understood his death on the Cross as a unique blood sacrifice for all the sins of mankind forever. His resurrection constituted proof of his identity — his oneness with the omnipotent, all-knowing, perfectly just, eternal "Father in Heaven" who created the cosmos and everything in it — who willed a blood sacrifice of part of himself "made flesh" (Jesus of Nazareth) to redeem human beings from their sins, once and for all, through faith in the risen Jesus Christ. Those who regard Jesus in this way, as the Messiah of Jewish prophecy, believe his willing, sacrificial death on the Cross and resurrection from death allows human beings to connect with him through faith in his eternal being and live in and with him, both now and forever. Belief in this meaning of Christ's death and resurrection has made Christianity the compelling worldwide religion which it is today.

According to Christian belief (see particularly the New Testament Gospel According to John), the only thing required for redemption from sin and death is faith in Jesus Christ as the "Son of God" and in his death on the Cross as an eternal sin offering. In other words, acceptance of Jesus as one's personal savior sent by the Creator of everything seen and unseen. Whoever believes Christ gave his life in loving and willing sacrifice for one's sins is redeemed from them and can hope to live eternally in heaven with God the Father and Christ. Faithful believers in Christ's redemptive death and glorious resurrection establish a connection with him which overcomes all disturbances of bodily misery and fear of death in one's life on earth.

Jews and Christians do not believe in a God man has created in man's image. Rather, they believe the opposite: that God has created man in *his* image (Genesis 1:26–27). Thus, man has a radically different nature from the other animals God created. What does the distinction mean? Perhaps it means that God has given human beings a semblance of his own freedom to freely do good. Such an interpretation is suggested by the fact that God after each of his successive acts of creation as reported in the first book of the Bible (Genesis 1: 4, 10, 12, 18, 21, 25, 31) declares each act "good." But, of course, man's freedom to do good is not cosmic and infallibly good, as God's actions are. Man, after all, is not God. He lacks his Creator's infinite understanding and unerring justice. Still, man does have freedom to do good, and yearns to do it.

Jesus of Nazareth, the Christ, was a Jewish prophet and teacher who knew, because of the perfect oneness of his being with God's being, that man cannot save himself from his mortality and sinfulness. No human effort or sacrificial offering could possibly atone for the sins of a human being and confer redemption from these defects on him or her. No one can, on his own, will a redemptive oneness with the Creator. To accomplish that requires an act of grace on God's part. No perfection of study and desire to conform one's thoughts and actions to God's moral laws, no propitiatory "sin offering" on the part of a human being, can obtain salvation from death or absolve one of sin. Salvation from sin and death can only be gained through faith in God's loving sacrifice on the Cross of a part of himself made flesh. Only through faith in that act of God's grace can mankind find salvation from sin and death.

The Bible tells us over and over that the ways of God are not the ways of man. This is one of this holy book's most profound truths. In both Judaism and its offshoot Christianity, God is entirely different from his creations (i.e. "holy"). Man resembles God only in having been endowed by him with a semblance of his ability to do good consciously and freely. But this capacity does not make human beings divine. It only reflects the human yearning to know their Creator, to want to be connected with his transcendence. Jews and Christians who dedicate their entire lives to the pursuit of sanctity never attain God's holiness. Rather, what they appear to attain by their earnest striving is a more complete awareness of how different God's nature is from theirs (God's holiness). The attempts of men and women to attain holiness seem to lead mainly to a humbling awareness of their need for God's grace.

Cultural Marxism does not believe in holiness or salvation through the mercy of God's love, because to a Marxist there is no God and human beings are only another species of animal having no traits that distinguish them from other species of animals. Marxists insist on this, that there is no human characteristic that cannot be found elsewhere in the animal kingdom. That is their faith. Karl Marx was not concerned with spiritual realities because he did not believe in a spiritual reality that transcends the material reality. He believed only in materialistic determinism. Marxists do not attempt to explain material existence in terms of God's prior, eternal existence, as the Judeo-Christian Bible does. For Marxists, there is no transcendent spiritual reality, no Creator. Material realities simply are, and all the laws which govern and order them simply are. Nothing exists except what is material.

The "miracles" of science in the last three centuries (my open-heart surgery in 2006, for example, which has extended my bodily existence)have canceled for Marxists the authority of Judeo-Christian teachings. But in contemplating and being thankful for the wonderful discoveries of modern science, we ought always to be mindful that science has not created any of its discoveries. When a Jew or a Christian speaks of "the glory of God," it is the infinite wonderfulness of God's laws and their inexorable power he is referring to, the full glory of which we cannot possibly comprehend but only have an intimation of.

Christ's willingness to sacrifice his corporeal being on the Cross and undergo the agony of that sacrifice, out of love for mankind, and his subsequent resurrection from the dead as a sign of his divinity, mean nothing to Marxists and other atheists. They dismiss the evidence of Jesus' resurrection reported in the books of the New Testament as self-serving lies. Faithful Jews who are certainly *not* atheists, likewise refuse to believe these reports of the resurrection of Jesus of Nazareth and regard them as self-serving lies rather than evidence that he was the expected Messiah, the savior of the world, whose coming was foretold by the ancient Hebrew prophets.

The disciples of Jesus of Nazareth after witnessing his crucifixion were in shock. They could not understand the significance of such a shameful public execution because his resurrection had not yet happened. They were cowering behind locked doors, in fear of the Jewish authorities who had manipulated their Roman overlord Pontius Pilate into executing Jesus. This fear lasted some forty hours — from the hour of the death of Jesus on the Cross through the remaining hours of that day; all the next day; and the early hours of the third day. But on that third day, the grief and the fear the disciples of Jesus were experiencing suddenly and entirely vanished, and were replaced with consummate joy.

How did this complete change come about? How could it have happened?

What caused that sudden, total change was seeing their slain rabbi *alive*. He had appeared to them! They *knew* he had risen from the dead because they had seen him, spoken with him, eaten with him, touched him. There was no doubt among Christ's followers in Jerusalem from the third day after his crucifixion that he was alive, that his death on the Cross had not annihilated him. It was that certainty which overcame their fear of death and replaced their grief with joy. There is no way we can account for this change in Peter, Andrew, John, James, and the other followers of Jesus of Nazareth in Jerusalem unless we see things as the New Testament Gospel reports them. Only by seeing things as the disciples themselves saw them can we explain how they went from fear to joy, from despair to a willingness to die for their conviction that Jesus of Nazareth was the Messiah or Christ. "Jesus lives!" they told each other in ecstatic amazement. "Whoever believes in him shall never die but have eternal life with him and the Father in Heaven!" They were quite willing to die for that certainty, and many did, starting with Stephen (Acts 7: 54–60). It is difficult to understand how the reports of Jesus' resurrection from the dead could have been "self-serving lies" when so many of his disciples, like Stephen, were killed because they professed their belief in his resurrection and willingly gave their lives (as countless martyrs have over the centuries since Jesus's resurrection) rather than deny what they knew to be true. From persons disoriented by fear and grief, the disciples of Jesus of Nazareth suddenly became fearless, focused, confident preachers of the "Good News" of the Risen Christ. Naturally, for the Roman and Jewish rulers in Jerusalem, the "Good News" which filled the hearts of Christians with such exultant certainty and gratitude for God's love was an insult to their authority. Likewise, today the hearts of strict materialists are hardened against beliefs which differ from theirs — no matter how spectacular the evidence for those beliefs might be.

Starting in Jerusalem the day after the resurrection of Jesus Christ, his disciples began preaching that he was the Christ, until today there is hardly a place of human habitation on earth, no matter how remote and isolated it may be, that has not heard that "Good News." Since Christ's life, death, and resurrection two millennia ago, no one can say how many Christians have accepted being killed rather than renounce their faith in the Risen Christ. The news of eternal life through faith in Jesus Christ's oneness with God, as manifested in his resurrection, has been spread throughout the world by the witness of those who live in that faith and in the presence of the Holy Spirit Christ transferred to his followers in Jerusalem before his ascension to the Father in heaven, the spirit which they and their followers transferred to the rest of mankind in obedience to his order to do so.

But with the advent of modern science in the seventeenth and eighteenth centuries, an exclusive faith in materialistic determinism — a new "religion" unprecedented in human history in being devoid of any trace of belief in transcendent realities — took root in Europe and has spread to other continents. The sublime Hebraic faith in the one, true, eternal God, the maker of all that is seen and unseen, and the laws which govern all that is, by whom Christ was sent into the world, no longer prevails unchallenged in Western civilization. Materialistic determinism and scientism jealously attack the belief of Jews and Christians in the God Moses and Jesus prayed to.

The first eruption of the new "religion" was the French Revolution in the final decade of the eighteenth century which was immediately suppressed by force. The totalitarian socialist regimes in twentieth-century Russia, Germany, and China were the second, third, and fourth major manifestations of the "religion" of godless materialism. Of these, Nazi Germany and the Soviet Union have been wiped from the face of the earth, leaving Red China. What will finally happen there is uncertain. For the dogmas of Cultural Marxism to be established as a culture in China, the next ten years will be decisive because of the four-generation rule in the formation of cultures. Marxism will have to be established as a culture in China before 2030, or it is not going to become the culture of China. And, Chinese Marxists in permitting the practice of a form of capitalism in China have already opened a path for further deviation from orthodox Marxism. Moreover, faith in the Risen Christ has taken root in China, despite opposition from the current Marxist rulers of China, and is now competing with strict materialism for adherents. Will Marxism in China continue to be modified in the direction of Western civilization in the next ten years and form a set of beliefs which will eventually be acted on for more than four generations to produce in China a culture with a religious element? We can only pray that it will and support as best we can the Christians already living the faith in China.

Cultural Marxism claims that man is only another animal species. Yet at the same time, Cultural Marxism is also preaching that man can be "his own creator" through science. These two assertions are at odds with each other. For if man is entirely and only a physical being and no different from other animals in his basic nature, and if all forms of life "evolved" from a single primordial cell (Darwin's theory) which somehow acquired the ability to reproduce itself (no one knows how), Marxists cannot also say human beings can be their own creator. For if man is only another animal, he cannot be his own creator.

It behooves us to keep in mind the results of materialistic determinism. In the last one hundred years (1917–2017) in the Soviet Union and Nazi Germany, the People's Republic of China, and other countries where the "religion" of materialistic determinism and scientism has either "come to power" or made significant headway toward that goal (including in the United States), the number of human lives snuffed out trying to establish Cultural Marxism makes the sixteenth-century Aztec priests in Mexico who killed only tens of thousand of human beings on the altars of their religion look good by comparison. *The Black Book of Communism* puts the number of human sacrifices on the altars of Marxism's materialistic determinism at approximately one hundred million. The death toll from Nazi materialistic determinism in the 1930s and 40s would probably add close to another ten million to that total. The extermination of human lives through wholesale abortion — a consequence of considering human beings as only another species of animal — has added tens of millions more to the death toll. Having come to doubt the existence of God and the special sanctity of human life as made in the image of God, the twentieth century saw a slaughter of human beings on a stupendous scale, a slaughter which scientific knowledge made possible.

This has been true in the United States as well as other places, as the snuffing out of human life in the womb just mentioned followed from the U.S. Supreme Court's decision in 1973 that a woman had the right to exterminate the separate human life developing in her womb. That "de-sanctification" of human life, which has been going on in Western countries ever since the rise of scientism began, led the twentieth-century American poet T. S. Eliot to write that human life in the Christian countries was, in his judgment, becoming only a matter of "Birth, copulation, death" — an existence no different from the existence of other animal species.

The worst effects of deterministic materialism and scientism are still in progress in countries like Cuba, North Korea, and Venezuela where a Marxist regime is ruthlessly resorting to starvation as a political tactic to establish itself against the will of the Venezuelan people with the aid of Russian state security police and a contingent of soldiers from Marxist Cuba that could be as large as 20,000. However, in the colonies the Soviet Union established in Central Europe after World War II, the countries of Eastern Europe, and other countries in the former Soviet Empire, the "religion" of materialistic determinism and scientism has been repudiated. We may therefore hope the same thing will happen wherever Marxists today either govern or appear to be on the way to dominance, including perhaps in the United States.

Please note, if you will, that after the Soviet state collapsed in 1991, the first large restoration project undertaken by the people of Moscow was the rebuilding of their city's most glorious pre-revolution place of worship, the basilica of Christ the Savior, which the Soviet dictator Stalin had leveled. For an account of Stalin's sacrilege and the rebuilding of this cathedral after the Soviet collapse, see pages 95–108 of *Imperium* (1995), a book by the internationally renown Polish journalist Ryszard Kapuscinski. According to one verbal report which has come to my attention, vocations to the Christian priesthood in Russia in the post-Soviet era are robust. In 1980 there were sixteen countries in the world with communist governments (see map, pp. viii–ix, in *The Rise and Fall of Communism* published in 2009 by Archie Brown, an emeritus professor of politics Oxford University). Today there are less than half that number in the world, and only one of them (Cuba) is outside of Asia.

Whether the wounds the new "religion" of materialistic determinism is inflicting on the human spirit can be healed or whether they are terminal injuries is as yet somewhat uncertain. But the collapse of the Soviet Union, where government based on materialistic determinism and scientism had its first extended trial, suggests that men and women will reject the new "religion" of materialism and scientism. In the Soviet Union, man's need for some sort of transcendent spiritual connection — that is, a connection to God — clearly proved greater than the attractiveness of materialistic determinism.

American culture has particularly deep religious roots. It was created by generations of men and women willing to brave the perils of crossing the North Atlantic in the seventeenth and eighteenth centuries in cramped, unsanitary, leaky wooden sailing ships on which the passenger death toll averaged ten percent: a decimation which in any military conflict would be considered tremendous battlefield loses. Many of these immigrants in the seventeenth and eighteenth centuries, and well into the nineteenth century, continued on, after arriving in America, into the unknown wilderness farther west to confront its dangers, which also required extraordinary faith in God. These facts inform us, as no others could, that the men and women who formed America's culture trusted in God.

The importance religion has had for Americans is also evident in the argument of the Declaration of Independence and the fact that the First and Second Continental Congresses which organized and achieved America's independence from Europe opened their sessions with prayer. The Founding Fathers believed God's providence brought about America's victory over British arms in the War for Independence and guided the writing and ratification of the U.S. Constitution, despite the deep political differences that then existed among American patriots. One sees the same belief in God in the images the Founders put on the Great Seal of the United States and the many references to God and his providence in the American poem that provided the lyrics for America's National Anthem. Faith in God is likewise evident in Lincoln's four citations of the Bible in his Second Inaugural Address, in the phrase "one nation under God" in America's "Pledge of Allegiance," and in the national motto "In God we Trust."

(For further proofs of the shaping influence of American belief in God in American history, see Michael Medved's *The American Miracle: Divine Providence in the Rise of the Republic*, 2016.)

The argument the Second Continental Congress made for American independence from Britain states that because God created man and endowed human beings with an "unalienable" birthright to freedom, no government which violates that divine birthright can be tolerated. The Declaration of Independence argues that American independence from Britain was in accordance with "the Laws of Nature and of Nature's God." America's charter of nationhood is steeped in faith in the Creator of the Universe.

As noted earlier, Antonio Gramsci (1891–1937), one of the founders of the Communist Party of Italy, rightly said that Marxism and belief in the Risen Christ are incompatible. In his opinion, before Cultural Marxism could be established anywhere where Christianity exists, Christianity would have to be destroyed.

Everywhere in agitprop's campaign against America's Christian culture during the past half-century, we see evidence of Gramsci's analysis. The campaign has won major victories in its war against religion in America by manipulating the power of U.S. courts. (1) The dogma of Separation of Church and State has been established through the federal courts. (2) The customary brief prayers in the public schools at the beginning of each school day which taught young Americans to believe in God's existence have been judicially abolished. (3) The Bible readings which gave American school kids an inkling of God's providence have been judicially removed. (4) The Ten Commandments proclaiming the Judeo-Christian moral heritage, including the commandment to tell the truth (not to "bear false witness"), have been judicially removed from the public schools of America and U.S. courthouses.

PC Marxism's successful attacks on the Christian basis of America's culture have all been made by invoking freedom of religion! That's why they have succeeded so well. Agitprop is destroying respect for Judeo-Christian morality in America. The strategy for doing this in one of the most deeply Christian nations in the world was quite simple. The strategy has two parts. (1) The simple prayers, Bible reading exercises, and displays of the Ten Commandments that were allowed in the public schools before the 1960s were declared *offensive* to atheists and persons of certain religious denominations. (2) Then it was argued that to offend anyone's religious views, even the views of atheists who deny the existence of God, was un-constitutional. This argument has been made over and over again in the federal courts. Gramsci who died in 1937 would have been proud of the effectiveness of these attacks on religion in America.

The Bill of Rights established freedom of worship as a positive right of believers in America. It did not oblige the government of the United States to protect the feelings of atheists — or, for that matter, the feelings of any American — including a Christian American whose religious feelings may differ from those of other Christians. Nowhere in the Constitution of the United States is the protection of feelings represented as an obligation of the general government, even if such an obligation was feasible in a country of over 300 million inhabitants.

In 1805, the third president of the United States at the end of his Second Inaugural Address fervently declared that he would need, during his second term of office, "the favor of that Being in whose hands we are, who led our fathers, as Israel of old, from their native land and planted them in a country flowing with all the necessaries and comforts of life." In the middle of the Address, Thomas Jefferson said everything that needs to be said regarding religious freedom in America: "In matters of religion I have considered that its free exercise is placed by the Constitution independent of the powers of the General Government." This was the most comprehensive, most public, and most emphatic pronouncement on freedom of religion in America Jefferson ever made. It states the basic truth about religious freedom in America: the federal government has no constitutional authority in matters of religion. Governmental jurisdiction in the

United States over religious freedom rests entirely with the States of the United States.

After decades of agitprop in America, freedom of religion is now at the mercy of whomever goes into a federal court and claims to be offended by someone's exercise of their freedom of religion. The offense an atheist's attacks on religion gives believers is never considered because agitprop has created a double standard in the United States regarding religion. If someone is offended by an atheist's expression of his beliefs, the atheist's feelings nowadays have priority. But what is the First Amendment guarantee of religious freedom worth when it is restricted to gatherings of like-minded believers where it can offend no one? What would free speech be worth if its exercise were limited to gatherings of like-minded persons?

The religious clauses in the Bill of Rights — the Establishment Clause and the Free Exercise Clause — were put in the Constitution, as Thomas Jefferson said in 1805, to exclude the federal government from having any jurisdiction in matters of religion. The whole point of the Bill of Rights was, and remains, not only to enumerate personal liberties of the people of the States but to protect them from encroachments by the federal government. The foremost of these personal liberties is freedom of religion because it has the most to do with the perpetuation of American culture.

# Conclusion

GITPROP HAS BEEN imposing on America the seven alien ideas just discussed. Biological Class Consciousness. "Social" Justice. Mandatory "Diversity." A Standard of Double Standards. "Sensitivity" Above All. "Correct" Free Speech. A Culture without Belief in God. These un-American concepts have a common denominator: hypocrisy.

A Standard of Double Standards is pure hypocrisy. Hypocrisy is also evident in the idea that the feelings of a PC Marxist must never be offended, whereas the sensibilities of everyone else can be offended. PC agitators and propagandists likewise demonstrate their hypocrisy in condemning the right of Americans to express Christian views in the public square while asserting for themselves freedom to express their atheism. Similarly, PC Marxists claim that burning the American flag while screaming anti-American obscenities is just "free speech" while they denounce criticism of whatever they support as "hate speech." Hypocrisy is manifested also in the Marxist idea of mandatory "diversity" which requires giving some biological classes special privileges while denying those privileges to other classes. Legislation promoting the Marxist dogma of "social" justice in the "War on Poverty" has devastated the Negro American family while claiming to benefit Negro Americans. In looking only to the past while pretending to be creating a better future, agitprop is being monumentally hypocritical.

For the past fifty years, Marxist agitprop in America has devalued human life and Christian marriage (the union of one woman and one man for the responsible procreation and nurturing of children) by insisting that a woman has an absolute right to destroy a developing human life in her body at any stage. (The "bioethicist" Peter Singer claims a woman has a postpartum right to destroy a "defective" child of hers for two years after the child's birth.) Marxist agitprop promotes "single-parenting," equates homosexual unions with Christian marriage, makes pornography a matter of free speech, supports "no fault" divorce laws, and claims abortion is just a woman's "right to choose," without any consideration of what is being chosen.

In all these ways, the hypocrisy of agitprop is making a mockery of the belief-behaviors of American culture and destroying them.

PART IV

# THE FUTURE OF CULTURAL MARXISM IN AMERICA

# The Failure of Marxism in the USSR and Successes of PC Marxism in America

I N CONSIDERING in this concluding part of the book, the odds of
PC Marxists finally being able to destroy American culture and
establish Cultural Marxism in its place, two indisputable facts
must be addressed.

**(1)** The movement which began in the 1960s on American college
campuses calling itself "the Counter Culture" — which its opponents in the 1970s renamed "Political Correctness" because of its
similarity to Mao Zedong's "cultural revolution" in China whose
politics Mao designated with the same title — has done immense
damage to the culture of America without obliterating it. The CC/
PC Movement even managed in 2008, after decades of agitprop
harping on racism in America, to install a Negro American
who was a PC Marxist in the White House, and by means of his
abuses of his office to reelect him in 2012. In the 2016 presidential
campaign, however, PC Marxists mistakenly thought they would
be able to elect a female PC Marxist to succeed their "African
American" president. If that had happened, the replacement of
American culture by Cultural Marxism might have been carried
through. As it is, the election of Donald Trump in 2016 instead of

Mrs. Clinton indicates that the people of the States of the United States are waking up to the dire threat which Political Correctness poses to the American way of life.

**(2)** The collapse of the USSR a quarter-century ago likewise does not bode well for the construction of Cultural Marxism in America. But, still, the question of whether half a century of agitprop in America has so weakened American culture and alienated so many Americans from their cultural heritage that the culture's replacement by Cultural Marxism is only a matter of time, is quite real. That replacement would be the "transformation" Barack Obama predicted his election in 2008 ensured, but in the event did not. Again, it must be emphasized that Trump's election is an omen of defeat for those anti-America Americans who have been working so hard to build Cultural Marxism in America, because, as I've said, Trump's election indicates that a great many middle-class American voters are becoming aware of the growing alien threat in their midst.

Let us examine the significance of the Soviet Union's collapse first.

When World War II ended in Europe in May 1945 with the unconditional surrender of Nazi Germany, the continuation of the Union of Soviet Socialist Republics that Lenin established in 1922 seemed absolutely assured. No one then thought the USSR would no longer be on the world's political map forty-seven years later in 1992. The disintegration of the Soviet Union took every "Sovietologist" in the West by surprise, although six years prior to its occurrence, President Ronald Reagan in a public speech spoke of the possibility that the USSR was in its final years. The failure of Western "experts" to predict the Soviet Union's disintegration, along with the disappearance of the supposedly omnipotent Communist Party of the Soviet Union, is akin to the failure of political experts in the United States in 2016 to predict Donald Trump's election to the U.S. presidency. These monumental failures call into question the competence of so-called pundits on the Left in the United States and suggest they have been so influenced by fifty years of agitprop in America that their judgment is no longer trustworthy; that it represents little more than the politically correct "Party line."

To truly grasp the stupendous significance of the Soviet Union's disappearance, it is first necessary to understand how total the Communist Party's control of Soviet society was. From the time that Lenin created the USSR in 1922 until its collapse in December 1991, the Party's spies and state security police supervised every aspect of life in the Soviet Empire with a thoroughness no normal American can comprehend. In the end, however, Party "discipline" and the power of the Soviet state to enforce "the Party line" were insufficient to sustain the Soviet Empire. In the end, the human desire for freedom and self-determination proved more powerful than the Communist Party of the Soviet Union and the totalitarian government it ran.

During the Soviet Union's comparatively brief existence of seventy years (1922–1991), it was a one-party police state maintaining a vast array of punishment camps ("the Gulag") to make the peoples of the Soviet empire afraid to disobey the Party and its dictates, which were administered through the Soviet state, with the Red Army held in reserve as the ultimate deterrent to rebellion. Soviet operatives in foreign lands were engaged in subverting governments not yet under communist control. Nothing of interest to the Party occurred any-where in the vast empire called the Union of Soviet Socialist Republics or the rest of the world which was not reported to Moscow, the nerve center of the empire and the Communist Party of the Soviet Union. But none of that prevented the fall of the USSR and the CPSU. Indeed, the extreme concentration of power in Moscow probably contributed to the Soviet state's collapse.

The leaders of the Communist Party of the Soviet Union did not, as they claimed they did, command a "superpower." To be sure, the USSR was super big, the largest contiguous empire of conquered nations centered in Europe ever known, the legacy of centuries of conquests by Russian czars. And, the Soviet Union had an impressive array of nuclear weapons and the missiles to deliver them intercontinentally, which the Party leaders were fond of displaying to the world via television every May Day in Moscow's Red Square. But these things did not make the USSR a "superpower," because the Soviet regime had severe moral and spiritual deficiencies.

For one thing, Soviet leaders as Marxists had no respect for truth or morality, two imperatives of normal human life. Morality and truth to Marxists were whatever served the Party's interests. Nor did the Party's leaders respect "the masses" they governed. To them, human beings were merely cogs in the machinery for creating communist governments around the world. The Party governed "the masses" of the former Russian empire by manipulating the lowest human motivators: fear and self-preservation. ("Take from me what you will, just don't kill or punish me or those closest to me, and I'll do whatever you say.") And all the while they were reducing those they governed to this groveling subservience, the rulers of the Soviet empire pretended to be governing in the name of democracy, "social" justice, and the loftiest humanitarianism. In truth, only the Party bigwigs and their crucial supporters — the chiefs of the security police, the Red Army's principal commanders, and high-ranking bureaucrats — had access to consistent supplies of good quality consumer goods, abundant good-quality food, first-rate medical care, and genuine education. Other Soviet citizens received indoctrination in Marxist dogmas, technological training, and whatever goods and food might be available, provided they "compl[ied] with the standards of socialist conduct" (Article 59 of the Constitution of Union of Soviet Socialist Republics in effect when the USSR collapsed).

Another inherent defect of the Soviet Union was that none of the persons who controlled the "organs" of Soviet government believed in God, the Creator of everything seen and unseen. Every functionary of the Soviet state had to be an atheist or, if a believer, had to keep his faith a closely guarded secret because atheism is a requirement of Marxist true believers. The refusal to acknowledge any power higher than the state made the rulers of the Soviet Union ruthless. Of course, the Marxist policies of the Communist Party of the Soviet Union did not regard man as a creature of God having a unique inner capacity to do either good or evil. Instead of God, the Party's leaders put their faith in their philosophy of materialistic determinism, the power of environment to compel behavior, and the Party's ability to terrify human beings into compliance with whatever directives it considered necessary to issue. As dedicated Marxists, the Party's leaders were absolutely convinced that human beings, like all animals, were the result of a process of interaction with environmental conditions, and they believed the socio-economic-political environment determined the behavior of "the human animal." But to treat men and women as if they are just another species of animal and the product of their environment is not a formula for creating anything that could be thought of as "super."

Ultimately, the Soviet plan for "the human animal" was to control its "environment" on a worldwide scale. Once that had been done and the planet's resources were under comprehensive Marxist management, "social" justice and universal peace would reign forever. That was the Marxist version of heaven on earth. In this plan for restructuring the world and creating "Soviet Man," human beings were analogous to Pavlov's dogs: creatures that could be environmentally programmed to behave as their masters wanted them to act. Humanity had no inherent value.

Marx and his followers scorned the insights of the Jewish prophets of old who communed with God, perceived his infinite glory and eternal holiness and the lawfulness with which he governed his creations. The Marxist plan for human happiness was incompatible with the intuition men and women have of their difference from the rest of the animal kingdom. True, man's organic being is essentially the same as that of other creatures God has created, but man additionally has a vivid awareness of good and evil and his freedom to choose between them. Humans desire to transcend the physical world to which their bodies belong.

These profound errors in Marxist theory and practical politics would have been sufficient in themselves to have caused the down-fall of the regime Lenin erected when he created the USSR. But they were not the sum of the reasons the USSR collapsed. The generation of Marxists who produced the Soviet Union and bequeathed their project for world dominance to their ideological heirs to complete, never understood that their plan for total control of the planet by one political party was neither feasible nor desirable. They were hyper-materialists and megalomaniacs who mistakenly imagined that they and their Party were capable of the omniscient acumen and infallible executive prowess which their plan would need to achieve fruition. Their confidence in the adequacy of their economic dogma "state-ownership of the means of production" was yet another flaw in their grandiose scheme which led to the Soviet debacle in 1991.

There came a moment in the 1980s, at the outset of the fourth generation after the founding of the Soviet state, when the leaders then "in power" in the USSR had to make a crucial decision which was becoming more urgent with every passing month. Could the project of "building communism" worldwide be continued or would it have to be abandoned because it was proving too costly? The leaders of the Soviet state in the 1980s could not ignore this question. The Central Committee of the Communist Party of the Soviet Union had to be aware that statistics indicated that the lifespan of Soviet citizens was *declining*. Should Marxism's universal project of destroying non-Marxist regimes world wide and rebuilding them as Marxist regimes go forward, regardless of cost, or should it be abandoned? Of course, the hubris and self-interest of the Party leaders in the Soviet Union compelled them to continue "building communism" at home and abroad.

But subsidizing subversion abroad and maintaining the costly police apparatus, bureaucracy, and military forces to sustain the authority of the Communist Party of the Soviet Union (CPSU) at home could
not all continue to be financed at the same time. There just wasn't
enough money, and the Soviet state had no credit-worthiness on the
international money market by which to borrow money. Another
dilemma even more fundamental existed: was the Party capable of
producing enough *food* for the people of the Soviet Empire through
its state-owned-and-run collective farms? And, could the Soviet state
propaganda apparatus sustain its myth that Marxism was succeeding
wonderfully in the USSR? Perhaps the most urgent question of all was,
did the members of the Central Committee of the Communist Party
of the Soviet Union, especially its general-secretary, have the stomach
to continue leading the Soviet Union down the yellow-brick road to
global socialism, regardless of the toll in lives and suffering that was
exacting?

Especially troublesome for Soviet leaders was their inability to quell
the recurring rebelliousness in the Soviet colonies that Josef Stalin
established in Central Europe after World War II, which were setting a
bad example of disobedience to Soviet authority. Soviet propaganda of
course referred to these Soviet colonies in Central Europe — Poland,
Hungary, Czechoslovakia (the present Czech Republic and Slovakia),
East Germany — as "Eastern Europe" to make it seem they were lo-
cated within Russia's historic "sphere of influence," which was Eastern
Europe, whereas these nations are in Central Europe, all of them lying
*west of* Europe's central meridian (25 degrees east longitude).

The Soviet colonies in Central Europe repeatedly required the application of military force to keep them in line. The year Josef Stalin
died (1953) East German workers were the first of the Soviet colonies
in Central Europe to rise up in violent protest against Soviet imperialism. Three years later, in the summer of 1956, Polish workers took
to the streets of Poznan, a city near the post-World War II German-
Polish border, to demonstrate against communist rule; and in October

of that same year, 1956, public protests by workers and university students in Budapest spread throughout Hungary and turned violent. A lot of killing by Soviet tanks had been necessary in Hungary to bring the Hungarians to their senses and show them who their imperial master was. In 1968, massive but peaceful demonstrations against Soviet imperialism in Czechoslovakia again necessitated the use of the Red Army to remind the Czechs and the Slovaks of their colonial status. In Poland, serious political disturbances occurred again in 1968, 1970, and 1976 requiring shows of military force to suppress.

Then in 1978, the most unpredictable, worst thing possible for the Central Committee of the Communist Party of the Soviet Union happened. An important leader of the Christian church in Poland was elected head of the Roman Catholic Church, the largest denomination of Christians in the world. This was extremely bad news for the Soviets because Poland was their largest colony in Central Europe and the only communist-ruled nation in Europe in which Christianity remained institutionally strong. The election of Karol Wojtyla to the papacy (he took the name John Paul II as pope) caused a lot of joy in his homeland and a lot of angst in the Kremlin and communist party headquarters in Warsaw. The new Pope, the first non-Italian pontiff in five centuries, had to be allowed to visit his native country, where more than ninety percent of the people were professing Roman Catholics; and during his papal tour of Poland in June 1979, John Paul II went from one large Polish city to another preaching to immense outdoor congregations the dignity of man as God's creation while presiding over the distribution of Christ's body to these huge crowds. He spoke of the dignity of Christian labor and the need for non-violent protest against materialistic determinism. These public reprimands of Marxism's animating philosophy, materialistic determinism, were galling to the communist rulers in Moscow and Warsaw.

Nevertheless, a Christian labor union, inspired by the visit of John Paul II to his native country, was organized by Polish workers. Membership in this national labor union which became the focus of the Polish aspiration for the restoration of their national independence grew by leaps and bounds despite all efforts by the Polish communist party to suppress the movement's disruptive nonsense about God's existence, man's dignity as his creation, and the right of workers to organize a labor union independent of Marxist theory. Most galling to Moscow and Warsaw, this unauthorized labor union — which was unique in the history of organized labor in that it enrolled in one union 85% of the wage and salary workers of an entire nation, from ballerinas, clerks, and electricians to miners, teachers, and zoo keepers — took the Marxist idea of workers' "Solidarity" as its name. Besides being an authentic labor union fundamentally interested in better pay and working conditions, Solidarity was also a non-violent, Christian freedom movement.

Finally, an attempt was made in 1981 to eliminate the influence of the Polish pope by assassinating him. From the Marxist point of view, this attempt had to be made because John Paul II was stirring up too much trouble among the Soviet colonies in Central Europe. In 1981, there was also an attempt to kill the president of the United States, Ronald Reagan, who likewise endorsed and supported the movement in Poland called Solidarity and was giving it moral and material support. Neither of these assassination attempts succeeded, and neither was traceable to the Kremlin which was undoubtedly the instigator of both.

The crisis for the Central Committee of the Communist Party of the Soviet Union came in November 1989 when the Berlin Wall, the symbol of Soviet authority in Central Europe, which had been constructed under orders from the Kremlin in 1961 to keep German workers from fleeing the workers' paradise being built for them in the name of Karl Marx, was breached by Germans living on both sides of it. For the first time in the history of the Soviet Union, the Central Committee of the CPSU did not order the suppression and punishment by military force of an act of overt rebellion in the Soviet empire. That failure proved fatal to the Soviet state. Within two years of the fall of the Berlin Wall, the Union of Soviet Socialist Republics fell apart, and with its disintegration the Communist Party of the Soviet Union also disintegrated. (With no Soviet Union, there could of course no longer be a Communist Party of the Soviet Union.)

The familiar flag of the Soviet Union — a crossed golden sickle and hammer against a uniform red background — was lowered for the last time from the ramparts of the Kremlin in Moscow, the ancient citadel of the Russian czars, the last week of December 1991. The project of building communism in the former empire of the Russian czars (the northern half of Asia and the eastern third of Europe and, under Stalin's leadership, half of Central Europe) came to an irrevocable end. The Soviet state. The Party. Government by fear. The superpower myth. The economics of central planning. The hallowed Marxist slogans "State ownership of the means of production" and "From each according to his ability, to each according to his needs." All gone. Shattered like a stack of dinner plates on a defective shelf that pulls away from a wall and crashes onto a tile floor. It was not an armed uprising that did it but a non-violent repudiation of Marxism by city dwellers, farmers, and factory workers tired of propaganda as a substitute for freedom and bread.

Hitting only the highlights, that is the story of Marxism's failure in the Soviet Union. The experiment lasted a decade short of four generations. The human cost? The "liquidation" of no fewer than thirty million lives: a human slaughter five times greater than that of the Nazi death camps, since Hitler's imperial ambitions never got outside of Europe and were defeated on the battlefield in six years, whereas Soviet communism spanned two continents and lasted seventy years. Neither of these totalitarian socialist regimes — one national (the Nazis) and one international (the Marxists) — produced anything lasting except memories of their evil behavior, though Hollywood movies insist on portraying only the Nazis as evil. The Russian and the German versions of totalitarian socialism had much in common. The Marxist version was the dogma of "social" justice married to state terrorism. The Nazis version was the dogma of "racial" superiority married to state terrorism.

❧

Let us now examine the achievements of politically correct Marxism in the United States. What have five decades of PC agitprop in America wrought? What have anti-America Americans accomplished by pushing their Marxist dogmas that every human problem is material and human beings are only another species of animal whose environment determines their behavior? The agitprop that there is no God who created the cosmos and everything in it, including the laws which govern it, and who loves the human race; that the purpose of government is to create and maintain a correct environment; that anyone who disagrees with these propositions is an enemy of mankind and deserves to be crushed — what have PC Marxists produced in America with their agitprop?

PC Marxists in the United States have been successful in promoting and increasing the use of destructive addictive drugs among middle-class Americans. They have succeeded in making prostitution, promiscuity, pornography, and divorce more common among middle-class Americans than ever before. They have successfully transformed the concept of marriage and transformed abortion into nothing more than a woman's right to choose, regardless of the fact that she is choosing to exterminate the human life developing in her womb. PC Marxists have assigned higher value to the habitats of "endangered" squirrels, insects, minnows, and plants than human uses of nature. They have introduced to America Marxist class consciousness and class struggle. They have made "nationalism" (i.e. patriotism) a dirty word and glamorized "thinking globally." They have made many middle-class Americans dependent on Big Government subsidies who never were before. They have removed the prayers acknowledging God from the public schools of America, along with Bible-reading exercises and displays of the Ten Commandments, and have

converted the public schools of America into centers for indoctrination in Political Correctness. And, they have made many Americans
in three successive generations wonder whether America would not
be better off as a socialist regime with one, politically correct party
that "got things done."

These are among the achievements of agitprop in America.

Also in the past half-century, Soviet-style Big Government has
flourished. The executive branch of the federal government has
nearly doubled in size, going from eight cabinet-level departments
to fifteen. Under the Obama administration, the number of regulations issued by the government increased by some 23,000 a year, at
an average annual administrative cost-increase of over $120 billion
(Diane Katz, Heritage Foundation, February 14, 2017). These federal "regulations" were, in effect, laws which Americans had to obey,
even though they were not called laws and were not enacted by the
constitutionally lawful legislators the people of the States elected to
make the nation's laws. Article I, Section 1 of "the supreme Law of the
Land" (Article VI, second paragraph, the U.S. Constitution) declares
unequivocally: "All legislative Powers herein granted shall be vested
in a Congress of the United States, which shall consist of a Senate
and House of Representatives." That First Section of the First Article
of the Constitution does not permit Congress to delegate its legislative obligation, which is a constitutional responsibility that only the
Senate and the House of Representatives acting together in accordance with the prescriptions laid out in Article I of the Constitution
can exercise. The truth is that the Congress of the United States in the
twentieth century has become so corrupt in its departures from the
requirements of the Constitution that it has even forsaken the main
principle in the Constitution, which is the separation of the legislative, executive, and judicial powers of the general government and
the separation of the general government's powers from the powers
of the State governments (see Amendment Ten in the Bill of Rights).
Congress, as just indicated, is illicitly sharing its exclusive legislative

responsibility with the executive branch of the government in violation of Article I, Section 1. The Supreme Court has usurped from the
States their constitutionally exclusive jurisdiction over the personal
liberties of Americans, in violation of Amendment X in the Bill of
Rights and Article V prohibiting the federal government from altering
the Constitution. In place of those wise separations of governmental
powers which protect liberty, Congress has created, illicitly and willy-
nilly, and in conjunction with the executive and judicial branches of
the general government, an "Administrate State" in total contradiction
of the Constitution.

Allowing executive-branch bureaucrats to make federal laws
called regulations not only violates the Constitution but has led to
enormous increases in federal expenditures and national debt (deficit
spending) because U.S. taxpayers would not tolerate the increases in
taxes which would be required to pay for the programs the Congress
wants but does not want to take responsibility for creating, so it
locates responsibility for creating them in the executive branch of
the federal government which funds the programs through massive
borrowing. By the end of the Obama administration, half of every
dollar the federal government was spending was borrowed money.
Obama as president doubled the size of the national debt, which now
has soared to an inconceivable *twenty trillion dollars*. (When federal
spending rises to that level, it is impossible to actually account for
what the money is being spent on.) Federal authorizations or commitments to provide funds for future expenditures are now something
like six times the current U.S. national debt. This unimaginable
extravaganza of irresponsible authorizations of spending cannot be
maintained. Half a century ago, in 1965, when agitprop was gearing
up to transform America into a socialist country (the so-called "Great
Society" of President Johnson), the national debt stood at 1.5 trillion
dollars instead of today's 20 trillion dollars; and federal commitments
for massive future expenditures for which no funding was provided
were unknown.

Fifty years of incessant agitprop in America for "social" justice have "deconstructed" much of the emphasis which American culture puts on personal independence and self-reliance and have moved the United States in the direction of becoming what the Soviet Union was on the eve of its dissolution: a big country with more obligations than it could afford. Too much of America's wealth and its credit-worthiness are now devoted to supporting Soviet-style "social" justice. Too many Americans today depend on Big Government for "social" security. Furthermore, during the eight years of Obama's presidency, a large portion of the American middle class acquired a huge amount of individual debt while the national debt rocketed into the stratosphere. This individual debt is especially evident among college-educated Americans whom the government is "helping" and has "helped."

It is crucial for Americans to understand how the country and so many Americans during the Obama administration fell into so much debt. It happened because *PC Marxists are transforming America into a country of Big Government socialism. And they are achieving their goal by appealing to and manipulating the values and beliefs of American culture.* PC Marxist agitprop became more intense and widespread under Obama's presidency which made Americans feel that being po-litically correct was synonymous with being upstanding Americans. Agitprop has used, for example, the value middle-class Americans put on Christian charity and the common American middle-class sym-pathy for the underdog to demand expansion of government "entitle-ment" programs. The deeply rooted belief of the people of the States in freedom has also been played upon to justify abortion mills (the redefinition of abortion as freedom of choice) which have been killing human beings in various stages of prenatal development at a rate that every five years since 1980 exceeds the six million lives exterminated in the death camps in Hitler's Nazi Germany. This scale of death is destroying America's cultural belief in the sacredness of human life and replacing it with the Marxist idea that human life is no different from other animal life, and that the same ethical standards which apply to the treatment of animals should apply to human beings ("bioethics"). Similarly, PC agitprop is transforming the American cultural belief in the God-given birthright to pursue happiness into a socialist demand for government-delivered "entitlements" for "victimized" classes of people for whom "social" justice must be assured. Likewise, agitprop has appealed to the American cultural belief in equality to make the oxymoronic concept of homosexual marriage ("same-sex marriage") seem identical to Christian marriage and has thus redefined the essential social institution of Western civilization. By rewriting American history as an across-the-board Marxist tale of "victimization," PC Marxists have made a country whose freedom-loving, law-abiding, and opportunity-rich culture has attracted tens of millions of ambitious immigrants from every part of the world into a land of oppression unworthy of respect or devotion. No one need be grateful for living in the country Marxists claim America has been and currently is.

But how, I ask you, could America have produced the world's largest, wealthiest middle class if it was just another location, no different than any other in the world, where the Marxian concept of history as the exploitation of "the have nots" by "the haves" has been played out? If that were true, how did America's enormous, collectively wealthy middle class get created? Naturally, sin and evil have been features of America's history. After all, America is populated by human beings. But where in the annals of human history has that not been the case? In the Soviet Union? In Red China? In Communist Cuba? Don't make me laugh. Tell me of another society apart from the United States that has shown greater compassion, both private and public, toward Marx's "have-nots." Show me another country where so much opportunity for individual initiative and enterprise to exert their creative powers has been so much in evidence. Show me another large nation with a greater level of personal success. Under the influence of agitprop, America's history of individuals taking responsibility for their lives has been rewritten as a narrative of Marxian class struggle, the story of a biologically defined ruling class of Straight Euro-American Males (SEAMs) "victimizing" non-SEAMs. Which doesn't even make sense since there are millionaires in America who are women, Negro Americans, members of ethnic minorities, and homosexuals.

During the eight years of the Obama administration, America saw drastic changes in how the United States was governed and how Americans regard themselves and their country. Historically, the United States has always had two main political parties whose names have varied over the years but which in their general outlook were "conservative" and "liberal." While they differed in emphasis, these were American political parties with a common allegiance to America's culture which acted on the historic beliefs of that culture. For most of the twentieth century, the Republicans may be said to have emphasized fiscal restraint and limiting the federal government to the powers granted it in the Constitution. The Democrats were the party of deficit spending in peacetime and the permissive interpretation of the Constitution which they dubbed "the Living Constitution" doctrine. Up until the 1960s, American foreign policy was for the most part bipartisan. These two political parties vied in national elections for control of Congress and the presidency, but generally kept the good of the nation uppermost in their actions. That no longer seems to be the case. Now, advancing the aims of PC Marxism seems to be the chief consideration of most Democrats, irrespective of the good of the country.

The Democrats of today have become loyal adherents of Political Correctness, and many Republicans have joined them in that loyalty. PC dogmas now dominate the thinking of Democrat leaders and a good many of the leaders in the Republican establishment. Before Donald Trump came on the political scene, Political Correctness had attained such dominance in America that openly and vigorously opposing its agenda and policies was not something that either Democrat and Republican leaders considered possible or cared to undertake.

That the Democrat Party is completely enthralled by the "narrative" of Political Correctness is evident in the disappearance of conservative Democrats from Congress. Not one is left. The Democrat Party now supports and elects only PC candidates. A kind of Soviet-style party discipline now pervades the Democrat Party that exists today, whose members vote as a bloc for whatever their party's leaders tell them to vote for. The good of the country embodied in the principles, procedures, prohibitions, and provisions of the Constitution is no longer the foremost consideration in their thinking. The Republican Party establishment is only somewhat less enthralled by Political Correctness.

The fear of opposing Political Correctness was evident in the pass given Barack Obama's violations of his presidential oath to "preserve, protect, and defend the Constitution" (Article II, Section 1) and his duty as president to "take Care that the Laws be faithfully executed" (Article II, Section 3). As president, he falsely claimed to have the authority to decide which laws he would execute and which he would not, thus assigning himself an absolute veto over the entire corpus of federal law, something the Constitution does not allow a U.S. president to have. Presidents of the United States do have a veto, but it is limited to legislation in the process of being enacting and is not an absolute veto. Congress by a two-thirds vote of both houses can override a presidential veto (Article I, Section 7, Para. 2). But when a president of the United States claims as Obama did the power to not execute a law that has been constitutionally enacted, he is claiming to have an absolute veto. Obama also exercised an unconstitutional power to amend, by a stroke of the pen, a law that had been duly enacted but not yet executed. Obama did this some twenty times to the text of his healthcare bill after it had been enacted and before he in his capacity as president had executed it.

The most consequential legislation of Obama's administration, his healthcare law imposed a tax; yet under his direction it originated in the Democrat-controlled Senate, and then went to the

Democrat-controlled House, despite the unequivocal stipulation in Article I, Section 7, Paragraph 1 of the Constitution that, "All Bills for raising Revenue shall originate in the House of Representative." And it was the Senate version of the bill (the administration's version) which was enacted into law by Obama and his Democrat-controlled Congress without being reconciled with the House version as the rules of Congress require. (The Democrat leaders in Congress simply declared the Senate and the House versions of the bill had been "virtually reconciled.")

Obama acted in the White House like a dictator not limited by the requirements of the Constitution he had sworn to obey when he took office as president of the United States. Yet despite Barack Obama's violations of the Constitution, Congress went along with whatever he did. That is, Republican leaders in Congress grumbled about his behavior sometimes but made no attempt to curb his unconstitutional actions. (See David Freddoso, *Gangster Government: Barack Obama and the Washington Thugocracy*, Regnery Publishing, 2011, and Aaron Klein and Brenda J. Elliott, *Impeachable Offenses: The Case for Removing Barack Obama from Office*, WND Books, 2013.)

Moreover, Republican leaders in Congress said they were helpless to repeal "Obamacare" as long as Democrats controlled both houses of Congress. When voters gave the Republicans majorities in both houses in 2015, they said they could do nothing as long as a Democrat sat in the White House. But in 2017, when a Republican president had been sworn into office and Republicans had a majority in both houses of Congress, Obama's healthcare legislation, which Republican members of Congress had for years vowed to repeal, was still not repealed. That's how fearful of the wrath of Political Correctness the Republican establishment has become.

Because of the fear of Political Correctness (one might call it "PC-phobia"), concern for America's national interest has plummeted in Washington, D.C. Political Correctness is now the dominant concern inside the Washington Beltway, which is why the approval ratings of

Congress with the American public are so abysmally low — under 10% in some polls in recent years. The people of the States, however, are not politically correct the way Congress is. Nor is Donald Trump, which is why the people of the States elected him president, and why the PC Democrats in Congress are "resisting" him and why some Republicans are too. American voters of all political affiliations — Democrats, Independents and Republicans — put Trump in the White House, particularly those of religious sensibilities who have not seen much point in going to the polls to vote in recent elections. Trump's candidacy gave them something to vote for besides one of two flavors of Political Correctness. The people of the States who find Political Correctness disgusting responded to Trump's candidacy enthusiastically because ordinary Americans of all political persuasions want the cultural beliefs which have made America a great country to live in restored to their full authority.

The fact that a highly successful American businessman would even present himself as a candidate for president of the United States is significant. When such a man decides to leave private life to devote his time, intelligence, and fortune to something as arduous as running for the highest elective office in the United States and serving as president, it indicates the degree of his alarm over the condition his country is in and demonstrates an uncommon degree of patriotism.

The pervasive effect of PC Marxism on the Democrat Party was evident in the 1960s when the 88th Congress (a twenty-two-seat Democrat majority in the Senate; an eighty-three-seat majority in the House) passed a series of laws making the federal government responsible for eliminating poverty in America. Called the "War on Poverty" by its Democrat sponsors and the media, these federal programs in 1964 marked the beginning of decades of federal redistribution of wealth in America, a procedure the Constitution does not authorize, and would have to be amended to legitimately authorize. Lyndon B. Johnson — elected to the House of Representative in 1937 as a "New Deal" Democrat who, twenty-six years later as vice-president succeeded President John F. Kennedy when he was assassinated — sponsored the "War on Poverty" which was an enormous Marxification of America *in the name of supposedly living up to the beliefs of American culture.*

The economic context for this massive legislative initiative was quite different from the "New Deal" of Franklin Roosevelt in the 1930s when in some cities and regions of America, unemployment was higher than 25% of the workforce as white and blue collar workers stood in long lines together outside soup kitchens to get a meal. No such severe economic conditions afflicted America in the 1960s. The "War on Poverty" was an ideological endeavor. It was an agitprop assault on the American cultural belief in self-determination. The "War on Poverty" put the United States on its present, accelerating downward spin toward socialism.

Worst of all, the "War on Poverty" has done comparatively little to reduce poverty in the United States, considering how many trillions of dollars have been spent on its proliferating programs in the past half a century. The "War on Poverty" is administering more than ninety federal anti-poverty programs, for instance, which now require hundreds of billions of dollars a year to sustain. Despite such astronomical, ever-increasing expenditures over the last five decades, poverty in the United States as defined by the government has not been reduced in a way commensurate with such outlays. All that has really happened since Johnson's "Great Society" was instituted is (1) the executive branch of the government has gotten much bigger and more powerful and (2) Congress has lost all restraint about borrowing and spending unlimited amounts of money ("deficit spending").

Today, costly full-page ads in glossy American magazines, featuring glamorous movie actresses, decry hunger in America with headlines like, "One in Five American Children Go Hungry." (See for example the *WSJ. Magazine* for May 2017, p. 129.) Such declarations bear no relation to the reality of the federal government's nation-wide school breakfast and lunch programs — the tens of millions of

Americans on federal food stamps — the private "food banks" and "pantries" for alleviating hunger in every fair-size city throughout the country — and the myriad churches and other private organizations in America which conduct "food drives" for the hungry. Given all of this, how can one out of five American kids be experiencing something agitprop calls "food insecurity"? This is Soviet-style propaganda declaring capitalism a failure in the United States because it can't feed the children.

But consider this: 18.8 percent of the current U.S. population of approximately 324 million is under the age of fifteen (*The World Almanac and Book of Facts 2017*, p. 848). For twenty percent of these kids to be suffering from "food insecurity," twelve to twelve and a half million American youngsters would have to be anxious about where their next meal is coming from, despite the government's aforesaid school breakfasts and lunches, federal food stamps, and the myriad private charities in America that provide the needy with food. In addition to the federal and private efforts, the States of the United States also help the poor. And why should beautiful actresses be needed in the hunger ads if there are so many kids lacking food in America? If the problem is so widespread, isn't there a picture somewhere of one hungry-looking kid in a country of over 300 million? And what about the obesity problem among American kids? How can child hunger be such a problem in a nation where overweight children are so much in evidence?

Ever since the 1960s, the decade which saw the beginning of agitprop in America, attacks on American capitalism, one of the pillars of American culture, have been incessant. According to PC Marxists, American capitalism has made no contribution to the prosperity and well-being of America. The agitprop to get rid of capitalist "greed" has become intense in America while PC Marxists offer no explanation of how the United States acquired the largest and wealthiest middle class in world history. Agitprop harps on the "income gap" in America, the sins of capitalism, and the need to create more federal "entitlements."

Agitprop insists that more government aid is urgently needed in America and that the urgency is getting more acute.

Has welfare spending in America decreased when economic times were good? No. Has it continually increased since the "War on Poverty" began in 1964? Yes. Welfare spending has fluctuated, sometimes being greater than at other times, but it has inexorably risen since the 1960s as more and more candidates for handouts have been proposed by PC Marxists and more and more "entitlements" of various kinds have been enacted. This plethora of federal activities has moved America steadily down the road to full-blown socialism. Once an "entitlement" gets established, it is never diminished or canceled. It just gets bigger. Though federal welfare rolls were reduced in 1997–2001 when the Republican Party, under the leadership of Speaker of the House Newt Gingrich (R-GA), managed to win a majority of seats in the Congress, no permanent, wholesale reduction in federal "entitlements," no elimination of entire programs of the "War on Poverty," has ever occurred because too many congressmen fear doing that would upset the PC Marxists and jeopardize their chances of re-election.

# Unsustainable Borrowing, Spending, and Deficits

FEDERAL WELFARE PROGRAMS have been ingeniously designated "entitlements" by PC Marxists to imply that the Constitution requires them. And the government is borrowing the money to pay for these handouts. It is not paying for them from government revenues because American taxpayers would not tolerate for more than one election cycle the taxes which would be necessary to fund the War on Poverty. Any congressman who voted for such gigantic tax increases would be turned out of office the next time he stood for re-election. Therefore, the money to run the U.S. government's "entitlement" programs is borrowed. It's pretend money that no one is accountable for. It's borrowed and there's plenty more when that came from. It's "Monopoly money." The government of the United States today is run on "Monopoly money." And with every year of such government that passes, the government of the United States becomes a less serious, less respectable common enterprise.

There is supposed to be a "debt limit" the government cannot exceed. But that's a fiction. There is no debt limit. As soon as Congress runs out of borrowed money to fund 'entitlements," it simply passes a bill, which both Republican and Democrat presidents show no reluctant about signing, increasing the nation's debt limit so more money can be borrowed for "entitlements." Republicans participate in this scam as well as Democrats.

Were the size of the national debt really limited, Congress would either have to increase taxes steeply to pay for "entitlements" which would be political suicide or massively cut spending which would also be political suicide. Either way, the Entitlement Industry, which is to say the redistribution of wealth in America by the federal government, would collapse, and there might be an unacceptably large turnover in the members of Congress. Under the influence of PC agitprop, the distribution of wealth in America has become a government industry run by and mostly for the benefit of congressmen. The wealth being redistributed is borrowed and is being given not just to the poor but to a growing segment of middle-class American voters. The government's definition of "poverty" in 2015 was an income of $24,257 for a family of four, yet Obama's 2010 healthcare bill made federal subsidies for health care available to families with incomes of $97,000.

The national debt is out of control. Indeed, the entire federal government is out of control, all three branches. Even the judiciary seems to have bought into the Marxian idea of "social" justice requiring massive programs of "entitlements." The cultural idea of limited government, which is the Constitution's most obvious, main principle, is being abandoned and replaced by politically correct "social" justice being funded in the United States (unlike in the Soviet Union) with borrowed money.

Most members of Congress, it seems, once they are elected make staying in office their foremost priority. Being in Congress has become the ambition of a lifetime and the main business of congressmen. And a large part of getting re-elected these days appears to be making sure federal handouts reach one's constituents and that voters know their representatives in Congress "fought" for everyone who could use an "entitlement" to get one. If this means circumventing the Constitution to enhance one's image as a compassionate congressman, so be it. The boondoggles to assure staying in office must continue. In this way, gradually but steadily over the past half-century, stimulated by the drumbeat of PC Marxism's hostility to the United States and its culture of independence and self-determination, a Soviet-style, cradle-to-grave socialism (America's present "entitlement" system) is being put in place, while America's historic set of belief-behaviors (its culture) is being destroyed. Should the dogmas of Cultural Marxism ever completely replace America's cultural belief in self-determination, the United States would no longer be an attractive place for enterprising immigrants from all over the world to come to and work in to fulfill their aspirations.

Federal debt to fund "entitlements" for "social" justice is also destroying America's future-oriented way of life. And if you think the United States of America is too big to suffer a total economic debacle, remember the fate of the financially over-committed and bureaucratically overburdened Soviet government, which the United States is coming to resemble more and more as ever-larger segments of the American middle class become dependent on "entitlements." And while this is happening, another destructive trend is developing: the portion of Americans paying federal taxes is dwindling. During Obama's administration, it was reduced to 47%. (Being excused from paying federal taxes is the equivalent of receiving an "entitlement.") Today roughly half the country no longer has a stake in how the government spends their federal taxes because they don't pay any. Their interest lies in receiving payments from the government. To put the matter another way, half the adult population of America today is subsidizing the other half.

This *danse macabre* or Dance of Death known as "deficit spending" (one might also term it the Dance of Debt) makes future generations of Americans debtors before they are even born. They have no consent in the matter. They are born in debt, but unlike other Americans have not derived any benefit from the national debt. The borrowed money was spent before they were born. Instead of being benefited by "deficit spending," they will be responsible for paying interest on the immense loans that are currently funding the government Entitlement Industry.

There's a name for this condition. It's called peonage, which *The Columbia Desk Encyclopedia* defines as a "system of involuntary servitude based on the indebtedness of the laborer (the peon) to his creditor." The indebtedness is involuntary because it is *inherited* from one's forebears. The escalating U.S. national debt is transforming the next generation of American workers into peons *encumbered by inherited debt*. In 1930, three years before President Franklin Roosevelt initiated the first unconstitutional welfare programs which he and his most ardent followers proudly referred to as "the New Deal," the share of the national debt owed by every American — man, woman, and child — was $131. The share of the national debt every man, woman, and child in the United States now owes is over $49,000. If "unfunded mandates" are taken into account — that is, government obligations to make payments in the future for which no money is currently available — the per capita share of the national debt is in the range of hundreds of thousands of dollars. Young Americans inherit this burden of debt at birth and are responsible for paying the interest on it.

The most ominous symptom of the effect agitprop is having on America is the recent reversal of U.S. statistics on longevity. For the last one hundred years, the trend toward longer life for Americans of both genders has been steadily upward. Americans on the whole have been living longer. But now statistics on longevity in America are starting to decline. The American population is no longer living longer with every passing year. Life-expectancy dropped in 2015; then stabilized, and in 2018 dropped again. This disturbing reversal in longevity is being attributed to an increase in suicides (see Associated Press article by Mike Strobbe in the *Arizona Daily Star*, November 30, 2018, p. A4). Despair is the general cause of people killing themselves, while participation in loving family relations and healthy cultures are the chief factors offsetting such deadly despair. (Life expectancy, you will recall, was declining in the Soviet Union in the years before its collapse.) In 2019, U.S. life expectancy rose slightly.

Why has America been doing this Dance of Death called "deficit spending"? The U.S. government — influenced by PC agitprop and the special interest congressmen have in staying in office — is being run on borrowed money to finance the Marxian dogma of "social" justice. Big Government "entitlements" is why the peacetime national debt of the United States is soaring.

Congressmen have found that "entitlements" paid for by "deficit spending" can garner votes. No need to beat the bushes as much for campaign funds. Just tell the folks back home that you're "fighting" to maintain their "entitlements" and keep them informed of your sterling record of "compassion." Congress seems to have decided there's no problem in borrowing unlimited amounts of money to finance "social" justice. Congress seems to believe the credit of America is inexhaustible, given the historical reputation of the American middle class for productivity and never reneging on its debts. But there has already been one disturbing sign that behavior based on the idea that borrowing can go on and on, without limit, can have adverse consequences. During the Obama administration profligate borrowing caused the credit rating of the United States on the international money market to be downgraded from AAA+ to AAA.

Members of Congress regularly complain about "special interests." But the interest most congressmen have in staying in office until retirement or death, whichever comes first, represents one of the most destructive special interests in existence in America today, because congressmen have a constitutional power to borrow at their discretion and to spend the borrowed money however they see fit. Congress can, therefore, indulge its present reckless behavior of "deficit spending" by constantly raising the limit on borrowing and refusing to cut back on spending. This problem could be solved by adding a clause to the Constitution that Congress must obtain the consent of two-thirds of the States to raise the national debt limit. Reckless "deficit spending" resembles the insanity of a man living off his credit cards instead of his income. As far as Congress is concerned, it seems, borrowing money to pay for "entitlements" to subsidize staying in office is a good thing, because it avoids raising taxes, which voters don't like, while still serving the interest congressmen have of handing out "entitlements" to stay in office.

The continual increase in spending on "entitlements" and the constantly escalating national debt are parts of the same problem. They must be separated if spending and the national debt are to be reduced, as they must be sooner or later unless you think the Tooth Fairy will fund increases in U.S. government spending without limit. And the way to separate the upward spiral of "entitlements" and the constantly increasing national debt, of course, is through term limits for congressmen.

Term limits would have an immediate, permanent effect on the character of Congress and a long-range effect on congressional spending habits. Instead of Congresses whose priority is staying in office through stoking the support of voters by providing them with handouts, term limits would produce Congresses interested in their oath of office to uphold constitutional representative government. But the term limit would have to be significantly less than the twenty-some years in Congress that is not uncommon now. The term would have to be the minimum possible to make it worth the honor of being a U.S. Senator or member of the U.S. House of Representatives but not so long a time in office that the person elected to Congress would develop saleable personal power. A six-year maximum might do the trick; that is one term for Senators instead of the three or four that is now a plausible expectation or the six or seven terms that the "Old Bulls" in the Senate are commonly in office, which attracts "special" interests to them to get their legislative support. For members of the House, a six-year term limit would mean a maximum of three terms. There should be no combination of service in the two houses of Congress. A member would serve either a total of six years in the House or a total of six years in the Senate.

It goes almost without saying that some related further provisions would have to be included in the Term-Limit Amendment.

The amendment should prohibit, under severe criminal penalty, congressmen from profiting while in office from information they receive as members of Congress and prohibit them after their service in Congress from ever becoming a congressional lobbyist or having any post-service congressional privileges.

Of course, retirement benefits would be prohibited for serving a mere six years in Congress. Most importantly, the Term-Limit Amendment for service in Congress should require the State which elects a member of Congress to pay their salary while in office and necessary expenses, such as travel or staffing, related to being in office. Receiving a monthly pay check from Hartford, Columbia, Frankfort, Baton Rouge, Austin, Lincoln, Santa Fe, Helena, Carson City, Sacramento, Juneau, or whatever the capital of the State is from which they are elected would be a positive, constant reminder to members of Congress that they work for the people of the State that elects them, which is, after all, the definition of a constitutional republic.

When the Constitution was written and ratified, term limits made little sense because the whole population of the United States then was just under four million persons, and the State populations from which candidates for Congress were chosen were comparatively small. Today, half the individual States in the United States have populations larger than four million which means that every one of them has an ample supply of qualified persons to choose from to serve six years in Congress and there is sufficient wealth in every State to pay the expenses of their congressional delegations.

Moreover, when the maximum term in Congress is restricted to six years, the required minimum qualifying age for service in the House of Representative and the Senate should be raised to thirty-five and forty-five years respectively to assure that congressmen are more mature and experienced for the required six-year term. The original, comparative low qualifying ages for serving in the House and the Senate were set when the average lifespan of Americans was perhaps thirty years less than it is now.

One of the most important improvements that a six-year maximum term in Congress would bring about is the elimination of nonstop campaign fund raising while in office. The present multiple terms in Congress makes nonstop fund raising while in office almost a prerequisite of office. Under the proposed Term-Limit Amendment, that would no longer be the case. The present nonstop, in-office fund raising is a serious impediment to carrying out a congressman's duties.

Congress has refused to face up to its shameless and irresponsible "deficit spending," which will eventually bankrupt the United States unless it is curbed. The problem is essentially that the U.S. government is spending far too much money. Entire agencies and departments in the executive branch of the federal government need to be eliminated. Unneeded components of the United States government certainly exist. The U.S. Department of Agriculture (every State has one). The U.S. Department of Commerce. The U.S. Department of Education; every State has one of these (triple star this department for elimination). The U.S. Department of Energy. The U.S. Department of Labor. The U.S. Department of Health and Human Services ("Human Services" seems just a bit vague and too all-inclusive, don't you think?). The National Endowment for the Humanities. The National Endowment for the Arts. National Public Radio. Certainly those ninety-some federal job training programs that are part of the "War on Poverty" could be laid on the table for elimination. (Why does the federal government have to train workers?) The process of reducing the size of the present federal behemoth, and thus the size of its spending, once begun would quickly acquire momentum.

Gargantuan waste has been created in Washington by the federal government taking on unconstitutional responsibility for regulating the lives of Americans and redistributing the nation's wealth. Let the

States of the Union be responsible for helping their citizens, if the people of a State decide they need such help. U.S. departments like Commerce and Labor are little more than special-interest lobbies funded by the government to influence itself. Certainly, government bureaus like the National Endowment for the Arts and the National Endowment for the Humanities are inappropriate in undertaking responsibilities government ought not to have. Let individuals or private corporations support the arts or the humanities if they must be subsidized. And let us hear no more talk regarding the funding of any part of the federal government, that "it's really not much money, just a few million dollars a year." That's the kind of talk — a million here, a billion there — that has produced federal spending that has escalated into the trillions of dollars annually. Even the richest man who thinks he can increase his spending as much as he wants to on anything he fancies, simply because he's rich and has an excellent credit rating, will eventually find himself head over heels in debt. Why is there a federal department having the catchall designation "Human Services"? Nonessential programs are too expensive regardless of the size of their budgets.

*Let the general government do only what a State cannot do for itself* ought to be the rule for conducting the desperately needed reform of reducing government services which must be undertaken if we are to lessen the government intrusions into our lives and reduce our now out-of-control national debt. The elimination of unnecessary federal activities will reduce federal spending and debt. It's the only way to address the problem of "deficit spending." The debate in Congress over which parts of the present federal government could be eliminated would develop rationales for putting the kibosh on a lot of needless activities and expense in the future. It would also develop standards to restrain the temptation to instigate future superfluous expenditures.

An amendment limiting the terms of congressmen must become part of the Constitution of the United States before any federal agency or department can be eliminated. Congress without term limits is too invested in Big Government and "entitlement" spending. As long as congressmen can use the power of their office to stay in office, government spending will never decrease, but only increase.

A term-limited Congress could return to writing comprehensive annual budgets as Congress once did, instead of lurching from one "Continuing Resolution" to another. If federal spending were greatly reduced, then it might be possible to know how much federal money was being spent on what. When half the money Congress spends is borrowed, no one much cares what it's spent on or how much more money has to be borrowed.

The biggest savings of all will come from the three branches of the federal government obeying each and every principle, procedure, prohibition, and provision of the Constitution of the United States of America which was conceived to be an instrument for *limiting* the general government rather than permitting it to become a government that intrudes into the lives of Americans and tramples on the constitutional prerogatives of the State governments. The meaning of the American refrain, "A Government of Laws Rather than Men," which is as old as the republic, should once more be taken seriously.

Yet another way to achieve federal savings would be to turn over to the States federal lands within the States, which the States could then sell, lease, or otherwise use as they considered best and the federal government would no longer have the responsibility and expense of administering. Almost without exception, federal lands still inside the States are west of the Mississippi. Why were the western States not given the federal land within their boundaries when they joined the Union, the way the eastern States were? Is it fair that 41% of Arizona's 114,000 square miles is federally owned? I don't think so.

The main thing to be considered in this discussion of drastically reducing the size of the federal government is the fact that half the money the federal government is spending is borrowed. This atrocity against future generations of Americans must be eliminated by cutting federal spending in half. Congress must be stripped of its present constitutional authority to borrow money without the consent of the people of the States and members of Congress should be more closely tied to the States which elect them by limiting their terms and having their States, rather than the federal government, pay their salaries.

Unless federal spending is reduced drastically, which means (1) eliminating entire federal agencies and departments and (2) reducing "entitlements," it is only a question of time, and probably not very much, before the United States experiences an economic catastrophe of unimaginably destructive consequences. A continually increasing national debt cannot be tolerated, especially not when the portion of the American population paying federal income taxes is in decline.

Again, let me say: the demands of politically correct "social" justice are destroying the set of historical belief-behaviors that is America's culture. One of those beliefs is that everyone must work, and manual work is respectable. Young Americans today are being fed an outdated, European line of snobbery. Get a college degree, they are being told and get a white-collar job. Don't work at a manual job because that's demeaning. And while young Americans are being encouraged not to make their livings by taking a blue collar job, hordes of manual workers are being allowed across the U.S. border with Mexico and are being told by PC agitators and propagandists that they don't have to assimilate into America's culture but can keep their native culture while living illegally in the United States. If however, the PC dogma of "multiculturalism," which would have everyone believe every culture is as good as every other, were really true, why are hordes of illegal immigrants trying to get into the United States? Might it be that American culture has given human life and the rule of law more sanctity than many other cultures do and that human beings in the United States have historically had more freedom and opportunity for personal success than elsewhere? PC Marxists answer these questions in the negative, saying there's nothing about American culture that is more worthy than what is available under every other culture's auspices, which is patently false. (Indeed, PC Marxists claim

American culture is deplorable compared to other cultures because it is so greedy and so "victimizing.")

Socialism however you want to define or evaluate it is essentially dependence on government. The increasing dependence of Americans on Big Government which PC agitprop is promoting is making a fundamental change to the American way of life. The word "victimization" which plays so prominent a part in the language of agitprop serves to justify the need for government "entitlements." Agitprop wants Americans to think government must take care of people, that they can't take care of themselves, and don't want to take care of themselves.

Americans used to be notably more future-oriented and independent of government. Before the last fifty years of PC agitprop, they wanted to leave to posterity a prosperous country, only reasonably encumbered by debt, for the next generation to improve further. But that hope no longer seems to exist. Congress's current out-of-control "deficit spending" is burdening posterity with a level of debt perhaps best characterized as evil. "Deficit spending" is not "investing in the future" as PC Marxists say it is. "Deficit spending" is ruining a great nation, something PC Marxists have long wanted to see happen. The destruction of America's culture and its replacement by Cultural Marxism are goals they have been pursuing for fifty years.

In the past, the size of the federal government and the national debt increased markedly only when the U.S. was in a major war (World War I, World War II, Korea, Vietnam) and a lot more money was needed to pay for the war effort. But since the advent of agitprop in the 1960s, the federal government just keeps getting bigger and more costly whether the country is at war or not. Which is undoubtedly why the "War on Poverty" was called a *war*: to justify wartime levels of "deficit spending" in peacetime.

Today's Congress resembles a deranged man who habitually spends half again more than his annual income, year after year, and goes to a bank he controls (despite his deranged behavior) to borrow money enough to make up the difference between his income and his profligate spending habits. This man, whose "deficit spending" grows worse by the year, tells himself he's not behaving recklessly because his heirs will be strong enough economically to bear every burden he is imposing on them. But how can they be when they are responsible for paying so much interest on borrowed money, money they did not themselves borrow or benefit from and which is a dead loss to them? Unless the government's "deficit spending" is reduced — not just a little or temporarily but drastically and permanently — America has no future as a notably great and free nation.

Instead of an honest government living within its means, the United States today has a politically correct, corrupt government which is forcing destructive levels of debt on future generations of Americans. The U.S. government is becoming a deceitful, bloated, crooked regime not unlike the USSR was at the time of its collapse, a regime which cares more about staying "in power" and maintaining a facade of "Political Correctness" than about being either lawful or responsible.

The United States today is a debtor nation because Marxian social-ism is being "built" in America on a foundation of debt. The solution requires getting rid of socialist "entitlements" and restoring the full rigor of American culture's belief in self-determination — with a "safety net" only for truly hard-luck cases and nobody else.

All this talk today about the United States being a "superpower" is malarkey. The United States is not a superpower. No nation with as much chronic and ever-growing peacetime debt as the United States has, is financial sound enough to be called a superpower. Because of the pernicious influence of agitprop, the government lacks the will to be fiscally sound. The U.S. government isn't healthy. Like the USSR in the 1980s, it is over-committed.

During and following the Second World War, America was a superpower. It fought simultaneous major wars on opposite sides of the planet; recruited and equipped huge armies, navies, and air forces manned by twelve million Americans, which the government trained, while at the same time providing its allies immense quantities of food and military supplies. The production of military equipment by the United States during World War II reached astonishing levels. For example, launching a seaworthy cargo ship within a few days of laying its keel in the shipyard and rolling a ready-to-fly B-24 bomber off the assembly line every sixty-three minutes at just one U.S. aircraft factory. Such stupendous feats of productivity by American factory workers, miners, and farmers during World War II signified America's superb combination of exceptional cultural resources with exceptional natural resources.

America was indeed a superpower during World War II and for a couple of decades afterward — say the thirty years from 1942 through the early 1970s — when citizen-soldiers provided the bulk of America's frontline military forces. After abolishing the draft as a result of the agitprop surrounding the Vietnam War and converting to all-professional armed forces, America's military strength has waned, as indicated by the strain the U.S. Army has been under in fighting recent small wars in Iraq and Afghanistan against irregular but diehard local forces. These small military engagements have dragged on and on without resolution. Except for the manpower furnished by State militias, the professional U.S. military forces today would have had a hard time deploying even the moderate forces it has deployed in Afghanistan and Iraq. One gets the impression that there is too high a ratio of "support personnel" to combat troops in the U.S. military today and too many generals and admirals in relation to the number of soldiers, marines, airmen, sailors, and coastguardsmen. And that there's too much folderal in the military services in deference to the dogmas of Political Correctness. Is it time to go back to congressionally declared wars only? Not until Congress is term-limited would that be advisable. Should the draft be restored and the idea of an all-professional force abandoned? Perhaps. What is clear is that we must have military forces equipped with high-tech weapons and that robust budgets for military research and development are therefore necessary. Infantry capable of rapid deployment to serve America's vital interests are also advisable. But most of all, it seems, we must renounce the pernicious development of Congresses comprised of majorities of lifetime officeholders who determine their own compensation and the amount of money they can borrow for increasing "deficit spending."

And consider this, please. Does America need to be a so-called "superpower" everywhere in the world all the time? I would say not, and I would add to that observation that America should not have a military presence in Europe at all. We have been subsidizing Europe's military defense far too long when the nations of Europe collectively have a much larger population than the United States and collectively a larger gross domestic product than the United States. World War II ended in victory for Western civilization in 1945. The Cold War with the Soviet Union ended in victory for the West in 1991. Europe recovered from the devastation of World War II a long, long time ago, and is now capable of defending itself from an external or intra-continental enemy. If it isn't, then the question must be raised, does Europe deserve to survive? A similar blunt question must also be asked regarding the United States. Does America deserve to survive if it continues to tolerate a corrupt, unconstitutional general government and allows itself to be dominated by PC Marxism?

# American Imperialism

S TARTING IN THE 1960S, Marxist agitprop incessantly pummeled Americans with the accusation that the United States was an "imperialist" country. Marxists denied that America's fabulous national wealth was the result of its exceptional abundance of natural resources in combination with an extraordinarily strong cultural belief in work among its uniquely large middle class, whose members put a premium on supporting themselves and providing for their families. Marxist agitprop disagreed. It attributed America's fabulous wealth to "American imperialism." The United States was immensely wealthy, Marxists in America and elsewhere said, because it robbed other nations and kept them poor. That's why America was the richest nation in world history. The United States was responsible for global poverty, the Marxists yammered. Just look at the import-export figures, they argued. U.S. exports were larger than its imports. Obviously, America was "exploiting" the countries it traded with, and the imbalance in its trade with them showed precisely how much it was exploiting them.

A new sort of "global economy," a "new world order," was needed which would eliminate "American imperialism" and the "exploitation" of other nations, agitprop in America clamored. American manufacturing jobs should be sent to poor countries where workers would work for less pay, thus benefiting both American capitalists and also American consumers through cheap imports while at the same time improving the standard of living of the foreign workers, who would eventually become customers for U.S. goods. That would be a "win-win" situation. Moving American manufacturing to China in the 1970s was the first important step in implementing this Marxist "scenario" or "narrative."

Let's examine the result of this plan for redeeming the United States from its "imperialism." Before 1975, the balance of trade between the United States and other countries varied of course from year to year but did favor America, which is to say the value of goods the United States imported following the end of World War II (1945) was consistently less than the value of goods it exported. But starting in the mid-1970s, about a decade after agitprop started beating the drum about "American imperialism," the yearly balance of trade in America's favor disappeared and then was reversed. The United States went from being a nation that exported between three and twelve billion dollars more each year to other countries than it imported from them to being a nation whose imports exceeded its exports *by hundreds of billions of dollars annually.* By 1985 the difference in U.S. imports over exports was nearly $122 billion: ten times more than the maximum balance of trade in America's favor prior to then. Fifteen years later, in 2000, the discrepancy of U.S. imports over exports had risen to $372.5 billion; five years after that, it was a mind-numbing $714 billion dollars. Since 2005, the annual U.S. trade deficit has lessened but remains in the range of hundreds of billions of dollars against America a year; and China now rivals the U.S. as the world's richest nation, and holds the largest part of the U.S. debt.

The PC agitprop of the 1960s and 1970s about "American imperialism" was the first instance of relentless name-calling changing American behavior, as Americans sought to avoid a slur that they found obnoxious. Accusing the U.S. of "imperialism" illustrates yet again one of the basic principles of propaganda: the more mendacious the lie, the less difficulty getting people to believe it.

The distinction PC propaganda makes between an American consumer and an American producer is, of course, another example of malarkey. The American worker is the American consumer. That was Henry Ford's secret of success: pay your factory line workers a high wage and they can buy the cars they make, and the Ford Motor Company will get rich. Which it did. Very rich. Henry Ford's philosophy made automobiles a common possession of the American working class, which is to say a big part of the American middle class. What is the benefit of cheap imports if American workers have no robust paycheck (or any at all) or are just scraping by on one or two part-time family paychecks, and don't have the wherewithal to be free and easy consumers? The American "standard of living" once so much vaunted was eroded during Obama's presidency by his slow-to-no-recovery from recession, anemic economic growth, promotion of Big Government, fixation on "social" justice and "entitlements," widespread underemployment, and burgeoning debt both for college graduates and the nation. Obama produced more middle-class dependence on government and advocated more national and private debt than it is healthy for America to have.

From the time of America's beginnings in the early seventeenth century to the present, the most important single belief of American culture, apart from belief in God, has been, "Everyone must work, and manual work is respectable." Under Obama's administration of the federal government, that belief was weakened by too many Americans who wanted a full-time job being unable to find one after years of diligently searching. These despairing workers who finally gave up looking for work were not even counted in the government statistics as unemployed because only men and women still looking for work are counted in the government's statistics as unemployed.

Not surprisingly, unemployment and underemployment became chronic during the presidency of a PC Marxist who spoke of "a new normal," of consuming less, setting the thermostat lower, and being frugal in the use of toilet paper: a president whose wife said with palpable sincerity that she had never been proud to be an American until her husband was nominated to run for president. As both presidential candidate and president, this Saul Alinsky follower, Barack Obama, who attended for years the Rev. Jeremiah Wright's Liberation Theology church in Chicago where America was vehemently and repeatedly damned from the pulpit, kept his disdain for America well hidden. He had to: otherwise, he could never have gotten elected president of the United States twice. Obama had an engaging wonderful smile and a natural aptitude for deception. He could project a remarkable appearance of sincerity. Under his presidency, the Marxist agenda for destroying America proceeded on all fronts without even appearing to exist. As a former teacher of Alinsky's rules for radicals, he was a deceiver to whom hypocrisy was second nature.

Interestingly, the years of Obama's presidency, when unemployment and underemployment in America were chronic, were also years of agitprop about the need for the government to help young Americans attend college, which led to such massive loan debt for American college students that the socialist idea of government-paid-for college education began to be seriously considered. Another PC agitprop theme of Obama's presidency was that "migrants" (i.e. illegal aliens) had to be allowed across the southern border of the United States because Americans wouldn't perform hard manual work. But if that were so, how did Americans civilize a continent-size expanse of Stone Age wilderness in record time?

What America needs at present is a return to an economy that puts American jobs first. It cannot be emphasized too much or too often that in America's cultural history one of the foremost belief-behaviors has been that *everyone must work and manual work is respectable.* Work has a central significance to American culture and is a defining element of what it means to be an American, which is why Americans always want to know on becoming acquainted with someone, "What do you do?" and don't feel altogether comfortable until they do know what the new acquaintance's work is. Work is an integral part of American culture and the American identity.

In the past fifty years, agitprop in America has succeeded in reducing a self-governing, self-respecting, future-oriented, exceptionally confident, highly successful nation into a backward-looking, guilt-ridden, self-doubting, debtor nation with a crooked government and a citizenry that is increasingly semi-literate and increasingly divided into warring camps. Obviously, a marked deterioration of America's culture has occurred in the past five decades. (But it is not an irredeemable decline.) Condemning America and its history has become intellectually fashionable at U.S. institutions of higher learning, and U.S. public schools have been in too many cases converted into incubators of PC Marxism. American history is being rewritten and taught from a Marxian point of view: Karl Marx's conspiratorial narrative of "the haves" exploiting, robbing, and killing off "have nots." Political Correctness now dominates the Democrat Party, a significant segment of the Republican Party, American higher education and the public schools, and almost the entire U.S. media and much of the entertainment industry. Even many American ministers, priests, and rabbis have become politically correct.

The above-mentioned institutions, particularly the public schools, exert an enormous influence on the way Americans perceive themselves and their history. Because of PC agitprop, many Americans have gone from regarding their country as the greatest nation in history to seeing it as a land of remorseless oppression which is the Marxist "line" about America. PC Marxism is now so common in the public schools, colleges, and universities of America that any expression of gratitude for being an American is likely to be greeted with derision by PC Marxists and their sympathizers, who tend to regard love of America as a sign of either stupidity or "naivety." The term "white nationalist" is the term du jour of the PC agitators and propagandists for American patriots, especially the patriot now in the White House.

# PC Marxist Dominance
# in U.S. Public Schools

B
Y FAR THE MOST important U.S. institution in its influence on American attitudes toward American history are the public schools of the United States, where most Americans get their only study of U.S. history. Our nation's history is now (significantly) being referred to in the public schools as "social studies" because it's being taught mostly from the perspective of socialism, specifically the perspective which sees America's history in terms of Karl Marx's concept of history as class struggle and the conspiracy of the rich against the poor.

By way of illustrating the anti-American views of PC Marxists, here is a sampling of remarks made after the sneak aerial attacks on Manhattan and Washington by Islamic terrorists on September 11, 2001. These coordinated attacks were the deadliest by a foreign enemy on U.S. soil since Japanese naval aviators bombed the American naval base at Pearl Harbor in a sneak air attack on December 7, 1941. On September 11, 2001, nineteen Islamic suicide bombers hijacked four fully fueled transcontinental airliners and used them as mega-bombs to kill as many Americans as were killed at Pearl Harbor.

*The Nation* (a leftist journal) said that any military retaliation by the U.S. government for these attacks would "reinforce the worse elements in our society—the flag-wavers, and bigots, and militarists."

Barbara Kingsolver said something quite similar, that the American flag stands for "intimidation, censorship, violence, bigotry, sexism, homophobia, and shoving the Constitution through the paper shredder." Columbia University professor Eric Foner was unsure which was worse: "the horror that engulfed New York City [on September 11, 2001] or the apocalyptic rhetoric emanating daily from the [George Bush] White House." MIT Professor Noam Chomsky, whose high-toned anti-American vitriol has been a prominent feature of his rhetoric since and before his days as a "protester" against the Vietnam War, instead of finding fault with the nineteen Islamic terrorists accused the government of the United States of having killed "maybe a million civilians in Iraq and maybe half a million children." Chomsky's "maybe" accusation, that America had committed far worse slaughters in other nations than the September 11 massacre of Americans, was a recurring theme in PC remarks on the Islamic terror attacks.

At the University of New Mexico, history professor Richard A. Berthold told his class, "Anyone who can blow up the Pentagon has my vote." That was protected free speech. But when political science professor Kenneth Hearlson declared, "I want to see the Arab world stand up and say, 'This is wrong,'" administrators at Orange Coast College in California where he taught reprimanded him for being "insensitive." Similarly, when an Arab-speaking student at San Diego State University overheard Arab students praising the acts of the Islamic terrorists and reported what he heard to school officials, he was put "on warning" by administrators for making his report. In New York City, the location of the worst slaughter and destruction, the president of ABC News, David Westin, told his newscasters not to wear American-flag lapel pins on camera because that would be "taking sides." Administrators at Brown University in Rhode Island issued guidelines to the faculty for discussing with Brown students why the United States is hated around the world, which was evidently what mattered to these politically correct academic "trolls."

The full context for these and further examples of anti-American-ism by PC Marxists can be found in Mona Charen, *Useful Idiots: How Liberals Got It Wrong in the Cold War and Still Blame America First* (Regnery, 2003); Daniel J. Flynn, *Intellectual Morons: How Ideology Makes Smart People Fall For Stupid Ideas* (Three Rivers Press, 2004); Brad Miner, *Smear Tactics: The Liberal Campaign to Defame America* (Harper, 2007); Jason Mattera, *Obama Zombies: How the Liberal Machine Brainwashed My Generation* (Threshold Editions, 2010); and Paul Kengor, *Dupes: How America's Adversaries Have Manipulated Progressives for a Century* (ISI Books, 2010). See also David Horowitz and Jacob Laksin, *One-Party Classroom: How Radical Professors at America's Top Colleges Indoctrinate Students* (Crown Forum, 2009).

To PC Marxists and their sympathizers, there is no positive mean-ing in the fact that more human beings have chosen to immigrate to the United States than to any other place on earth. That fact goes undiscussed. But surely the statistics on immigration suggest that America is *not* what PC agitators and propagandists say it is: a land of unmitigated oppression. Surely the reasons America has been at-tractive to immigrants are worth considering in the classrooms of America's public schools.

Another aspect of America's exceptional history which is being neglected in American education is the fact that in just four centuries America grew from a settlement of 107 colonists which was barely surviving on the edge of a continental expanse of Stone Age wilder-ness (Jamestown, Virginia) into the world's third-largest political entity in size (the Russian Federation is first, Canada second) and the third-largest nation in population after China and India.

The principal reason for this astonishing growth was, of course, the continual influx generation after generation of large numbers of hardworking, future-oriented, ambitious immigrants who in America found the freedom and opportunities which allowed them to exert their maximum efforts to attain their dreams of achievement. Their American-born descendants imitated their parents by also working diligently to accomplish their ambitions. The immigrants and their descendants were encouraged to do their utmost because the scarcity of workers for hire in America made hired laborers better paid. (Labor for hire was comparatively scarce because workers in America, being comparatively well-paid, were continually leaving the labor-for-hire market to become property owners and employers of labor.) Without the constant influx of diligent workers, America's rapid development would not have occurred, and without a continual high volume of legal immigration today, the U.S. population would be in the same condition as the populations of Europe and Japan. Instead, because of a high volume of legal immigration, America's population continues to grow.

Another prominent feature of U.S. history that needs to be appreciated is the invention of a way to write and ratify constitutions to institute government by "Consent of the Governed." This breakthrough in self-government is not getting the attention it should have today in America's public schools, colleges, and universities.

(In the last fifty years, immigrants to America have offset to some extent anti-American PC agitprop by informing their children of how much better conditions in America are compared to conditions in the countries they left behind. Thus, a patriotic gratitude for the American way of life has been instilled in the minds and hearts of the offspring of immigrants who have come to live and work in America.)

The anti-American Marxists in America say the United States has always been and will always be a land of oppression run by cruel racists and greedy capitalists until the dogmas of Cultural Marxist prevail and transform it. PC Marxists like Al Gore call the repetition of the same thing over and over again "staying on message." The purpose of such messaging is indicated by a character in Lewis Carroll's comic poem *The Hunting of the Snark* (1876) who says, "What I tell you three times is true." The falsehood that America is, was, and always will be a land of oppression has been repeated so many times in America's classrooms, lecture halls, and media outlets in the past fifty years that it has begun to convince some Americans of good will.

The first Soviet agents sent by the Communist Party of the Soviet Union to the United States in the 1920s to foment revolution in America invented the word exceptionalism. It was the term they used to ridicule the American claim that America's history was different from that of other nations. Marxists had to ridicule that claim because to let it stand unchallenged would have jeopardized Marx's theory of history as "science" since the truth of science is the same everywhere, no exceptions. Americans of all political persuasions in the 1920s, including liberals, believed in America's uniqueness, as can be seen in the memoir on the 20s by the American liberal novelist John Dos Passos (1896–1970), *The Best of Times* (1966), in which he says: "The Marxist codifiers had long since labeled our heresy [that America's history is different] American Exceptionalism." The only child of a highly successful Portuguese immigrant, Dos Passos was reclassified by his liberal friends in the 1950s as a conservative because he remained true to the values and beliefs of American culture as they moved leftward toward PC Marxism.

Perhaps you recall that a reporter once asked Barack Obama when he was president if he considered America an exceptional nation. As a PC Marxist, he replied that lots of people consider their nation's history exceptional, citing the people of Greece as an example. Obama evidently forgot Americans invented the word OK, Coca-Cola, and a billed cap which can be adjusted to fit any size head. No other country in the world has invented a universally used word, beverage, and headgear. These are matters of pop culture, to be sure. But on a more consequential note, before America became known during World War II as an exceptionally great nation, only half a dozen nations had written constitutions as the United States did. Now, few nations lack such constitutions. That's an American contribution of great cultural significance. But Obama when asked if he considered America an exceptional nation could think of no exceptional contribution America had made.

Agitprop has made U.S. public schools centers for anti-American agitprop. American public school students need therefore to hear some rousingly patriotic perspectives on America's history to offset the Marxist perspective which is the mainstay of "social studies" in U.S. public schools. The three accomplishments in American history just mentioned: America's immigration history; America's unprecedented rate of development; the American invention of ways to write and ratify constitutions for self-government come readily to mind as suitable topics for study to offset the PC message of American imperialism, genocide, racism, etc. which is called "social studies" in U.S. public schools today.

We do not want teachers in our public schools to tell young Americans that the history of their country is an uninterrupted tale of immaculate civic virtue and invariable Judeo-Christian morality from the settlement at Jamestown in 1607 until the American astronaut Neil Armstrong stepped on the surface of the moon 362 years later, because that would not be true. But neither is the rata-tat-tat of telling American kids to be ashamed of their country's history true. We need graduates from our public high schools who have at least some knowledge of why they can be grateful to be an American.

As I've said, the fact that studying U.S. history in America's high schools today is referred to as "social studies" suggests the prevalence of the Marxist point of view in them, but so too does the idea of "social promotion" in the schools, which is incompatible with American culture's emphasis on personal not class responsibility. Teaching in the public schools the skills and knowledge which enable young Americans to lead self-determining lives seems to be taking a backseat to indoctrination in "social" justice. It is likewise worth noting that PC Marxists refer to the restructuring of the United States which they are attempting as "social engineering," another term also in common use today in America.

What's not being taught in the public schools of America that should be? How about the Constitution of the United States as the only law in America ever approved by the people of every one of the fifty States? Young Americans in the public schools are not getting the knowledge of how this charter for government was intended to limit the power of the general government while still providing for the "general Welfare" of the States. American public school students need to understand the principle of the separation of powers in the Constitution evident in Article I, Sections 8, 9, and 10; Article II, Section 2; Article III, Section 2; Articles IV, V, and VI; and the Bill of Rights. American school kids need to thoroughly understand the reasons for these many separations of power. They need to be able to recite the principle of the separation of powers and to answer detailed questions about it in writing. They need to know how different this principle is in comparison to the British constitution and to the Administrative or "deep" state which has been developed in Washington, D.C. in the last fifty years and which unconstitutionally abolishes the separation of powers principle by combining all three functions of government in itself.

Students in the public schools also need to be able to read beyond a fourth-grade level. In too many of the schools today, that skill is not being learned, even though the ability to read beyond a fourth-grade level is essential to participating in the U.S. economy and to performing the duties of U.S. citizenship. Too many American school kids today are not attaining the ability to read that they must have to lead self-determining lives. Too many are being promoted from grade to grade on the basis of the biological class they happen to belong to ("social" promotion), without being required to improve their ability to read. Such "social" promotions defeat the purpose of the public schools because they are based on considerations other than a student's skills and knowledge. These unearned "social" promotions from grade to grade benefit neither the students who receive them nor the society that has at great expense established the schools and maintains them. "Social" promotion produces too many semi-literate high school graduates, the future citizens of the United States. In too many cases, these semi-literate eighteen-year-olds will be only semi-competent and semi-successful. Semi-literacy has, however, great value for PC Marxism by making the future citizens of the United States more susceptible to the deceits of agitprop.

The failure of U.S. public schools to teach more than rudimentary reading skills is so widespread that common-sense, patriotic Americans who understand that a semi-literate America will be only semi-free and semi-prosperous have organized programs throughout the country to teach reading. In 1995, for instance, the several Rotary Clubs in my hometown, Tucson, Arizona, population half a million, started "Reading Seed" to supplement the teaching of reading in the public schools. Sixteen years farther on, in 2011, "Reading Seed" merged with four other groups in Tucson with a like purpose ("Literacy Volunteers of Tucson," "Reach Out and Read, Southern Arizona," "Literacy for Life Coalition," and "Stories That Soar!") to ensure that the necessary level of literacy is attained by the school-age young adults of this one American city. The more comprehensive reading program has been named "Literacy Connects." Many such volunteer-taught reading programs have been organized by civic-minded Americans across the United States. They would be unnecessary if the public schools were doing their job.

There have also been initiatives by devoted patriots like the late Barbara Bush, wife of the 41st president of the United States, who stated in her *Memoir* that the purpose of the Barbara Bush Foundation for Family Literacy is to "establish literacy as a value in every family in America by helping every family in the nation understand that the home is the child's first school, that the parent is the child's first teacher, and that reading is the child's first subject" (p. 565). This mission statement suggests that responsibility for literacy in America lies primarily with the family, a suggestion which lets the public schools and the teachers' unions off the hook.

In the late nineteenth century, when America was inundated by massive waves of immigrants who did not speak English, the public schools stepped up to meet the challenge. They did not rely on Rotary Clubs or private foundations like Mrs. Bush's to do their job for them. Obviously, those millions of non-English-speaking parents couldn't teach their children to read English in the home because they didn't themselves know English. In fact, it seems the children of these immigrants often taught their parents the English reading and speaking skills they themselves learned in school. Where are the "educationists" of the public schools of America today? They're busy blaming the parents of their students for their children's failure to read English competently. They do not blame themselves.

The alarming underperformance of the public schools today in teaching reading above a fourth-grade level and the alarming tendency of the schools to teach American government and history from the point of view of socialism reflect the same thing: the dominance of Political Correctness in the schools.

This development has coincided with the two major institutional developments in public education that took place in the United States in the 1970s: the establishment of the U.S. Department of Education and the organization of national teachers' unions. The argument for these institutional innovations was the same in each case. Expert, professional supervision of public schools nationwide was needed to assure that the highest quality of primary and secondary education existed in every State and every community across the U.S. But the quality of public schooling in America has not improved since the U.S. Department of Education and the teachers' unions came on the national scene. The quality of the public schools has, instead, noticeably deteriorated.

If the complete takeover of the United States by Cultural Marxism is to be avoided, the U.S. Department of Education must be abolished, the influence of the teachers' unions must be firmly curtailed, if not eliminated, and control of the public schools must be returned to the States and local school boards. There is no need in the United States for a federal department of education. There is a department of education in every State. Moreover, the Tenth Amendment of the Bill of Rights ("The powers not delegated to the United States by the Constitution, nor prohibited by it to the States, are reserved to the States respectively, or to the people") prohibits the federal government from being involved in the education of children, just as it bars federal interference with the religious practices of the people of the States. However good an idea it may appear to be to have the federal government involved in the improvement of the public schools, the people of the States knew quite well in 1787–1791 what they we doing when they insisted that the Bill of Rights, with its Tenth Amendment, be added to the Constitution. Supervision of public education and jurisdiction over the personal liberties enumerated in the Bill of Right must be left to local and State authority.

The federalization of U.S. public schools in the 1970s opened the way to the politicization of the public schools. The U.S. Department of Education issued regulations to control the public schools by making federal money available to the school districts that complied with the regulations. The federalization of America's public schools has proven to be a thoroughly bad idea. It has made primary and secondary education in America vulnerable to centrally controlled curriculums and course content, and everything which such control produces by way of uniformity of thought.

Teachers unions were supposed to ensure that only knowledgeable teachers with a strong sense of professionalism would teach America's youth. But like every trade union, the teachers' unions put the economic well-being of their members at the top of their agenda. This is only natural. Teachers unions exist to promote job protection, better pay and working conditions, and more benefits for their members. Pay, working conditions, benefits, job tenure, are the bread and butter issues of unions. Educating America's youth is not the main concern. Albert Shanker, president of the second-largest national teachers union, the American Federation of Teachers (the National Educational Association is the largest), stated the matter quite frankly in a moment of unguarded truthfulness, "When children pay dues, I will represent the children."

Teachers unions protect the jobs of unfit teachers, as can be seen in the public schools of New York City. Since the advent of teachers' unions in that huge public school system, teachers barred by school administrators from having classroom contact with students because of some gross ignorance or egregious delinquency cannot be dismissed for cause because of their union contracts. Instead, they must be kept on the public payroll — sometimes for quite a while — as the complicated process for hearing their case which their union contract establishes runs its pettifogging course. During that protracted process, these unfit "teachers" report to special locations for the same number of hours they would work if they were still classroom teachers, and are paid as if they were still working. They pass their time reading, watching television, gossiping, playing electronic games, and working on their computers. These holding pens have fittingly been nicknamed "rubber rooms," the nickname used for the padded cells in insane asylums where out-of-control inmates are kept to prevent them from harming themselves and others.

Eliminating union protection of unfit teachers is probably the most urgent priority in any effort to improve the quality of public schooling in the United States. Having only knowledgeable teachers of good character in the classroom is the only way the schools can turn out the number of skilled, knowledgeable high-school graduates of good character the country needs. I would likewise observe that ignorance and moral delinquency (if proven) are not the only cause for prompt dismissal of a teacher by a school board. The use of public school classrooms for propaganda and agitation (political indoctrination) also constitutes legitimate grounds for terminating a teacher. The public schools have been created and are maintained at great public expense not to dispense political indoctrination but to give young

Americans an adequate preparation for their future lives in the United States. Local school boards are the only practical custodians of the mission of the public schools because they represent the fundamental interests of the taxpayers who support the schools for the good of the students in them and the general good of American society.

That the public schools in the United States are failing in many instances to do the job they should be doing and are meant to do is clear. The commonness of high-school graduates who can't read above a fourth-grade level is only one symptom of the failure. Another is that twenty percent of the parents of school-age kids in America have chosen at considerable expense and inconvenience to educate their children outside the public school system. Three percent of American kids are being formally taught at home; six percent are being educated in charter schools; and twelve percent are being sent to private schools, most of which are not the expensive prep schools that that term conjures up but schools run and subsidized by churches who charge low tuition and admit students on a first come, first served basis. The administrative cost of these church-run schools per student is much lower than that of the unionized schools; yet students educated in the church-run schools generally outperform public school students on standardized tests of knowledgeable and skills.

Another sign of the failure of the public-school system is the high proportion of foreign students enrolled in the graduate programs of American colleges and universities in such demanding fields as math, engineering, and science. Without these enrollees from abroad, many of the science, math, and engineering graduate programs in America's institutions of higher learning today would dry up and blow away. Not long ago, the United States ranked third in the world behind Japan and Finland in the proportion of its public-school graduates who went on to college to take degrees in engineering. Now the United States ranks twenty-first in the world in that attainment. That's why there aren't enough American undergraduates to matriculate in graduate programs in demanding fields like math, engineering, and science. As public schooling in the U.S. has deteriorated, employers have gotten by on their in-house training programs, the skills and knowledge of kids educated at home and in private schools, charter schools, and the public schools that still manage one way or another to provide quality education.

What do private schools, charter schools, and home schooling have in common? (1) No interference from teachers' unions. (2) No interference from the U.S. Department of Education. (3) Political Correctness is not a factor in what is taught and how it is taught. Charter schools, church schools, and home-schooling parents are free to teach the skills and knowledge their students need to learn and to teach them in cost-effective and pedagogically sound ways. These schooling options can also teach belief in God because they do not fall under the U.S. Supreme Court's ban on teaching principles of Judeo-Christianity, as the public schools do.

The PC dogma "Separation of Church and State" which justified the Supreme Court's religious bans in the public schools would have astonished the Second Continental Congress which wrote the Declaration of Independence and opened its meetings with prayer asking for God's guidance and protection. Similarly, the First Congress to assemble under authority of the U.S. Constitution created an office of congressional chaplains to open Congress's meetings with prayer, an institution which continues to this day. That First Congress also established a chaplain service for the armed forces of the United States which has continued down to the present.

The federally imposed "secularization" of America's public schools in the 1960s has weakened belief in God which is the foundation of morality and culture in America. The sanctity of human life in America also derives from belief in God. Without belief in the God of Moses and Jesus, we cannot expect freedom, equality, and morality to last in American culture. Here is the text of the twenty-two-word prayer which the U.S. Supreme Court declared "unconstitutional" in 1962: "Almighty God, we acknowledge our dependence upon Thee, and we beg Thy blessings upon us, our parents, our teachers, and our Country" (*Engel v. Vitale*, 370 U.S. 421, 1962). A committee of pastors from various religions and Christian denominations had been commissioned by the school board of the State of New York to write a short prayer for voluntary use in the public schools of the State. The twenty-two-word prayer just quoted which they produced was not an establishment of religion because its recital did not result in any preferential treatment being bestowed on the students who recited it or their parents by the State of New York. A religious establishment invariably does bestow preferential governmental treatment. That is the whole purpose of a religious establishment, to confer special favors on one religion over all others because it is the one a government prefers its citizens or subjects to practice. Parents who objected to the simple religious exercise just cited, acknowledging God's existence and man's dependence on him, had their children automatically excused from it. But only a handful of parents did object. Almost all the parents of students in the public schools of the State wanted their children to acknowledge God's existence by reciting the prayer.

Belief in God is the premise for the Declaration of Independence's argument that America's independence from British rule was in accord with God's natural law. Moreover, the Declaration proclaims that God has made "Life, Liberty, and the Pursuit of Happiness" and government by "the Consent of the Governed" inalienable human rights. As Thomas Jefferson said in his *Notes on the State of Virginia*, if belief in God is ever lost in America, there will then be no foundation for the American form of government. Which is why, when Jefferson was president and there were too few churches in the nation's nascent capital to accommodate would-be worshippers, he allowed government buildings to be used as places of worship.

It should be noted here that the government of the Soviet Union did not permit public acknowledgment of God. Religion in the Soviet Union was considered strictly a "private matter" which is also the position the U.S. Supreme Court has taken. It did not satisfy the high

Court that the State of New York excused students from reciting the prayer produced by the interfaith committee of pastors if their parents objected to their participation. No, recitation of a non-denominational prayer on public property had to be *forbidden* altogether, to achieve a complete, Soviet-style "secularization" of the public schools. Religious American parents were blocked from having their children learn belief in God in the public schools. The Court was willing to protect the feelings of non-believing parents from being "offended," but not to accommodate the feelings of believing parents. Otherwise, the Supreme Court said in 1962, students who did not participate in the prayer exercise at the beginning of the school day would feel "left out," even though it was their parents' wish that they should be left out. The Court didn't think its religious ban was a violation of the Constitution's guarantee of the "free exercise" of religion in the Bill of Rights. The U.S. Supreme Court in handing down its 1962 school prayer decision sacrificed the wishes of the overwhelming majority of parents in the State of New York, and hence in all the other States of the Union as well, to the feelings of a tiny minority who were offended by the voluntary recitation of a twenty-two-word non-denominational prayer acknowledging the existence of God and man's dependence on him.

The Pledge of Allegiance to the American flag at the beginning of each school day has also been subjected to the same sort of unconstitutional interference by federal courts. The Supreme Court excused Seventh Day Adventist students from participating in the Pledge; then granted all students, for the sake of uniformity, the right to refuse to say the Pledge of Allegiance to the flag so they wouldn't feel "different" from Seventh-Day Adventist students. In banning voluntary religious exercises in the schools and the requirement to recite the Pledge of Allegiance, beliefs of American culture are being suppressed by the federal government *in the name of upholding religious freedom.* As pointed out in Part III above, the First and Tenth Amendments of the Constitution exclude the federal government from having any jurisdiction in religious matters, a view which Thomas Jefferson endorsed in his Second Inaugural Address.

The secular self-esteem now being taught in America's public schools is a weak substitute for teaching American school kids that they are creations of the Creator of the universe who made them "in his own image." Secular "self-esteem" consists of repeatedly telling students "You're special," which is an assertion without an explanation. The Judeo-Christian belief that God created man in "his own image" explains *why* human beings should respect themselves and other human beings. Being told "You're special" promotes self-centeredness and indifference toward other human beings.

Another insidious development in America's public schools is that pedagogy has been given a higher priority than the knowledge and skills pedagogy is supposed to convey. This is to say that how to teach (pedagogy) has been given a higher priority in hiring and promoting teachers than the knowledge and skills teachers have in the subjects they are being hired to teach. By allowing this switch in priorities, we have turned the educational process on its head. Both pedagogy and knowledge of the subjects to be taught are important, of course. But in any education worthy of the name the foremost consideration is the teacher's knowledge of what is to be taught. Inexperienced teachers can pick up all they need to know about how to teach (pedagogy) from a course or two on that aspect of education and by interacting with the veteran teachers in their schools with whom they have day-to-day contact. They don't need coursework in education as a process as much as they need courses in the subject they will be teaching.

Colleges of Education, of course, don't see things that way. They are in the business of teaching how to teach; so they have lobbied their State legislatures to pass laws to make courses in teaching the primary qualification for certifying and hiring teachers for the public schools and promoting them after they have been hired. Colleges of Education want teachers to take a maximum number of courses in education as a process. That's what keeps Colleges of Education in business. One of the most alarming educational statistics today is the drop in the percentage of public school teachers having advanced degrees in the subjects they teach. In the past thirty years, the percentage of public school teachers having Masters degrees in the subjects they teach has declined by two-thirds, from 17% in 1982 to 5% today. The emphasis Colleges of Education put on pedagogy is responsible for this decline.

Colleges of Education regard the numerous rules and regulations the U.S. Department of Education is issuing as an opportunity for them to expand their importance by introducing formal courses on how to cope with the large number of bureaucratic reporting requirements Washington now demands from the public schools if they are to receive federal money. The unionization of America's public school teachers has likewise created a need for public school administrators trained in the complexities of union contracts and how to negotiate with unions. Colleges of Education can meet that need also. Thus, the number of specialized administrators in the public schools is on the rise.

The U.S. Department of Education is motivating interest in novel teaching methods by offering financial grants to do research in new pedagogies. Among the federally sponsored pedagogies have been "the New Math," a highly complex approach to teaching mathematics, and "Psycholinguistics," a theory for teaching reading by recognizing whole words rather than memorizing the alphabet and its sounds and then sounding out the syllables of words, the traditional method of teaching reading known as Phonics. The appeal of the New Math and Psycholinguistics lies in the notion that since they're innovative they must be superior, the fallacy that new equals better. The U.S. Department of Education also promotes "Bilingual Education," the idea that the best way to teach English to students whose native tongue is not English is by means of their native language rather than by immersing them in English. Of course, the theory of bilingual education requires bilingual teachers, thus opening up a whole new field of training for Colleges of Education.

The practical effect of bilingual education is to encourage among non-English speaking students the continued use of their native tongue. From the perspective of Political Correctness, that's a desirable thing because it promotes "multiculturalism," the idea that all cultures have the same worth, although the number of legal immigrants and illegal aliens pouring into the United States would seem to disprove that contention. The multicultural argument helps to destroy American culture by putting it on the same level as the world's least prosperous and most authoritarian cultures.

American unilingualism whereby a single language has been *voluntarily* adopted throughout a nation the size of Europe with its many languages is one of the wonders of American history. The principal motive for the immigrants who came to America with their many languages to adopt the same language was, of course, that it maximized participation in America's economic dynamism and upward social mobility. The importance of voluntary unilingualism, or the use of one language, was articulated by John Dos Passos in the preface to his trilogy of novels *U.S.A.* published in 1937, in these terms:

> U.S.A. is the slice of a continent. U.S.A. is a group of holding companies, some aggregations of trade unions, a set of laws bound in calf, a radio network, a chain of moving picture theatres, ... a public library full of old newspapers and dogeared history books with protests scrawled on the margins in pencil. U.S.A. is the world's greatest river valley fringed with mountains and hills, U.S.A. is a set of loudmouth officials with too many bank accounts. U.S.A. is a lot of men buried in their uniforms in Arlington Cemetery. U.S.A. is the letters at the end of an address when you are away from home. But mostly U.S.A. is the speech of the people.

The ability to write good expository prose, once considered the hallmark of an educated person, is now taught by a pedagogy known as "Process Writing." The theory in this teaching method is that students will learn to write good English by practicing the writing of English. All those off-putting, boring drills in spelling, grammar, sentence structure, and paragraph coherence can be skipped. "Process Writing" gets right to the heart of the matter — which is, according to this new pedagogy, writing. It turns kids into like cool writers who can like communicate like, you know, real good and produces like lots of them like all the time. (The English heard in America these days is sometimes so burdened by a mania to include "like" in every utterance, that it's difficult at times to follow what is being said, never mind depending on students in the public schools to have enough literacy in the language to be able to teach each other how to write smooth, coherent, grammatical English.)

The teacher in a Process Writing class refrains from interfering with the process. The class is divided into "circles" to facilitate the methodology, and the teacher's involvement in the class consists principally in distributing a list of topics to write on for the students to choose from. The students share what they write with their "circle," consisting of perhaps six or seven classmates, to read and discuss it. For the teacher to make judgments on the efforts of the students in her Process Writing class would, it is theorized, inhibit the students' desire to write and thus thwart the defining concept of this pedagogy: the cliché "Practice makes perfect."

"Sex Education" is another addition to the politically correct public school curriculum which the U.S. Department of Education endorses. Undertaken ostensibly to teach students "how to have safe sex," and therefore avoid venereal diseases and unwanted pregnancies, "Sex Ed" promotes the PC dogma of "sexual orientation." "Sex Ed" encourages youngsters to explore their "sexual identity" and "experiment" to find out what it may be. The inevitable result is more kids having more sex, more deviant sex, and having it at an earlier age. "Sex Ed" makes the Judeo-Christian moral tradition irrelevant by rejecting the idea that some sexual behavior is wrong. It gives young Americans the radically different notion that having sex is just an animal need like breathing, with no right or wrong about it. "Sex Ed" generally presents abstaining from premarital sex as unnatural and unhealthy. It disassociates the act of sexual intercourse from having children in a faithful, lifelong marital partnership with a person of the opposite sex (Judeo-Christian marriage).

Recently, "Sex Ed" courses have started teaching young Americans that they have a constitutional right to choose their gender. This is a truly revolutionary concept. Indeed, endorsing the theory of "gender choice" appears to be one of the main purposes of today's politically correct sexual indoctrination in the public schools. It represents a new level of destruction in the campaign to destroy American culture, a destruction disguised as protecting the "rights" of "transgendered persons." Respect for (or, perhaps more accurately, recruitment for?) the Lesbian, Gay, Bisexual, and Transgender "community," also known as "the LGBTQ community" (the Q stands for "Questioning") is another major goal of "Sex Ed" today. In arguing for putting "Sex Ed" into the curriculum of America's public schools, it was said that young people will have sex regardless of what adults tell them; therefore, they should be taught to have it with the least amount of risk to their health and well-being. But when "Sex Ed" classes include making flavored condoms available to the students in a "sex ed" class, it would appear something besides safety is being encouraged.

Another matter that must be addressed if we are truly serious about improving America's public schools is the authority of classroom teachers. I say this because approximately one-third of all new teachers in the public schools leave the system after two years. Half are gone in five years.

Attitudes regarding the classroom authority of public school teachers have undergone a drastic change since PC agitprop came to the United States. Before the 1970s if a teacher had a problem with a student's behavior in class, the teacher could generally count on the student's parents, school administrators, and the school board for support. That is no longer true. Nowadays the teacher is likely to be considered in the wrong and to receive at best namby-pamby support from school authorities. In all likelihood, the teacher will end up being subjected to that onerous, unprecedented process of official bullying known as "sensitivity training," which is peculiar to Political Correctness. "Sensitivity training" is one of the chief means PC agit-prop has devised for imposing its dogmas on America.

Since the 1950s, student respect for public school teachers in the classroom has declined precipitously. Fifty years ago, the idea that a student would use disrespectful, or foul, language in addressing a teacher was unthinkable. Today, verbal assaults on teachers are not uncommon, and even physical assaults are not unknown nowadays. The authority of teachers in their classrooms must be restored, because classroom disorder undoubtedly plays a large part in the high turnover among public school teachers, which is highly detrimental to education in the public schools.

Vandalism and graffiti in the era of Political Correctness is commonplace, and new forms of violence against persons have also cropped up since prayers to God, Bible reading exercises, and teaching the belief that God has created human beings in his image have been banned from the public schools of America by the federal judiciary as "unconstitutional." An especially disturbing form of violence has afflicted America's public schools since school prayers, Bible reading exercises, and displays of the Ten Commandments disappeared from American public schools. Since those prohibitions went into effect in the 1960s, there have been recurring incidents of multiple murders by students at public schools. *No such episodes have occurred, however, at charter and private schools, where the Supreme Court's rulings have no judicial standing.* Given these undeniable facts: (1) No multiple murders ("school shootings") by students of students, teachers, or administrators at schools in America, whether public or private, occurred prior to the federal court bans on Judeo-Christian teachings in the public schools, and (2) No "school shootings" since those bans went into effect at public schools at schools where religious exercises are still permitted expressing Judeo-Christian teachings, only one conclusion is possible. Teaching Judeo-Christian precepts, even cursorily in the simple religious exercises and the display of the Ten Commandments used in the public schools prior to the 1960s, promotes self-esteem and respect for human life among students. School shootings occur only in schools where Judeo-Christian beliefs are no longer taught.

Here's another basic point about the public schools of today: the high turnover among teachers in the public schools cannot be attributed to low pay or poor expectations of better pay because the average teacher's salary in the United States these days for about nine months of work is more than fifty-seven thousand dollars (*World Almanac and Book of Facts 2018*, p. 377). Median annual compensation in the United States for all occupations is twenty-thousand dollars below that amount (same source, p. 104).

The failure of the public schools to graduate enough skilled, knowledgeable worker-citizens of good character (did I mention that cheating has become rampant in the public schools since federal judges outlawed displays of the Ten Commandments?) cannot be attributed to a lack of financial support for public schooling. The public schools of America receive on average $11,360 for each student in them (*World Almanac and Book of Facts 2018*, p. 377). Recent information provided by an aide to the governor of my home State is that 50–51% of Arizona's entire budget is expended on just one thing: K through 12 (kindergarten through high school) public schools.

The per-student expenditure in the United States for public schooling far exceeds that of any other nation in the world, and has for decades. Yet American public school students do not perform as well on standardized international tests of skills and knowledge as students from nations which spend a lot less per student than the United States does. In math proficiency, for instance, the United States in 2015 ranked below thirty-eight nations (*World Almanac and Book of Facts 2018*, p. 380) in this vital skill which trains students to think analytically and solve problems. Between 2000 and 2015 (the most recent year for which these statistics were available at the time this book was written), the proficiency of U.S. students in mathematics dropped 23 points, from 493 to 470.

However, the teachers' unions, being unions, claim that insufficient funding *is* the problem. Pay teachers more and give them fewer students to teach, the unions say, and by golly we'll graduate as many skilled, knowledgeable high school graduates as you want with the training to be self-supporting, responsible citizens. But the unions have been saying that for decades, ever since they came on the national educational scene.

Money is *not* the problem.

Not having enough teachers who have mastered the subjects they teach is the problem. Lack of local control over curriculum and too many impediments to getting rid of defective teachers is the problem. Federalized schools is the problem. Unionized teachers is the problem. The special interest of Colleges of Education is the problem. Too much time in the school day spent on indoctrination in the dogmas of Political Correctness is the problem. Too much of the budgets of public schools going to administrative costs is the problem. Not teaching the Judeo-Christian basis for self-respect and respect for the lives of others is the problem.

Defenders of the way the public schools are currently run blame critics of the system like me for wanting to "destroy" public schooling. But that's absurd. No one wants to do away with the public schools. People like me want them to be what they have to be for the good of the country and the students in them. We are not hostile to the idea of public schools. Public schools are a necessary American institution. But they are not being well run. They don't have the right priorities. They are not using the ample public funding they are receiving effectively.

I suspect most critics of the system like me graduated from public schools, which is one reason we care about public schooling and want it to be much better than it presently is. Critics of the public schools praise charter schools, home schooling, and private schools because they are doing the job public schools once did, and doing it, I might add, at considerably less cost per student. Critics of public schooling in the United States like me advocate school vouchers so parents can choose which school their child will attend and thus improve the system through competition for students. Randi Weingarten, president of the American Federation of Teachers, says people who advocate the use of school vouchers to give parents a choice about where their kids will attend school are motivated by "racism, sexism, classism, xenophobia and homophobia" (*Wall Street Journal*, July 24, 2017). All anyone can say about such a PC Marxist rant is, *wow*! It's not possible to respond to it rationally.

By the way, school vouchers save money for the States that use them because the per-pupil cost of education outside the unionized public schools is lower, and the States that issue vouchers to parents who want to send their children outside the public-school system get to keep the savings in educational cost for those students.

A sense of what public schools once were in America, when the curriculum in an American high school was equivalent to that in a junior college today, can be obtained from reading about the education a young American kid from Missouri named Harry Truman (1884–1972) got at the end of the nineteenth century and the beginning of the twentieth century in Independence, Missouri (see David M. McCullough's superb 1992 biography *Truman*, section IV, chap. 1). Truman had only a high-school education. But because the public schools the 33rd president of the United States attended had great teachers — smart, knowledgeable, demanding, dedicated — who nurtured his love of books, and because he had an unusually retentive memory and developed under the encouragement of his teachers an inclination to read meaty books, he was as well-read as John F. Kennedy, the 35th president of the United States, a rich man's son who attended private schools and Harvard University.

The measures which must be taken to remedy the deficiencies of America's public schools today are not as complicated as rocket science or brain surgery. To implement them requires only enough parents and other concerned citizens who understand what ails the public schools of America and enough courage to overcome the fear of going up against Political Correctness which currently afflicts so much of American life, especially in public schooling.

One thing is quite certain: public schooling in the United States cannot be allowed to continue on its present course because it is a fiasco for too many of the students in the schools and for the society the schools are supposed to be serving. Public schooling in the United States has not been for more than forty years what it has to be to serve the needs of the students in them and the needs of the nation. Reforms have not been carried out, only because dogmatic PC Marxists and their sympathizers have worked their way into positions of control over the public-school system and want the schools to remain nurseries for Political Correctness.

I seem to hear in the background a loud, angry voice shouting, "Conspiracy nut! This guy's a conspiracy nut!" OK. I am saying the special interests of the teachers' unions, the Colleges of Education, the U.S. Department of Education, and Political Correctness coincide and are having a negative effect on public schooling in America; and I am saying politically correct Americans are running the Department of Education, the Colleges of Education, and the national and State unions of public school teachers. But answer me this. If my analysis is wrong and I'm just a "conspiracy nut," what is your explanation of why the proficiency scores of U.S. students on international math tests dropped twenty-three points between 2000 and 2015, and why are students in thirty-eight nations around the world now more proficient in math than U.S. students, even though the United States spends far more money per student on public schooling than they do? Please answer that question to your own satisfaction, if my analysis offends you.

I concede that it doesn't seem possible that a movement has been underway in America for two generations which wants to reduce the number of competent, upstanding graduates from America's public schools. Yet a presidential commission of eminent Americans from a variety of professions and both major political parties, when charged with examining and reporting on the condition of America's public schools in the early 1980s, titled their report "A Nation at Risk." That 1983 report said U.S. public schools were so deficient that if an enemy of the United States had been allowed to construct a public-school system to weaken America, a more effective system for achieving that goal could not have been devised than the curriculum and pedagogy then in use in America. And the public schools have not improved since 1983.

Americans have been misled into believing the U.S. Department of Education, the teachers' unions, and the Colleges of Education have the best interests of the nation and America's youth at heart. They do not. They have their own interests at heart. Advocates of Political Correctness are in charge of the nation's public schools. They must not be allowed to continue in charge. If public schools continue down the road they are currently on, the complete destruction of America's culture and the triumph of Cultural Marxism in America are assured.

ॐ

On January 21, 1960, the first month of the first decade in which agitprop made a strong showing on America's college campuses, a decorated combat veteran of World War II, John F. Kennedy, who received the Purple Heart and the Navy and Marine Corps Medal for his service during World War II in the Pacific, was elected president of the United States. In his Inaugural Address as president, he declared that the torch of national government had been passed to a new generation of Americans "proud of our ancient heritage, and unwilling to witness or permit the slow undoing of those human rights to which this Nation has always been committed." Nevertheless, a slow undoing of American culture has occurred despite John Kennedy's vow that his generation would not permit that to happen. But he was assassinated in 1963, and his brother Robert, who would most likely have become the presidential nominee of the Democrat Party, when it was still an

American political party instead of the party of Political Correctness, was assassinated the day he won the 1968 California presidential primary. That same fateful year, 1968, Martin Luther King, Jr. was also assassinated. I was still a registered Democrat when these political murders occurred.

In the 1960s, Nikita Khrushchev — Stalin's successor as General Secretary of the Communist Party of the Soviet Union — boasted in an address he made to the United Nations that Marxism was going to "bury the United States" and America would "buy the shovel." The PC agitprop launched in America in the 60s was a big part of Khrushchev's boastful confidence, I think; and America's culture, the source of America's strength, *is* being destroyed, with the U.S. government funding the destruction.

In the last two centuries, successive attitudes regarding the government created by the Constitution of the United States have prevailed among federal officeholders. The prevailing attitude in Washington before the Civil War of 1861–1865 seems to have been that federal officeholders could generally do whatever the Constitution's principles, procedures, prohibitions, and provisions positively allowed them to do. Following the cataclysm of the American Civil War, a different general concept of the Constitution emerged: the idea that officeholders could do whatever the Constitution does not explicitly forbid them to do, a permissive idea which has allowed abuses of power and corruption in the federal government to become commonplace. With this permissive attitude toward the Constitution came the suppression of the Tenth Amendment, the clearest, most emphatic clause in the Constitution stipulating that the federal government does not have unbridled power: "The powers not delegated to the United States by the Constitution, nor prohibited by it to the States, are reserved to the States respectively, or to the people." As the Tenth Amendment says, the general government has only those powers specifically granted to it, while the people of the States and their governments retain the powers not touched upon in the Constitution. The government in Washington was not intended to have unlimited powers.

In the 1930s, with the election of Franklin Roosevelt to the presidency, backed by tremendous majorities of his political party in both houses of Congress, a third and much more pernicious idea of the government took hold of the thinking of federal officeholders in Washington. Roosevelt was fond of calling his administration "the New Deal" because it was his notion that the political party which has the White House and big majorities in both houses of Congress possesses "a mandate" to do whatever the head of that party, the elected president, considers in the best interests of "the American people," and has the authority to exercise this "mandate" regardless of the Constitution which the people of all the States have approved. This new doctrine, known as the "Living Constitution," boils down to the idea of a government of partisan men and women rather than a government of laws. Or to put it another way: the political party that has the White House and lots of seats in both houses of Congress is the ultimate law of the United States, just as the Communist Party of the Soviet Union was the ultimate law in the USSR from 1922 to 1991. This idea of a "Living Constitution" has permitted Congress to transfer a large part of its legislative responsibility to the executive branch of the government. It has also allowed the legislative, executive, and judicial branches of the government, in direct violation of Article V of the Constitution, to amend the Constitution through legislation, "executive orders," and court decisions. With the "Living Constitution" doctrine in place, virtually the only limitation on what federal officeholders can do is the limit imposed by their imagination and their ability to get their fellow officeholders to go along with whatever they imagine they can do.

Though most Americans still think of the Constitution as the supreme law of the land, it seems to have lost that status among federal officeholders in Washington, D.C. The doctrine of the "Living Constitution" offers too many political benefits to federal officeholders for them to abandon it. The idea of the "Living Constitution" has restructured the government of the United States, and the people of the States don't like the result and want to return, it seems, to the previous ideas on the Constitution which the people of the States have approved. The people of the States are rebelling against the "living Constitution" doctrine.

The "Living Constitution" is quite congenial, however, to PC Marxists, because it so much resembles the government the Soviet Union had before it collapsed, in which the leaders of the Communist Party of the Soviet Union were the *de facto* government of the USSR, before majorities of the elected legislative representatives of the people of the Soviet Socialist Republic of Russia under the brave leadership of Boris Yeltsin, the elected legislative representatives of the people of the Soviet Socialist Republic of Byelorussia, and the elected legislative representatives of the people of the Soviet Socialist Republic of the Ukraine voted to dissolve their ties with the USSR and thus caused the collapse of the Soviet Union and the Communist Party of the Soviet Union. The restoration of the U.S. Constitution's rightful claim to the status of the supreme law of the United States will happen only when the Tenth Amendment and Article V of the U.S. Constitution are once again obeyed by the overwhelming majority of officeholders in Washington.

# The Significance of the 2016 Presidential Election

**D**ONALD TRUMP's election as the 45th president of the United States on November 8, 2016 signified the rebellion of the people of the States against Political Correctness and the idea of a "Living Constitution." Not a few Americans regard Trump's election as an answer to prayers for the restoration of the American republic to what it was before Marxist agitprop in America began destroying America's culture and building Cultural Marxism (see Stephen E. Strang, *God and Donald Trump*, Front Line, 2017). When one contemplates the odds against Trump's election, perhaps the idea of divine intervention is not too far off the mark. He certainly confronted what seemed to be insurmountable odds. Not only did he have to overcome his PC Marxist opponent Hillary Clinton and her party's financial clout, he also faced the opposition of most of the leaders of the Republican Party who correctly saw him as a threat to their Political Correctness. Donald Trump likewise had to contend with the nearly unanimous opposition of America's academics, the American media, the political pundits, and nearly every Hollywood celebrity with a PC message to voice. All he had going for him was the support of ordinary Americans in the States, and that proved quite enough to give him the presidency.

With the people of the States behind him, Donald Trump won the Republican presidential nomination with the largest number of votes ever cast in a Republican presidential nomination. What is perhaps more astounding, he won the nomination by spending less money than any of his Republican rivals. In the general election, he also won by spending less than his Democrat opponent. The election of 2016 demonstrated that in the present rebellion in the United States against Political Correctness and the "Living Constitution" doctrine, it is more important to have voter support than the support of millionaires.

Donald Trump defied the predictions of pollsters, editorial writers, television commentators, and the so-called political experts who were all but unanimous in forecasting his defeat. In forecasting his defeat, they said he was too blunt, too politically inexperienced, too untutored in campaign strategies and politics. He had too many rough edges. He spoke in a weird, repetitive way and was fond of communicating in messages of 149 characters ("tweeting") which though highly effective (and often amusing) was said to be "unpresidential" (whatever that means).

He promised to reduce U.S. corporate taxes (the highest in the world) and expressed other anti-PC views that would surely torpedo his candidacy for president, it was predicted. He insisted, for instance, that a wall be built across the southern border of the United States to keep illegal aliens out; that immigrants from Moslem countries who sponsor international terrorism be halted temporarily until provisions could be put in place for properly vetting them; that the North American Free Trade Agreement (NAFTA) and other international trade agreements which he characterized as "dumb" had to be renegotiated. He promised to stop the flow of jobs out of America, to "drain the swamp" in Washington, to put American interests first, and to "make America great again." The political experts predicted he could never be nominated on a political platform like that; and if, by some miracle, he was nominated, he would surely be trounced by his Democrat opponent. But he was not going to get the chance to lose to Hillary Clinton. He wasn't going to be nominated to represent the Republican Party in the 2016 presidential contest, the experts said with a good deal of confidence and disdain. But the experts did not perceive the country's rebellious anti-Political Correctness, anti-"Living Constitution" mood.

This non-endorsement by most establishment Republicans did not faze Donald Trump, who was indifferent to the taboos of Political Correctness which the entire leadership of the Democrat Party, as well as most Republican leaders, feared. Trump's rapport with the consistently large crowds that turned out for his rallies (not a few of whose members appeared to be disgruntled Democrats) was uncanny and consistent. Yard signs bearing his campaign motto "Make America Great Again" sprang up in neighborhoods all over the country; and the issues he raised, what he said about them, and how he said it met with enthusiastic approval at his well-attended rallies. People liked his bluntness and opposition to Political Correctness, which he made fun of when he wasn't insulting it in a worse way by ignoring it. Voters liked that he was not feeding them the usual political pabulum but talking to them straight in words they could truly understand and saying things they could sink their teeth into, which meant a lot to them.

For all these reasons, he knocked off his sixteen Republican rivals one after the other, won the Republican nomination, and defeated his Democrat opponent handily by taking a majority of votes in more than one State which had gone Democrat, i.e. politically correct, in recent presidential elections. The day before the people of the States went to the polls, *The New York Times*, the most aggressively anti-Trump big-city newspaper in the United States, predicted he would certainly lose to Hillary Clinton. Almost every American newspaper echoed that prediction. The election was going to be an Electoral College blowout for Clinton. Trump was not going to be president. It was simply unthinkable.

But the unthinkable happened. The people of the States defied the predictions and elected Trump. He was voted in not only by Iowa, Florida, and Ohio — States he had to win — but by Pennsylvania, Michigan, and Wisconsin — States that even his most ardent supporters in many cases doubted he could win. The people of the States were for him. The election was a blowout for Donald John Trump. He bettered the 2012 tally of the Republican presidential candidate in Ohio by almost 180,000 votes and got a lot bigger vote tally than Barack Obama got in that State in 2008. Likewise, in Florida, Trump's vote exceeded Obama's vote in 2008. His margin of victory in Pennsylvania was almost 300,000 more votes than the Republican candidate in 2012, who lost the State. In the home state of the 2012 Republican candidate, Michigan, his vote was 164,000 more than Mitt Romney's had been in 2012. (These details are from Joe Pollack's and Larry Schweikart's enlightening *How Trump Won*, Regnery, 2017.)

If the popular vote in California — where millions of persons illegally in the United States undoubtedly voted — is discounted, Trump very likely won the popular vote as well as the Electoral College vote, which went to him 306 to 232 even with Hillary Clinton's 55 California electoral votes of dubious validity.

Permit me to give you some information on voter fraud in the United States, which everyone influenced by agitprop says doesn't exist in any significant sense. Some years ago, a wealthy Spanish friend of ours who owned rental properties in Tucson and came over from Madrid almost every year to check on his investments decided to get an Arizona driver's license to use during his nearly annual visits. Being a highly intelligent, multi-lingual man who had driven automobiles all his life, he passed both the written and the driving parts of the examination on his first try. When he stopped by our house to see me and my wife to tell us how he had done, he said that after he was told he had passed the test and would be issued his Arizona license, the Department of Motor Vehicles clerk asked if he would like to register to vote. An honest man, Juan Manuel Cremades, a citizen of Spain and resident of Madrid, informed the DMV clerk that he couldn't vote in U.S. elections because he wasn't a citizen of the United States. The DMV clerk replied, "It doesn't matter." Those were the exact words Juan Manuel reported to us: "It doesn't matter."

You see, in 1993 a Democrat Congress during the presidency of Bill Clinton passed what was called the National Voter Registration Act, which Clinton eagerly signed into law. This nefarious federal statute was promoted by its Democrat backers as a law to make it easier for "minorities" to register to vote. But that was only a smokescreen. What the National Voter Registration Act actually did was make it easy as pie for non-U.S.-citizens to vote in American elections. Had our friend from Madrid, Spain been a scofflaw — as all illegal aliens in the United States are, since they're here in violation of U.S. immigration laws — he could have registered to vote in American elections. The Voter Registration Act, or "Motor Voter Law" as it was affectionately nicknamed by its Democrat enactors, is why California's Democrat legislature has passed a law requiring every illegal alien in California to get a driver's license — and thus be offered the opportunity to register to vote. Because of the federal voter registration law, the millions of illegal aliens throughout the United States, if they get a driver's license, can register to vote. Hillary Clinton's "popular majority" came from millions of illegal aliens going to the polls casting ballots in the 2016 national election.

What does Donald Trump's election to the presidency of the United States mean? It means PC Marxism has been ousted from the White House and can't get back in until January 2021 at the earliest, if then. It signifies that Cultural Marxism is not a sure thing to take over America.

But make no mistake. Trump's 2016 election means only that the culture of the United States, the historical values and beliefs Americans have lived by, has a chance to get up off the canvas and fight for its survival. Trump's election does *not* mean the innumerable gains of PC Marxism in the culture war of the last five decades have been wiped away and the historical greatness of America's culture has been restored overnight by this one momentous victory at the polls. Most significantly, it means, I think, that the many deeply religious Americans who have been sitting on the sidelines in recent national elections, have finally wakened up to the fact that they had better enter the political fray because PC Marxism is threatening to replace America's Christian culture. If the beliefs of America's culture should be completely destroyed and replaced by the dogmas of Cultural Marxism, belief in the God of Moses and Christ will no longer provide the necessary moral compass for America.

In Donald Trump, American voters saw a patriot grateful to be an American; a man who gives America's interests higher priority than the PC ideology of "globalism." PC Marxists and their sympathizers view Donald Trump not as the elected president of the United States but as the embodiment of everything they despise and find "deplorable." Which is why they are hell-bent on trashing his presidency and why they call him a "fascist," the strongest epithet of condemnation in their vocabulary, which derives from the titanic life-and-death struggle in Europe between Marxism and fascism in the 1930s and 40s.

Two days after Trump's election, I happened to be scheduled to give a talk on American culture to a small group of patriots in Tucson, Arizona, the local chapter of a national organization named Act for America. Before starting my talk, I handed out 3x5 note cards to those in attendance and asked them to write a sentence or two on why they thought Trump had won the election. I was curious to know what such a group might have to say on this question. There was considerable unanimity in their responses.

"Trump won because he always told the truth, didn't play political games, and spoke to middle America." "Donald Trump said what ordinary Americans really felt and told the truth without fear of Political Correctness." "Donald Trump won because he wasn't afraid to speak the truth about anything or any topic. He had the backbone the rest of us wanted to have but didn't." "Donald Trump won the election because he told the truth about everything average Americans have been angry about for the past eight years and longer. Americans have been fed up, and he provided a focus for their frustrations." "He showed strength by fighting back against lies." "Trump won because he said out loud what we were all thinking and because he is not from Washington, D.C."

The rest of the responses from this group of earnest American patriots closely followed the Trump-told-the-truth theme. "He communicated directly with the people and ignored the media." "Donald Trump stood up to the establishment and was unapologetic, which people liked." "I believe he won the election because America is tired of the evil, lying Democratic Party. We deserve to have a hard working, honest man leading our country." "He won because people wanted an outsider." "Americans were outraged by the antagonizing behavior of Obama and his associates toward anyone outside their elite group." "He got to the hearts of the people and made them see the corruption of the Democratic Party." "He was a strong businessman and was going to make America strong again." One respondent gave as the reason Trump won, "It was God's will. The church woke up."

The perpetrators of today's nonstop agitprop attacks on Donald Trump inside the Washington Beltway call what they're doing "the Resistance" in an attempt to associate their actions with the heroic acts of sabotage committed during World War II by European civilians, at the risk of their lives, against Nazi troops occupying their countries. To liken the attacks on President Trump to that resistance to fascist occupiers is absurd. The saboteurs who are presently agitating against a constitutionally elected president of the United States are trying to eliminate his legitimate ability to function as president, and to prevent his opposition to their will. Their acts are *not* the moral equivalent of resisting fascist occupiers. The tactics Marxist regimes use to get rid of enemies (apart from incarceration and murder) are clearly visible in the agitprop employed against Trump: relentless character assassination, denunciations, and condemnation of whatever he says and does, including things he is only alleged to have done or said. Attacks on his wife, his older daughter, and his adolescent son have also been part of these unsuccessful, unprecedented attempts to distract and demoralize him.

On November 9, 2016, the day after a majority of voters in a majority of the States in the Union gave Donald Trump his wonderful electoral victory, *The New York Times* had no respectful news about him to print on its front page. No homage for a just-elected president and his family (particularly, in Trump's case, none for his European-educated, unusually glamorous wife); no admiring commentary on the uncommon vigor and consistent good judgment he displayed during his successful political campaign (his first bid ever for elective office); no impartial, informed analysis on whether his election might portend a huge reorientation in American politics. What was principally in evidence in the *Times* and almost all the U.S. media on November 9, 2016 was spiteful dismay that Donald J. Trump had been chosen by the people of the States to be president of the United States. The U.S. media has been thrumming with anti-Trump spite and resentment ever since.

PC Marxists like Maxine Waters (D-CA) began calling vehemently for Trump's impeachment before he was even sworn into office, and therefore before he even had the chance to do anything impeachable. She also raucously advocated all-out, in-your-face harassment and intimidation of Trump supporters in restaurants, on the streets, at their workplaces, and wherever they might be found. Hers was a simple, vicious message: make Trump supporters fear such bullying. Since Donald Trump became president, PC Marxists have repeatedly rejected the constitutional principle which stipulates electing U.S. presidents by States rather than by a majority of the nation's voters. This has been part of their attempt to undercut the legitimacy of his presidency. They have also shown an unequivocal scorn for the American custom of granting a degree of respect to political opponents. Speaker of the House Nancy Pelosi (D-CA), the PC Marxist mainly responsible for the baseless, fake "impeachment" of President Trump in December of 2019, has publicly declared she "doesn't care" whether the wholly partisan behavior of the Democrats in the U.S. House of Representatives under her control is regarded by congressional Republicans as non-constitutional.

Trump's predecessor in the White House seems to be taking a hand in directing the "Resistance" (Matthew Vadum, "Overthrow! Barack Obama's Treacherous War on President Trump!" available from frontpagemag.com). The "Never Trump" agitprop which started as soon as it became evident he might have a chance of being elected president has lasted longer than the agitprop attacks against President George W. Bush in 2003 and 2004, the second two years of Bush's first term in the White House. See Bryon York's 2005 book *The Vast Left Wing Conspiracy: The Untold Story of How Democratic Operatives, Eccentric Billionaires, Liberal Activists, and Assorted Celebrities Tried to Bring Down a President—and Why They'll Try Even Harder Next Time* and the confirmation of York's prediction, Gregg Jarrett's 2018 book *The Russia Hoax: The Illicit Scheme to Clear Hillary Clinton and Frame Donald Trump.*

In the three years since Trump entered the White House, leaders of the Democrat Party such as Barack Obama, Hillary Clinton, Maxine Waters, and Nancy Pelosi have clearly indicated that the United States is, in their thinking and feelings, an "oppressive," "racist," "greedy" nation in need of "transformation." Whoever disagrees with their PC assessment of America is dismissed as a "fascist," just as Donald Trump is. Such criticism of the United States is reminiscent of Soviet criticisms of the United States when the USSR existed.

Donald Trump's defeat of Hillary Clinton for the presidency, which averted a complete, perhaps irreversible takeover of the U.S. government by PC Marxists, plus Trump's categorical rejection of socialism, have produced the solid hate PC Marxists have for him. Because tens of millions of middle-class Americans find Trump's unmistakable love for America reassuring, his presence in the White House threatens the success of PC Marxism. Every tweet he sends or public remark he makes alluding to some anti-America aspect of Political Correctness diminishes the authority and influence of the Counter Culture/ Political Correctness Movement. Donald Trump is helping a great many Americans who are grateful to be Americans (still by far the largest portion of the U.S. population) to regain their confidence in America and their self-respect as Americans.

For the first time since Marxist agitprop came to America with the intent of accomplishing what Obama referred to as "the transformation" of the United States, Political Correctness is confronting a bold, indefatigable opponent in the most powerful office of the U.S. government. Moreover, President Trump seems to relish the political confrontations which hitherto only PC Marxists have shown much interest in or aptitude for. Prior to Trump, PC Marxists got away with making their opponents react to them. Now, he's forcing *them* to be "reactionaries," which is probably the main reason they loathe him.

Two closely related issues will be at stake in the election on November 3, 2020 in the United States: Will the people of the States keep in office an honest, tireless, America-First president who is grateful to be an American and has made good decisions of major benefit to Americans? And, will the people of the States put enough Trump supporters in Congress to make it possible for him to drain the swamp of corruption in the nation's capitol, finish building the border wall from California to the Gulf of Mexico, and restore in other ways the rule of law to America? Agitprop would have the people of the States believe the issue is the size of "Trump's base." But that is not truly the issue. The issue is the extent of *America's base*. It was *America's base* that elected Donald Trump in 2016 and will re-elect him in 2020. The Democrat presidential candidates of today bear little resemblance to any of the Democrats I voted for in the 1950s, 60s, and 70s as a registered member of the Democrat Party. The leaders of the Democrat Party today aren't grateful to be Americans.

❧

The motto of this book, "You can live with the loss of certainty,/But not belief," calls attention to the essential importance of beliefs to human society. It comes from a poem by Robert Rehder, an American professor who was teaching American poetry in England at Oxford University at the time he died. Bob and I met in 1953 when we were waiters in the undergraduate dining halls at Princeton University; we remained friends until his death in 2009. His poem which has provided the motto for this book also wisely observes, regarding the nature of words,

> They mean what they mean,
> Not what we do.

Having published his first poems when he was in high school in Iowa and a statewide debate champion, Bob knew from an early age what all debaters and poets know: trying to tell the truth is your only hope of lasting success. Words have meanings we don't give them, meanings which come from generations of use by the whole community of the language's users. Marxists don't recognize that bedrock truth about the nature of words. They think words mean whatever the leaders of their political Party say they mean.

When the Union of Soviet Socialist Republics collapsed in 1991, Mikhail Sergeyevich Gorbachev and the other members of the Central Committee of the Communist Party of the Soviet Union abruptly learned how unhelpful the Marxist idea of words is in the long run (think *glasnost*; think *perestroika*). The human reality in which words are grounded and "mean what they mean" is impervious to political dictates, even those which come from a totalitarian regime. Regardless of the impressive skill of Marxist propagandists in manipulating language, truth does not change and, invariably, eventually prevails as it did in the Soviet Union in 1991.

A one-party police state is not a "true democracy," as the Constitution of the Soviet Union said the USSR was; bestowing special privileges on classes of people does not beget "equality;" hateful agit-prop doesn't produce Marxist "social" justice, or any kind of justice at all for that matter. Language does not exist to serve political ends but to express truth. A father whose son has asked him for bread doesn't give him a stone (Matthew 7:9). The Soviet Union's disintegration was essentially caused by seventy years of programmatic lying (handing out stones and saying they were bread). The Counter Culture/Political Correctness Movement in America is likewise, I think, about to come apart under the accumulated weight of half a century of lying about America.

The theme of this book has been that American Marxists and their "fellow travelers" opened an agitprop front inside the United States in the 1960s as part of a worldwide Marxist effort to destroy America's culture, which was the basic reason the U.S. government formulated and could sustain its policy of containing communist expansion. The thesis derives from my experiences with Marxist regimes in Cuba and Poland and Marxian agitprop in the United States. My understanding of the nature of culture, and American culture in particular, has benefited from my traveling to all fifty States of the Union and the ten jobs I have held in four regions of the United States, my travels in thirteen other countries of the Americas and teaching in two of them, and my travels in fifteen nations of Europe and teaching in two of them.

Residences in Cuba (my wife's native country) before and after the Cuban Revolution taught me that Marxist regimes are built on a foundation of deceit and are governed through fear. Encounters with American Marxists in Durham, North Carolina, Madison, Wisconsin, and Tucson, Arizona corroborated those lessons from experience. But my most informative experience of Marxism was while teaching Polish university students from all over Poland at the English Seminar in Poznan and interviewing two officers of the Polish national labor union/Christian freedom movement Solidarity elected from the

Poznan district. These representative Polish workers and university students taught me, by their example and instruction, that when the great majority of persons living under a Marxist government get over their fear of reprisals and speak the truth about their experience with Marxism, such a government loses its ability to intimidate, and hence to govern. Poland's self-liberation from fear of Marxist government precipitated the collapse of the Soviet empire which, once it began to crack, fell with an amazing speed and completeness.

Marxism has yet to provide the basis for culture in any society on earth, because it's too elitist, too dependent on coercion, too hypo-critical, too dominated by Karl Marx's ideas of "class struggle" and history as a conspiracy of the rich against the poor. Marxism is too dogmatically opposed to the Judeo-Christian belief that God has cre-ated mankind in his own image, which is to say with a semblance of God's awareness of evil and ability to do good. Marxism is a delusion which forces men and women to act against their spiritual needs. It insists the human soul and the Creator do not exist and that only a benevolent state bureaucracy can provide sufficient compassion for "the masses." Marxists preach that the state should and must replace God and the family. They deny the existence of the need to know God and to love and be loved by other humans, needs which neither gov-ernment nor science can satisfy. Marxists likewise deny the need of human beings to exercise their God-given freedom.

# APPENDIX A

# Beliefs of American Culture

1. God created the universe and the laws for governing it, as well as man and the moral laws for guiding man's unique freedom.

2. God has given all human beings the same birthright of life, liberty, the pursuit of happiness, and government by consent of the governed.

3. To attain success and happiness, the moral laws the Creator has ordained must be freely obeyed.

4. Being responsible for one's own well-being is a law of God, but so is helping others.

5. The purpose of government is to protect human freedom.

6. Obedience to a written constitution, consented to by the people who are to live under it, safeguards freedom.

7. Everyone must work and manual work is respectable.

8. Society is a collection of individuals, and individual achievements determine social rank.

9. Freedom of speech and association are necessary to improve society.

# APPENDIX B

# Dogmas of Cultural Marxism

1. Human problems are entirely material because human beings are only another species of animal that has, like every species, evolved by chance without purpose or design.

2. Environment determines human behavior.

3. The purpose of government is to provide the correct environment.

4. Experts with scientific political views must control government to implement policies for the correct environment.

5. Any behavior which does not conform to these views must be suppressed.

# Some Further Relevant Reading

Alinsky, Saul D. *Rules for Radicals: A Pragmatic Primer for Realistic Radicals* (Vintage Books, 1989; first published 1971).

Ash, Timothy Garth. *The Magic Lantern: The Revolution of '89 Witnessed in Warsaw, Budapest, Berlin and Prague*, with a New Afterword by the Author (Vintage Books, 1999).

Beard, Henry and Christopher Cerf. *The Official Politically Correct Dictionary and Handbook* (Villard Books, 1992).

Behe, Michael J. *Darwin's Black Box: The Biochemical Challenge to Evolution* (Touchstone, 1996).

Berlinski, David. *The Devil's Delusion: Atheism and Its Scientific Pretensions* (Crown Forum, 2008).

Bernstein, Richard. *Dictatorship of Virtue: How the Battle over Multiculturalism Is Reshaping Our Schools, Our Country, Our Lives* (Vintage Books, 1995).

Bruce, Tammy. *The New Thought Police: Inside the Left's Assault on Free Speech and Free Minds* (Forum, 2001).

Chambers, Whittaker. *Witness* (Random House, 1952).

Collier, Peter and David Horowitz, eds. *Second Thoughts: Former Radicals Look Back at the Sixties* (Madison Books, 1989).

Conquest, Robert. *The Harvest of Sorrow: Soviet Collectivization and the Terror-Famine* (Oxford University Press, 1986).

Courtois, Stephane and Nicolas Werth, Jean-Louis Panné, Andrzej Paczkowski, Karel Bartošek, Jean-Louis Margolin. *The Black Book of Communism: Crimes, Terror, Repression*, translated by Jonathan Murphy and Mark Kramer. Consulting Editor Mark Kramer (Harvard University Press, 1999; first published in French, 1997).

Coulter, Ann. *Slander: Liberal Lies about the American Right* (Crown Publishers, 2002).

Darwin, Charles. *On the Origin of Species: By Means of Natural Selection, Or the Preservation of Favored Races in the Struggle for Life* (Modern Library, 1998; first published 1859).

Dewey, John. *Liberalism and Social Action* (Prometheus Books, 2000).

D'Souza, Dinesh. *America: Imagine a World without Her* (Regnery Publishing, 2014).

Elder, Larry. *The Ten Things You Can't Say in America* (St. Martin's Griffin, 2000).

Flynn, Daniel J. *Intellectual Morons: How Ideology Makes Smart People Fall for Stupid Ideas* (Crown Forum, 2001).

———. *Why the Left Hates America: Exposing the Lies That Have Obscured Our National Greatness* (Prima Publishing, 2006).

Fontova, Humberto. *Exposing the Real Che Guevara and the Useful Idiots Who Idolize Him* (Sentinel, 2007).

———. *The Longest Romance: The Mainstream Media and Fidel Castro* (Encounter Books, 2013).

Franklin, John Hope. *From Slavery to Freedom: A History of Negro Americans*, fifth edition (Alfred A. Knopf, 1980).

Freddoso, David. *Gangster Government: Barack Obama and the Washington Thugocracy* (Regnery Publishing, 2011).

Hardy, David T. *I'm From the Government and I'm Here To Kill You* (Skyhorse Publishing, 2017).

Haynes, John Earl and Harvey Klehr. *In Denial: Historians, Communism & Espionage* (Encounter Books, 2003).

Heller, Mikhail. *Cogs in the Wheel: The Formation of Soviet Man* (Alfred A. Knopf, 1988).

Horowitz, David. *The Professors: The 101 Most Dangerous Academics in America* (Regnery Publishing, 2006).

———. *Radicals: Portraits of a Destructive Passion* (Regnery Publishing, 2012).

Hunter, Edward. *Brainwashing: The Story of Men Who Defied It* (Pyramid Books, 1961).

Huntington, Samuel P. *Who Are We? The Challenges to America's National Identity* (Simon & Schuster, 2004).

Isserman, Maurice and Michael Kazin. *America Divided: The Civil War of the 1960s* (Oxford University Press, 2000).

Jarrett, Gregg. *The Russian Hoax: The Illicit Scheme to Clear Hillary Clinton and Frame Donald Trump* (Broadside Books, 2018).

Kengor, Paul. *Dupes: How America's Adversaries Have Manipulated Progressives for a Century* (ISI Books, 2010).

Koestler, Arthur and Ignazio Silone, Richard Wright, Andre Gide (forward by Dr. Enid Starkie), Louis Fischer, Stephen Spender. *The God That Failed*, Richard

Crossman, Editor; with a New Forward by David C. Engerman (Columbia University Press, 1950).

Lazo, Mario. *Dagger in the Heart: American Policy Failures in Cuba* (Twin Circle Publishing, 1968).

Loudon, Trevor. *The Enemies Within: Communists, Socialists, and Progressives in the U.S. Congress, 2013–2015 Edition* (Pacific Freedom Foundation, 2015).

McCarthy, Andrew C. *The Grand Jihad: How Islam and the Left Sabotage America* (Encounter Books, 2010).

McElhinney, Ann and Phelim McEleer. *Gosnell: The Untold Story of America's Most Prolific Serial Killer* (Regnery Publishing, 2017). [A case study of the abortion as choice syndrome.]

McElroy, John Harmon. *American Beliefs: What Keeps a Big Country and a Diverse People United* (Ivan R. Dee, 1999).

———. *Divided We Stand: The Rejection of American Culture since the 1960s* (Rowman & Littlefield, 2006).

Madison, James. *Notes of Debates in the Federal Convention of 1787* (W. W. Norton, 1987; first published 1840).

Meyer, Stephen C. *Signature in the Cell: DNA and the Evidence for Intelligent Design* (HarperOne, 2009).

Murray, William J. *Utopian Road to Hell: Enslaving America and the World with Central Planning* (WND, 2016).

O'Leary, Brad. *The Audacity of Deceit: Barack Obama's War on American Values* (WND, 2008).

Paloczi-Horveth, George. *The Undefeated* (Eland, 1993; first published 1959). [The colonization of Hungary by the Soviet Union and the Hungarian revolt of 1956.]

Parker, Star. *Uncle Sam's Plantation: How Big Government Enslaves America's Poor and What We Can Do About It*, revised and updated (Thomas Nelson, 2010).

Pipes, Richard. *Communism: A History* (Modern Library Chronicles Book, 2001).

*Poland Under Jaruzelski: A Comprehensive Sourcebook on Poland during and after Martial Law.* Edited by Leopold Labedz and the Staff of Survey Magazine (Charles Scribner's Sons, 1984).

Powers, Kirsten. *The Silencing: How the Left Is Killing Free Speech* (Regnery Publishing, 2015).

Ravitch, Diane. *The Language Police: How Pressure Groups Restrict What Students Learn* (Alfred A. Knopf, 2003).

Riley, Jason L. *Please Stop Helping Us: How Liberals Make It Harder for Blacks to Succeed* (Encounter Books, 2014).

Service, Robert. *The End of the Cold War 1985–1991* (Pan Books, 2016).

Shifrin, Avraham. *The First Guidebook to Prisons and Concentration Camps of the Soviet Union*, with 170 maps, photographs, and drawings (Bantam Books, 1982; second edition).

Singer, Peter. *Unsanctifying Human Life,* ed. Helga Kuhse (Blackwell Publishers, 2002).

Sowell, Thomas. *The Quest for Cosmic Justice* (The Free Press, 1999).

Strassel, Kimberley. *The Intimidation Game: How the Left Is Silencing Free Speech* (Twelve, 2016).

Strobel, Lee. *The Case for a Creator* (Zondervan, 2004).

Thomas, Clarence. *My Grandfather's Son: A Memoir* (Harpers, 2007).

Trump, Donald J. *Crippled America: How to Make America Great Again* (Threshold Editions, 2015).

Valladares, Armando. *Against All Hope: A Memoir of Life in Castro's Gulag*, translated by Andrew Hurley; originally published in Spain by Plaza & James Editores, 1985, as *Contra Toda Esperanza* (Encounter Books, 2001).

Vazsonyi, Balint. *America's Thirty Years War: Who Is Winning?* (Regnery Publishing, 1998).

Voegeli, William. *The Pity Party: A Mean-Spirited Diatribe against Liberal Compassion* (Broadside Books, 2014).

Washburn, Katharine and John Thornton, eds. Introduction by John Simon, *Dumbing Down: Essays on the Strip-Mining of American Culture* (W.W. Norton, 1996).

Washington, Booker T. *Up From Slavery: An Autobiography* (Lancer Press, 1968; first published 1901).

West, Diana. *American Betrayal: The Secret Assault on Our Nation's Character* (St. Martin's Griffin, 2013).

West, John G. *Darwin Day in America: How Our Politics and Culture Have Been Dehumanized in the Name of Science* (ISI Books, 2007).

Willis, Clint, ed. *The I Hate Ann Coulter, Bill O'Reilly, Rush Limbaugh, Michael Savage, Sean Hannity… Reader* (Thunder's Mouth Press, 2004).

York, Byron. *The Vast Left Wing Conspiracy: The Untold Story of How Democratic Operatives, Eccentric Billionaires, Liberal Activists, and Assorted Celebrities Tried to Bring Down a President — and Why They'll Try Even Harder Next Time* (Crown Forum, 2005).

# Acknowledgments

BECAUSE THE EXPERIENCES of a long life have gone into this book, it is impossible to thank everyone to whom I am truly indebted. The following persons contributed information to *Agitprop in America*. Bruce Ash. Larissa Blanco. Alan Bomberger. Michael and Rose Bird. Neil Clements, MD. Carolyn and Garland Cox. The late Blanca Rosa Diaz Rodriguez. Thomas Drake. Lech Dymarski. Tiernan Erickson. The late Louis Fanning, PhD. Col. Jon Gold U.S. Army (ret.). Charles Heller. The late Manuel Antonio Herrera Martinez. Ann Howard. Dave Hurley. Al and Sally Litwak. The late Helen S. and John H. McElroy. Lauren McElroy. Onyria Herrera McElroy, PhD. Capt. U.S. Merchant Marine (ret.) Al Melvin. Bill Netherton. Curt Pedersen. Krystyna and Olgried Palusinski, PhD. The late Juliusz and Zofia Pietrzak. Boris Shoshitaishvili, PhD. The late M. Solomon. Barry Webb. Tamas Zsitvay, PhD. None of these persons can be held accountable for anything I've said or how I've said it, or anything I've left unsaid which perhaps ought to have been said.

I also want to express my gratitude to William S. Lind for putting me in touch with Arktos, the publisher of this book and to John Bruce Leonard, Tor Westman, and others on the staff of Arktos for their patience and courtesy during the production of *Agitprop in America*.

JOHN HARMON MCELROY

# About the Author

JOHN HARMON MCELROY is a professor emeritus of the University of Arizona. He also taught at Clemson University, the University of Wisconsin-Madison and, as a Fulbright Professor of American Studies, at universities in Spain (Salamanca) and Brazil (Santa Catarina). In 1956–1958 he served aboard a U.S. Navy destroyer escort radar picket ship in the North Atlantic, stationed out of Newport, Rhode Island. His experiences with Marxism include being arrested and interrogated by communist state security police in Cuba in 1960, and in the summer of 1981 teaching in Poland under U.S. State Department auspices when the Christian freedom movement labor union Solidarity was challenging communist rule in Poland. In the 1980s, he was president of Solidarity Tucson, a citizens group he helped to found in support of Solidarity. In 1990–1992, he organized the planting of 500 *Sequoia sempervirens* (coastal redwoods) in northwest Spain to honor the 500th anniversary of Columbus's world-changing voyage. In 2006, he created "America's Fabric," a Sunday-morning radio series on American history and culture broadcast over KVOI in Tucson, which he produced and hosted until 2016. In 2010 at age seventy-six, he walked 430 miles of the Camino de Santiago, the medieval pilgrim road across northern Spain. He and Onyria Herrera Diaz, PhD, who writes best-selling Spanish-English medical dictionaries, were married in Havana, Cuba in 1957. They have four children, eight grandchildren, and two great-grandchildren. *Agitprop in America* is McElroy's fifth book on America's cultural history; his other three books include an historical detective novel featuring Benjamin Franklin, the first in a planned trilogy.

# NOTES

## OTHER BOOKS PUBLISHED BY ARKTOS

# OTHER BOOKS PUBLISHED BY ARKTOS

# OTHER BOOKS PUBLISHED BY ARKTOS

CPSIA information can be obtained
at www.ICGtesting.com
Printed in the USA
LVHW042203280720
661796LV00002B/617